Writer and critic Roz Kaveney was a contributing editor to *The Encyclopaedia of Fantasy* (1997). She has contributed to many publications, including *Flesh and the Mirror* (1993) and the *Cambridge Guide to Women Writers* (1999), as well as editing a number of science fiction anthologies. She is a regular reviewer for, among others, the *New Statesman*, the *Independent* and the *Times Literary Supplement*. She lives and works in London and watches *Buffy*. A lot.

This is for Paule
and for Michael and Elizabeth

READING the Vampire Slayer

An Unofficial Critical Companion to BUFFY and ANGEL

Edited by ROZ KAVENEY

TAURIS PARKE PAPERBACKS
LONDON • NEW YORK

Third impression reprinted in 2002 by I.B. Tauris & Co Ltd
6 Salem Road, London W2 4BU
175 Fifth Avenue, New York NY 10010
www.ibtauris.com

In the United States of America and Canada distributed by
Palgrave Macmillan a division of St. Martin's Press
175 Fifth Avenue, New York NY 10010

First published in 2001
Reprinted in 2001
Copyright © Roz Kaveney, 2001

The right of Roz Kaveney to be identified as the author of this work has
been asserted by the author in accordance with the Copyright, Designs and
Patent Act 1988.

ISBN 186064 762 6

A full CIP record for this book is available from the British Library
A full CIP record is available from the Library of Congress

Library of Congress Catalog Card Number: available

Project management by Steve Tribe, London
Manufactured in the United States of America

contents

acknowledgements

First of all, I have to thank all those with whom I have watched the shows, especially Paule. Tapes were lent to me or made for me by Graham Kent, Oliver Morton and Nancy Hynes, Anna Chen and Charles Shaar Murray – Charles also explained *Star Trek* to me. All of my friends have been endlessly tolerant of my obsession with *Buffy* and *Angel* over the last three years – and I thank them all for this.

I want especially to thank Lisa Brown, with whom I was originally going to collaborate on this book and who had to drop out because of ill-health; she suggested a number of contributors to me and acted as liaison with them. She and her partner Polly Richards have been a part of my intellectual support system on this project, along with all those mentioned above and the following – Tanja Kinkel, Ian Shuttleworth, Farah Mendlesohn, Mary Gentle, Alex Stewart, Helen Sterling Lane and the Battistas' gang. The late Lorna Sage encouraged me to write the book; Kate More made me explain large parts of the Buffy mythos to her; John Clute read a draft of my chapter and told me what I had failed to tell him.

Philippa Brewster and Susan Lawson have been a joy to work with, as have all at I.B.Tauris.

The chapter headings incorporate illustrations adapted from photographs by Ruth Thomas.

On-line, I have to thank the cix Buffy conferences, the late great Buffylist, JossBtVS, BRAXS, and IreUK_BAfans. In the Buffy and Angel slash communities, I have in particular to thank Dymphna, Dolores, Faithtastic, Lar and Te, but more generally the community associated with the UCSL list and chatroom – I would not have understood slash and fanfiction without you. I want also to thank

Jennifer Godwin for running BuffyNewsWire, Rayne for Buffylist and the Shooting Script Site, and Little Willow for her smooth moderation of the JossBtVS list, all of whom have been personally helpful.

My thanks are also due to the DSA PR Agency, the 20th Century Fox London Office, the United Talent Agency in LA and the committee of the Nocturnal3K Convention.

Resources

The online resources for researching matters related to *Buffy* and *Angel* are too plentiful to list; a few indispensable ones are listed below.

BuffyNewsWire (www.buffynewswire.com) is an almost unbelievably helpful site and updates service for casting, associative films, spoilers, picture galleries and so on,

Until recently, the Buffy and Angel Shooting Script site (www.mustreadtv.com/buffyscripts) had those scripts not available in book form available on line, often with deleted scenes and variants. Rayne miraculously – and helpfully for those of us who live outside the US – often managed to post new episodes within days of broadcast. Legal complications have now made the status of this site uncertain. An alternative, is www.psyche.kn_bremen.dc/buffy.html. Scripts for the first season, and by the time this goes to press, the first part of the second season, are now available in book form from Pocket Books.

The episode guides Buffyguide.com (www.buffyguide.com) and The Screening Room, Home of the Angelguide (www.sanctuary. digitalspace.net/screening/screeningrm.html) are excellent sources of quotage and pop culture references.

contributors

Anne Millard Daugherty is a research associate at the University of Kansas

Roz Kaveney is a freelance literary journalist and publisher's advisory reader.

Zoe-Jane Playden is a health service administrator attached to the University of London

Esther Saxey is working on a doctorate in Media Studies at the University of Sussex.

Karen Sayer teaches in the Department of Literary Studies at the University of Luton

Ian Shuttleworth reviews theatre for the *Financial Times*

Boyd Tonkin is Literary Editor of the *Independent*

Brian Wall is a doctoral candidate in the Department of English at the University of Western Ontario, completing a study of Samuel Beckett's works in electronic media.

Dave West writes extensively on East Asian cinema and martial arts.

Steve Wilson is a freelance journalist.

Michael Zryd is an Assistant Professor of Film Studies in the Department of English at the University of Western Ontario.

the regular, recurring or otherwise significant characters of buffy and angel

The Summers Family
Buffy Anne Summers, a vampire slayer, daughter of
Joyce Summers, a gallery owner, divorced from
Hank Summers, a neglectful father.
Dawn Summers, (Season Five onwards) apparently Buffy's sister and
    Joyce and Hank's child, actually the Key, a mystical pattern of
    energy given human form and memories.

Sunnydale High School
1. Faculty
Principal Flutie, eaten by pupils and replaced by
Principal Snyder, eaten by the Mayor at the end of Season Three.
Rupert Giles, known when young and wild as Ripper, school librarian
    and Buffy's watcher, in love with
Jenny Calendar, computer teacher and technopagan, actually Janna,
    agent of the Kalderash tribe.

Various doomed teachers.

2. Pupils
Willow Rosenberg, a computer nerd (later a witch) in love with
Xander Harris, who is in love with Buffy.
Oz (Daniel Osbourne), a guitarist in Dingoes Ate my Baby and a
    werewolf, in love with Willow.

Cordelia Chase, cheerleader and queen bitch, girlfriend of Xander.

Harmony Kendall, one of Cordelia's courtiers, latterly a vampire and girlfriend of Spike.

Jonathan Levinson, a shy unpopular short boy.

Devon, lead singer of Dingoes ate my Baby.

Amy Madison, aspiring cheerleader and witch.

Larry, football captain and in the closet.

Marcie, an invisible girl.

Various Cordettes, members of the swim team, stoners and variously doomed others.

The City of Sunnydale

Mayor Richard P. Wilkins the Third (also the First and the Second).

Deputy Mayor Allan Finch, a henchman.

Willie the Snitch, a bar owner.

Various doomed proprietors of the Magic Shop.

Slayers and The Watchers' Council

Kendra, a vampire slayer.

Faith, another vampire slayer.

Wesley Wyndham-Price, a Watcher.

Quentin Travers, a Senior Watcher.

Gwendolen Post, a renegade Watcher.

Various scholars and hit-men working for the Council.

Sunnydale University and The Initiative

Maggie Walsh, head of the Psychology deparment, actually head of the covert Government research facility the Initiative, commanding officer of, and in love with,

Riley, a teaching assistant and commando, in love with Buffy, commander of

Graham and
Forrest, posthumously in the service of
Adam, an experiment.

Kathy, a room-mate.
Parker Abrahams, a seducer.
Veruca, singer and werewolf.
Tara McLay, a witch, in love with Willow.
Sunday, a cool vampire.
Various students, some of them commandos, wiccans, partygoers or
    vampires.

Los Angeles
Kate Lockley, a policewoman.
Gunn, a vampire hunter.
David Nabbit, a millionaire.

Wolfram and Hart
Holland Manners, head of Special Projects, boss of
Lindsey McDonald, latterly in love with Darla, and
Lilah Morgan and
Lee Manners.
Nathan, Holland's boss.

Vampires and other supernatural entities
1. Sunnydale
The Master (of the Order of Aurelius), an ancient vampire whose
    acolytes include
Luke
Absalom
Colin, the Anointed One, and
Darla, the sire and lover of
Angelus (formerly Liam and latterly Angel after regaining his soul,
    losing it and getting it back), in love with Buffy, sire of

Drusilla, sire of
Spike (formerly William, a minor Victorian poet).

Kakistos (another ancient vampire).
Mr Trick, an African-American computer-literate vampire latterly in
     the service of the Mayor.
Dalton, a scholarly vampire in the service of Spike and Drusilla.

Machida, a snake demon.
Lurconis, another big snake.

Ethan Rayne, a sorcerer, Ripper's fellow-member in the demon-raising
     cult of Eyghon.
Whistler, a demon in the service of the Powers.

D'Hoffryn, master of vengeance demons.
Anyanka, patron demon of wronged women, latterly reduced to
     humanity as
Anya, lover of Xander.

Glory, a Hellgoddess imprisoned in the form of
Ben, an intern at Sunnydale Hospital, and served by
Jinx, Dreg and other minions.

2. Los Angeles
Doyle, a half-breed Brakken demon in the service of the Powers That
     Be, formerly married to Harry, a demonologist.

Merle, a demon stoolpigeon.
The Host, Lorne, a demon karaoke club owner.

The Oracles.

Fred, a missing librarian.

The Scooby Gang
Season One – Buffy, Giles, Willow, Xander
Seasons Two and Three– Buffy, Giles, Willow, Xander, Oz, Cordelia

Season Four – Buffy, Giles, Willow, Xander, Oz (prior to his departure)
  Riley, Anya

Season Five – Buffy, Giles, Willow, Xander, Riley (prior to his
  departure), Anya, Tara and (effectively) Spike.

Angel Investigations
Angel, Doyle (until his death), Cordelia, Wesley and, latterly, Gunn.

The Alternate Universe of the Wish
1. White Hats
Giles, Oz, Larry, Nancy
2. Vampires
The Master, Xander, Willow.

she saved the world. a lot

an introduction to the themes and structures of BUFFY and ANGEL

roz kaveney

I had never quite been seduced by a television show before.

There were British television drama series I liked, of course. Howard Schuman's *Rock Follies* had snappy one-liners and a few good songs. *Gangsters*, starting from the premise of multi-racial gang-warfare in 1970s Birmingham, kept inventively absurd twists and turns of the plot coming right up to the moment that the hero was killed by a Vietnamese martial artist who looked like W.C. Fields. *The Avengers*, in its Diana Rigg heyday, had visual style and sex appeal and a refusal to take itself entirely seriously.

Of American shows, *Twin Peaks* and *Babylon 5* both created their own worlds and endlessly recomplicated them; *Twin Peaks* also had weird music and an inventive lewdness in its writing. *The X-Files* had a great visual style, largely appropriated from Demme's *Silence of the Lambs*, and a central couple with a chemistry all the more intense for not being specifically sexual. *Due South*, though excessively cute, had a classy soundtrack that introduced me to some terrific blues bands and jazz singers like Holly Cole.

None of these ever became obsessions, because none of them did everything that I wanted a show to do.

Buffy the Vampire Slayer, though, just about had everything I wanted. Its central conceit – a bunch of high-school kids who fight supernatural evils that often map metaphorically over teenage preoccupations – was not automatically promising, but the comedy and the nightmarish horror kept brilliantly wrong-footing each other. There was romantic chemistry, both overt and subtextual, that scorched the screen. The show constantly tinkered with its own premises – important characters died or became evil; our sense of how the supernatural order works was endlessly complicated. The writing was snappy – high-school bitches and centenarian vampires alike got lines like 'What is your childhood trauma?' or 'I'm love's bitch, but at least I'm man enough to admit it.' The fight scenes were some of the most energetic and kinetic on television; the show's directors acquired visual flair as they went. As the show continued, it became apparent that its use of foreshadowing and echo across seasons indicated a real commitment to, and respect for, the intelligence of its viewers. And it had great live indie bands and a hyper-Romantic orchestral score. The spin-off show *Angel* was more of the same with extra noir and a more passionately perverse sexiness.

And I was not alone in my obsession: pre-teen fans buy posters of the shows, middle-aged writers and intellectuals discuss it over dinner. The vast internet fandom, which includes both lists that discuss spoilers, pedantic trivia and the shows' philosophical implications and a large amount of fan-fiction, much of it erotica that draws on the shows' polymorphously perverse subtext, is dominated by undergraduates and post-graduate students. Typically, people watch a few episodes and then go back to the beginning, watching video-tapes in order to pick up the complex story-lines.

I was lucky enough to start watching at the beginning and experience the conviction that this was something special slowly and as a personal discovery. I had written about revisionist fantasy,[1] fantasy that plays with standard genre tropes and makes different readings of them stand both for extra-textual real-world concerns and as a source of delight, so I knew pretty much from the start what I was watching. Sitting with friends watching and rewatching the shows on video made it clear that they were complex texts, the conceptual and verbal wit of the surface, the sheer loopy romanticism of the emotional plots and visceral excitement of the action plots, the range of cultural references high and pop, sustaining deep readings of the shows' underlying implied discussion of feminism, religion, politics and so on. The amount of offence they caused to the Religious Right, oddly more for their sexual libertarianism than for their inventively heretical treatment of theology, was also a point in their favour.

One crucial factor for me was the impressive performances of the large central stock company – by the fourth season, the shows' principal creator Joss Whedon could trust them with a script, 'Hush', (4.10), in which for half an hour or more they never uttered a word – fairytale monsters, the Gentlemen, having stolen the voices of everyone in town. It is also worth remarking that, even for a Hollywood series, the cast are for the most part staggeringly beautiful.

Above and beyond all this, though, there was, particularly from the second season of *Buffy* onwards, a sense of the shows as more than merely sharp individual episodes. Joss Whedon, the shows' creator and writer and director of many of the finest episodes, gradually built a stable of writers around him who fitted in with, and contributed to, his evolving vision; interviews indicate that the core writers have come to see the show as a collective enterprise with Whedon as its benign dictator. Perhaps because of this working method, the show developed its particular strengths, its complex clustering of characters and the solid formalized architecture of its seasons.

Definitions

Briefly, then, *Buffy* is a show which has run for five years and is contracted to run at least two more; it has generated one successful spin-off, *Angel*, and is likely to generate at least two more, one dealing with Buffy's mentor and Watcher Giles and the other an animated recap and expansion of the show's first year. Buffy is the Chosen One, the Slayer, one in a sequence of slayers extending back into the mists of human past. A teenager in 1990s California, she is called on the death of her predecessor, to cull vampires[2] and combat a variety of supernatural evils that congregate at the Hellmouth at Sunnydale. In the course of the show's five years, she has built up an impressive group of friends and allies, protected her class at Sunnydale High, averted six or more apocalypses and coped with a variety of personal traumas, culminating, at the end of Season Five, in her self-sacrificing death. There is no reason whatever to believe that she will stay dead; both show and actress are scheduled to reappear in Autumn 2001.[3]

Angel takes a selection of *Buffy* characters — Buffy's lover, Angel, the vampire cursed with a soul, a conscience and the memory of the atrocities he committed as the demonic Angelus, both before the curse and when it was temporarily lifted; Wesley, the Watcher who replaced Giles and badly failed both Buffy and her dark shadow, the rogue Slayer Faith, through cowardice and prissiness; Cordelia, queen bitch of Sunnydale High — and puts them to work fighting evil in Los Angeles and elsewhere. Most of the good characters in *Angel* have something to atone for; though *Buffy* has its fair share of moral ambiguity, *Angel* is so noir that almost everything takes place in shades of grey.

Both shows take place in something like real time — the first three seasons of *Buffy* were closely tied to the rhythms of the American High School Year, and latterly Buffy and her friends Willow and Tara attend Sunnydale University. The human characters have accordingly aged in something unusually close to real time for an American television show that is not formally a soap opera.

Character clusters

In most genre series, the relationships between the central core of characters are predetermined by status structures within an organization; the characters of the various *Star Trek* series are officers of Star Fleet, say, while Mulder and Scully are Special Agents of the FBI and have roles in a hierarchy represented by Skinner as their immediate boss, but ultimately determined by an elaborate and corrupt system. Though her original relationship with Giles, her Watcher, is supposed to operate within a hierarchical structure laid down by the Watcher's Council, Buffy's relationships are for the most part determined by emotional structures – Giles is eventually sacked by the Council for developing 'a father's love' for her.

These emotional structures have more in common with soap opera relationships than with most genre series – an original core of characters, which eventually becomes known as the Scooby gang, in homage to the cartoon series *Scooby Doo* which also features a group of young adventurers who fight what often appears to be supernatural evil, but is almost always rationalized away. This forms in the first episode around a mixture of affinity, attraction and mutual protection against both supernatural evil and high school. Giles is an adult, but as a rather stuffy Englishman adrift in Southern California is fairly vulnerable; Willow and Xander have already attained pariah-hood as bright geek and the class clown who hangs out with her. Buffy passes the test of coolness imposed on her by Cordelia, but chooses to hang out with Willow and Xander and Giles instead of joining Cordelia's coterie. Gradually, most especially in 'Out of Mind, Out of Sight' (1.11), Cordelia reveals the angst and loneliness that lies behind pursuit of popularity.

There is a strong element of family in all this – Buffy's mother Joyce may be queen of denial about her daughter's nocturnal activities, but, compared to Xander and Willow's respectively abusive and neglectful parents, she is a paragon. When she dies in 'The Body' (5.16) it is clear that all of the younger Scoobies, not just Buffy and her sister Dawn, have lost a parent – the thousand-year-old ex-demon Anya is as affected as any. Giles, of course, has lost a friend and – briefly and in extraordinary circumstances – lover; in 'Forever' (5.17), he drinks to Joyce's memory by himself and listens to the Cream track they once listened to together.

The original quartet of Buffy, Giles, Willow and Xander acquires Angel, Jenny, Oz and Cordelia as partners, all of whom are important for a time and then depart – Angel and Cordelia to become in their turn the core of a new group in a spin-off series. Joining up with the Scoobies demands the sacrifice of what they were before – Angel definitively breaks with his past by staking Darla, his vampire lover and sire; Cordelia quarrels, ultimately irrevocably, with her clique of snobbish Valley girls, often referred to as the Cordettes; loving Giles places Jenny in a conflict of interests between the Scoobies and her gypsy clan.

In the latter part of *Buffy* Season Three, Cordelia continues to help the Scoobies, but is endlessly malignant in her verbal treatment of them; Xander finds out about her poverty and uses his savings to buy her a Prom dress – this moment of grace and her equally graceful acceptance is a surprisingly touching closure. At the end of Season Three, she fights uncomplicatedly by their side, shares the moment of peace after the destruction of the Mayor, and departs for LA, hardly ever to speak to them again.

Oz is the exception here – his existing relationship with his band remains the same – but becoming a werewolf and being put down a year are serious enough disruptions of his life, even if not caused by his tie-up with the Scoobies. It is perhaps significant that, of the four, he is the one least caught up in hierarchies – his group, Dingoes Ate My Baby, does not even have roadies. Vampirism, as we see it in the first series, is very precisely seen as a hierarchy in which the dominance of the Master, a very old and cunning vampire trapped under Sunnydale, is endlessly enforced by terrible and counter-productive punishments of those who fail him; the Cordettes are seen by those they victimize socially as almost equally terrifying, like the KGB 'if they cared a lot about shoes.'

In due course, in Season Four, Buffy is involved with covert Government anti-demon commando Riley Finn. Xander with the former demon Anya and Willow with the shy lesbian witch Tara. Giles' rather shadowy relationship with Olivia, an old friend from England' never really amounts to much. Significantly all three are refugees from hierarchy of one sort of another – Riley from the Initiative, Anya from the demon dimension ruled callously by D'Hoffryn, ruler and recruiter of all vengeance demons, and Tara from a dysfunctional family whose males rule by lies. Riley leaves Buffy, ruler and recruiter of all vengeance demons, and the show half-way through Season Five; after developing a fixation on illicit 'suckjobs' from vampire whores, he returns to the Army.

The core group in *Angel* is slightly different, since what unites them is in large part exile, penance and redemption. Angel has no family because he is an immortal and because he killed them; he has left Sunnydale in order to reduce the risk posed by his relationship with Buffy – the perfect happiness caused by their one night of love broke his curse and returned him to evil.

Cordelia's family lost their money shortly after her traumatic break-up with Xander and she is aware of a need to atone for her earlier snobbery and callousness: she is also exiled by her desire to suceed as an actress and almost complete lack of talent. Doyle, a vision-haunted Irish drunk, half spike-faced Brakken demon, allowed a group of his demon kin to be massacred by the Scourge, a cadre of demon racists, and failed his human wife. He bequeaths to Cordelia the blinding head-aches that go with the visions and his role as Angel's link to the Powers That Be, the Buffyverse's rather shadowy equivalent of Providence.

Of the later additions, after Doyle's death Wesley, who briefly replaces Giles as Buffy and Faith's Watcher, is belatedly growing up out of his earlier persona as effete cowardly fop and coming to terms with his abusive treatment by his father; Gunn, leader of a small group of mostly African-American young homeless people, has fought vampires all his life to protect his sister, only to have to stake her when she is captured and turned into a vampire. (In *Buffy*'s mythology, vampires are made when a human is drained and then compelled to drink the blood of a vampire, who is referred to as the new vampire's sire irrespective of gender.) This dark disturbed group nonetheless become a family of sorts, with Angel first serving as the parent who cooks breakfast and then temporarily as the bad father who neglects his family for other loyalties.

The group of evil vampires we have come to know best are also, in their way, a family – and another one in which Angel is seen as untrustworthy patriarch. If this seems almost too human a trait, it is part of the package of human pleasures which Angelus and Darla, Angelus' sire, a Virginian whore sired in 1609 by the Master, chose along with each other when they walked away from the Master and his ascetic Order of Aurelius in 'Darla' (A2.7). Their objective in driving the young Victorian psychic and nun Drusilla mad and turning her was pure malice, but their relationship with the resulting vampire Drusilla is a blend of (highly incestuous) parental love, sado-masochism, amused tolerance and genuine affection. When Drusilla in her turn sires Spike, a street tough brawler of a vampire, whom we eventually learn to have been a failed poet, the older generation find him entirely infuriating; Spike's relationship to them is a mixture of mockery, hatred and adulation – when he belatedly finds out, in 'School Hard' (2.2), that Angel has become ensouled, his disillusion-ment is bitter.[4] Just as Drusilla is both Darla's grandchild and her mother, Spike is her child, her lover and her brother; vampire families are, after all, demonic.

Spike's subsequent status as a quasi-Scooby and as Buffy's suitor could thus be explained without the assumption that he is necessarily engaged in any process of redemption; he needs, as we saw in a poig-nant moment in 'Pangs' (4.8) when he stared in at a vampire feast like a Dickens orphan, a family to belong to. Buffy has enough darkness to her that he finds her attractive; when he talks of family and friends as keeping her from her deathwish, in 'Fool For Love' (5.7) the occa-sionally suicidal and often foolhardy Spike is also talking about himself.

Significantly, his other major relationship is with Harmony, a vampire formerly Cordelia's disloyal lieutenant and an abject failure at forming her own gang. His tragedy, and that of Darla and Drusilla, is that they are capable of passionate love, but not of the broader emotional register that goes with it on a quotidien level.

This group of vampires serves as one of the major focuses of the show's revisionist treatment of fantasy themes – the other principal ones being the figures of the Slayers themselves, and of the group of variously empowered humans that surround them, and the various one-off monsters and season villains. Spike and Angel, the latter posing as his earlier evil self, make jokes about Anne Rice vampires with tortured consciences – ironic, given what later happens to both of them.

There is a neat joke across the series about the social construction versus essentialism debate – the Master is evil because he regards it as his ascetic religious duty to be so, the younger Darla and Angelus out of a selfish aristocratic hedonism, Spike purely because he is a predator; the precise form evil takes recapitulates mediaevalism, the ancien regime and cutthroat capitalism.

Just as these three groups exist partly in opposition to each other, partly overlapping their memberships, so the relationships between individual characters are made even more complex by a set of shadow-double relationships. Characters are alternate versions of each other – Buffy and Cordelia (Buffy before her powers), Buffy and Faith (Buffy without family and friends) – or recapitulate aspects of each other's careers – Angel and Faith. Angel and Spike are not only related through their ties to Drusilla and to Buffy, but by being respectively dark and blond and by being originally called Liam and William. One of the reasons why the poet William becomes the streetfighter Spike is because the roisterer Liam has become the moody sadistic aesthete Angelus and the role of family intellectual is taken.[5]

The regular use of doppelganger plots – Willow and her evil twin in 'Doppelgangland' (3.16), the two Xanders in 'The Replacement' (5.3), the Faith/Buffy body switch in 'Who Are You' (4.16), Spike's acquisition of a Buffy robot for sexual purposes in 'Intervention' (5.18) – is only one special case of the ways in which these patterns of doubling and opposition are used to enhance the show's exploration of moral ambiguity, especially in the context of its almost obsessional reflexivity. One example will serve here – in the aftermath of Buffy's sleeping with Angel in 'Innocence' (2.14), he experiences agony and turns into Angelus, whereas in the aftermath of sleeping with Darla in 'Reprise', he experiences a similar agony but does not; both women, deeply confused by the behaviour of the man they love, utter the same line: 'Was I . . . was it . . . not good?'

Joss Whedon has said, partly in response to the erotic fan fiction, much of it dealing with imagined lesbian and gay relationships between the characters, 'All the relationships on the show are sort of romantic (Hence the B(ring) Y(our) O(wn) Subtext principle).' Other shows, such as those in the *Trek* franchise, have carefully avoided the implication that characters not formally in a relationship are attracted to each other; *Buffy* and *Angel* have consistently implied both heterosexual and homosexual relationships outside the show's official canon.

In a dream, 'Restless' (4.22) Willow writes out Sappho's invocation to the goddess on Tara's back, a love charm not neccessarily intended for her current woman lover. Xander flirts with every woman in the show and has, at one time or another, homosexual panic about every male in it – his reaction to the vast underground military base under Sunnydale when Buffy takes him there is 'I totally get it – can I sleep with Riley too?' Darla, necking with the ambivalently villainous lawyer Lindsay, says 'It's not me you want to screw, it's him (Angel).' And so on – it is almost easier to list character pairings in the show where there is no sexual chemistry than those where there is.

All of the large core of central characters have personal story arcs that develop consistently across time. Buffy, hitherto an only child, becomes steadily more self-centred – a habit of sacrificing yourself to save the world is not neccessarily good for the character – before having to take care of her sister, believing herself always to have had a sister, changes her; Willow loses her shyness and blossoms, losing the edge of resentment that, in 'Something Blue' (4.9) made her powers dangerous. In Season Five, the fight with Glory, a half-mad and incredibly powerful being in exile from her own dimension, forces her to become so powerful that her power becomes explicitly amoral – unlike the less powerful, more focussed Tara, she is not interested in limits. The unacademic Xander gradually acquires a sense of his own worth. Envy and (by strong implication) unrequited and unspoken lust for Buffy drive Faith to evil for a time. Cordelia gets so many moral lessons, particularly once she takes over from Doyle as Angel's personal clairvoyant, that it is tempting to suppose that the Powers take an especial interest in her.

Characters who do not fall into the central clusters, or the hier-archies which oppose them, are nonetheless often given a complex life of their own. The vampire wannabe Chanterelle in 'Lie to Me' (2.7) is just as drippy as the feckless streetperson Lily in 'Anne'(3.1) but grows into Anne, the savvy hard-bitten social activist of 'Blood Money' (A2.13) and 'The Thin Dead Line' (A2.15). Jonathan starts as an unnamed Sunnydale High student, evolves into a comic presence, becomes a central figure in one episode, 'Earshot' (3.18) and entirely dominates another show, even taking over the title credits, 'Superstar' (4.17). This is partly a matter of the writers responding to actors' performances and developing characters that work, partly the shows' fascination with human and inhuman personality.

Season structure

Most American TV drama series, especially those with strong genre elements, have an anthology format – characters apart from the regular cast hardly ever recur and the stories concerning them do not have to be told in any particular order. For purely practical and pragmatic reasons, any overall story arc takes a back seat to ensuring that there are strong guest star episodes at the time of contract renewals – the November and February sweeps. An important commercial objective has traditionally been to run for enough seasons that syndication and endless reruns are possible; issue on VHS and DVD has only become a commercial objective comparatively recently.

Star Trek Voyager or *The X-Files* have rather stronger story arcs – the attempt by Voyager to return from the far reaches of the galaxy to its home in the Alpha Quadrant in spite of its enemies, or Mulder and Scully's gradual uncovering of the conspiracy between government and aliens crop up at regular intervals in the course of a season. Nonetheless, the major premises of both produce single episode structures as a matter of course – Voyager finds a world or region of space that poses a threat or has a problem, and resolves the issue; Mulder and Scully investigate a case, discover something bizarre and deal with it. Individual episodes only occasionally have long-term continuity consequences, except for season endings which may well culminate in a cliff-hanger.

Babylon 5, particularly in its later seasons, with the Shadow War and the overthrow of the Earth dictatorship, has a very strong story arc indeed, with some elements that run throughout the five seasons; quite minor story elements occasionally turn out to be significant. Unfortunately, the decision, subsequently revoked, to end with the fourth season meant that a number of these storylines had their climaxes somewhat rushed; new story lines – the Drakh virus for example – which lacked some of the same mythic force, had to be invented for the eventual fifth season and the abortive spin-off series *Crusade*, and were left hanging when the latter was cancelled.

Buffy the Vampire Slayer and *Angel* get much of their strength as series from their stronger than usual season construction. The five seasons of *Buffy the Vampire Slayer* share a structural pattern as coherent as the statement, development, second statement, recapitulations and coda of sonata form. The extent to which each episode is crucial to this pattern varies; those which deal with a one-off monster or other menace generally include some elements from the main story arc, or from the romantic and other character-driven subplots. The five seasons are self-contained as to central plot; the story arcs that continue from season to season being for the most part those which deal in character development.

Season openings

In the first four season premieres, Buffy's status as the Slayer is affirmed or reaffirmed by her arrival in, or return to, Sunnydale. In 'Welcome to the Hellmouth' (1.1), she arrives at Sunnydale High determined to live down the events of her life in LA (which both are and are not those of the film *Buffy the Vampire Slayer*);[6] in 'When She was Bad' (2.1) she comes back from an extended stay with her father Hank in LA; in 'Anne' (3.1), she is working under an assumed name as a waitress in an unnamed metropolis and only returns to Sunnydale at the episode's end; in 'The Freshman' (4.1), she arrives at Sunnydale University and finds herself a fish out of water.

In each of these episodes, Buffy has to reaffirm herself and her Slayerhood. In 'Welcome to the Hellmouth' for example, she is appalled to discover that Giles, the School Librarian at Sunnydale High, is her new Watcher and that Sunnydale is even more infested with the supernatural than LA was, but resists the idea of taking up Slayerhood again. It is only when her new friends Willow, Xander and Jesse come under threat from Darla, Luke and the other servants of the Master that she fully recommits herself to the fight.

As a series as well as season premiere, 'Welcome to the Hellmouth' is a virtuoso introduction of the core of central characters – Giles, Xander and Willow, and to a lesser extent Cordelia, in her role as comic foil rather than the more interesting character she subsequently becomes, and Angel. Indeed, one shocking piece of trickery is the introduction of Jesse along with the others as if he were important and not to be first turned and then dusted (staked through the heart and turned to dust) in the following episode. Importantly for the world of Buffy as a whole, though not for Season One, one of the two first characters we meet is Darla, who allows a male pickup to tempt her inside Sunnydale High and then despatches him; the show announces in its first minutes that this is not a show where, as would be the stock assumption in slasher movies, a cute blonde with loose morals is necessarily going to be a victim.[7]

In 'When She was Bad', Buffy is still recovering from the trauma of her death at the hands of the Master in 'Prophesy Girl' (1.12) and behaves, as Willow says, 'like a complete b-i-t-c-h', using Xander to make Angel jealous and failing to understand until it is almost too late that her friends are in mortal danger. Here, it is not her vocation but her particular strength as Slayer, of loyalty to friends and family, that she has neglected; as the vampire Spike points out in 'Fool for Love' (5.7), it is her commitments that have so far muffled the death wish she shares with earlier Slayers.

'Anne' takes place in the aftermath of 'Becoming Part 2' (2.22), when Buffy was expelled from school and home, and had to send Angel to Hell to save the world from the demon Acathla; traumatized by this, she runs away to LA and works under her second name as a waitress. The street person Lily, whom Buffy knew and saved in Lily's earlier incarnation as vampire-wannabe Chanterelle in 'Lie To Me'(2.7), recognizes the Slayer and gets her involved with the disappearance of her boyfriend. When the demonic social worker Ken abducts them to a Hell where they are specifically condemned to anonymity, Buffy reclaims her name and calling and frees the slaves, iconically seizing a hammer and a sickle-shaped axe.[8]

After her return to Sunnydale, however, it takes the whole of the next episode – 'Dead Man's Party' (3.2) – before she is entirely at her ease with her mother and her friends and it is only at the end of 'Faith, Hope and Trick' (3.3) that she tells Giles and Willow exactly what happened between her and Angelus/Angel and lets go of the sorrow she has been repressing. She goes back to Angel's mansion and leaves the claddagh ring – an Irish token of friendship – he gave her there. It is never entirely clear whether his return from Hell is triggered by this act of renunciation, by the emotional resignation of which it is the trigger, by her earlier harrowing of Hell or merely happens at this point for the inscrutable reasons of the Powers That Be.

'The Freshman' sees Buffy and Willow arrive at Sunnydale University, where Buffy is at sea. She is 'off her game' and fighting 'like a girl', sure signs of supernatural skullduggery – we find in the following episode, 'Living Conditions' (4.2), that her room-mate Kathy has been stealing her soul. The super-cool campus bitch vampire Sunday mocks Buffy's clothes and hair; it is when her mockery extends to smashing the parasol given to Buffy by Sunnydale High students as Class Protector in 'The Prom' (3.20) that Buffy summons the will to fight back and win.

The partial exception is 'Buffy vs. Dracula' (5.1) in which a relaxed summer on the local beach and in the arms of her boyfriend Riley Finn, only marginally punctuated by rising from their bed to go out and kill some routine vampires, is broken by a change in the weather and the arrival of the Count himself. Here the return is to the seriousness of her vocation – she realizes that she needs to understand the darker aspects of being a Slayer, 'What you are, what you are to become,' (the cryptic remark made to her in turn by the dream version of Tara and by Dracula) and persuades Giles to return to his original status as her watcher at a point where he is considering leaving Sunnydale for good. At its end, the episode also introduces Buffy's younger sister Dawn; earlier explicit statements that Buffy is an only child and the 'flashy Gypsy tricks' of Dracula indicate that all is not entirely as it seems.

Big bads and emotional traumas

Early in each season, we get what appears to be a conclusive statement about the nature of the conflict and adversary Buffy is going to be involved in as the season's major story arc; and at about the half-way mark, there is some radical revision of the rules of that conflict. In each season, and particularly in its second half, there is also a more abstract enemy to be dealt with – an emotional atmosphere that pervades and enhances the storyline. These plot twists often coincide with the February sweeps – the week when viewing figures are closely assessed as a guide to shows' futures – or precede them by few enough episodes to have raised the emotional temperature to fever pitch in time for them.

Season One

In 'Never Kill a Boy on the First Date' (1.5), the Master, deprived of his massive aide Luke by Buffy in 'The Harvest' (1.2), creates the Anointed One; Buffy and Giles fail to realize that the Anointed One is not the crazed fundamentalist they kill in the local crematorium but a small child; in 'Angel' (1.7), we discover that the mysterious ally to whom Buffy has already started to feel herself attracted is himself a vampire, albeit one with a soul who is struggling with his past – his old vampire lover Darla – and his vampiric urges to side with Good.

'Angel' is also the point at which the series starts to explore the areas of moral ambiguity that have become its hallmark. Season One is about letting go of the illusions of childhood, the sense that the world is a safe place in which one's actions have no serious consequences. Cordelia starts her long journey away from entirely narcissistic solipsism when one of the victims of her sharp tongue turns on her violently in 'Out of Mind, Out of Sight' (1.11). In 'Prophesy Girl' (1.12), Xander realizes that not only can he not have Buffy, he cannot expect Willow to date him as his fallback. Childhood fears become deadly in 'Nightmares' (1.10) and Buffy has to come to terms with the strong possibility that what she has had of her life may be all there is – 'I'm sixteen years old. And I don't want to die' – acceptance of the fact of death is a definitive end of childhood illusions. Significantly, it is her rejected suitor Xander, not her idealized beloved Angel, who confounds prophesy by bringing her back from death with CPR (and by doing so, incidentally, changing destiny – see the demon

Whistler's remarks in 'Becoming Part Two'); life is as it is, not as we might wish it to be.[9]

Season Two

The Anointed One and his minions fail to resurrect the Master and there is a power vacuum among the forces of evil. The arrival in Sunnydale of Spike and Drusilla in 'School Hard' (2.1) and their irritated despatch of 'The Annoying One' indicates that a different kind of evil has come to Sunnydale; where the Master was concerned with bringing about mayhem and Apocalypse as a religious duty, Spike does so out of pure pragmatism, Drusilla out of insane whim – 'From now on,' Spike says,' there's going to be a lot less ritual and a lot more fun.' No audience could be seduced by the Nosferatu-like Master, but the bleached blond punk Spike and Gothish Drusilla brought evil in the show its own glamour, though not as much as we find in the second half of the season, when, after taking Buffy's virginity in 'Surprise' (2.13), Angel loses his soul in 'Innocence' (2.14) and reverts to being the charming murderous monster Angelus. Where Spike's determination to kill Buffy is purely a matter of self-preservation, Angelus hates her because she is what his ensouled self loved, and determines to destroy her a little at a time, just as he did Drusilla in the days when she was still human, eventually deciding to destroy the world primarily as a piece of spite against her.

Angelus is not only dangerous in and of himself; he is the principal representative of the menace posed by love gone rancid, a theme variously picked up in 'Bewitched, Bothered and Bewildered' (2.16) where Xander ill-advisedly casts a love spell which affects every female in Sunnydale, human and otherwise, except for Cordelia whom it was meant for, 'Passion' (2.17) and 'I Only Have Eyes for You' (2.19), where Buffy and Angelus find themselves possessed by the ghosts of another pair of doomed lovers.

Buffy is torn between her love for what Angel was and her duty to destroy what he has become, but is not the only representative in

Season Two of the conflict of love and duty. The technopagan computer teacher Jenny Calendar's possession by the highly sexualized and androgynous demon Eyghon in 'The Dark Age' (2.8) causes what ought to have been a temporary rift between her and Giles. (Both this episode and the earlier 'Halloween' (2.6) also reveal an intense, possibly sexual, past friendship between Giles in his rebellious 'Ripper' phase and the evil sorcerer Ethan Rayne). By the time Jenny is ready to forgive Giles, other issues have supervened.

Jenny is torn between her love for Giles and her real identity as Janna Kalderash, one of the clan who cursed Angelus and were in large measure destroyed for doing so; her uncle appears to remind her of her duty. She tries ineffectually to prevent Angel and Buffy consummating their love, but cannot bring herself to tell the truth and warn them that the curse will be annulled if Angel knows that one true moment of happiness. Jenny's particular story arc ends with her attempt in 'Passion' to reconcile love and duty by recasting the curse – Angelus finds out and kills her, but her research eventually helps destroy him when Willow finds the crucial computer disc he failed to destroy.

The conflict of love and duty has its satanic parody among the vampires; as early as 'Innocence', Spike and Drusilla were warned by the reassembled demon the Judge that their affection for each other was human and therefore, from a demonic perspective, corrupt. Even an ensouled Angel, captured and tortured in 'What's My Line Part Two' (2.10), teased Spike about his failure to give the sadomasochistic Drusilla everything she needs; Angelus, who drove Drusilla mad with his atrocities and then sired her, renews their relationship both because he can and as a way of tormenting both Spike and Buffy. Spike retaliates, in 'Becoming Part 2 (2.22), by betraying Angelus and Drusilla, by trading the life of his sire and lover Drusilla for Giles.

Buffy's reaction is a little unfair given the way her own sense of duty has got muddled by her relationship with Angel: 'the whole world could be sucked into Hell and you need my help cause your girlfriend's a big ho? Let me take this opportunity to *not care*.' Spike follows his heart, proving that a vampire can have one, but loses Drusilla by doing so (as we hear from him in 'Lover's Walk' (3.8) and see in 'Fool for Love' (5.7); Buffy follows the path of duty and breaks hers.

Season Three

We have known ever since 'School Hard' that Principal Snyder of Sunnydale High was well aware of the nature of Sunnydale, and that he and other parts of the town's power structure – at least some of the police – are consciously involved in covering up the depredations of e.g. vampires. Gradually we become aware of the importance to all of this of the unseen Mayor of Sunnydale, of whom Snyder is clearly frightened in 'I Only Have Eyes for You' (2 20) ringing him in 'Becoming Part 2' with the news that he has found a pretext for expelling Buffy.

When Mr Trick arrives in town in 'Faith Hope and Trick' and forms an alliance with the Mayor in 'Homecoming' (3.5), the pattern of Season Three appears to be emerging, but, in spite of some impressively sassy dialogue and his computer skills, Mr Trick never quite acquired the impact needed by a major Buffy villain, partly because every scene that contained them both was stolen by the effortless folksy charisma of Harry Groener as the Mayor.

The season's major twist was delayed until February and 'Consequences' (3.15) when Faith, after saving Buffy by staking Mr Trick, goes to the Mayor and offers to take Trick's place as the Mayor's hitman. Though Faith's motives are never made explicit, the extent to which her betrayal is motivated not only by envy of Buffy's ability to combine skill as slayer with a life but also by unrequited desire for Buffy is indicated in 'Consequences' by clear echoes of Angel in 'Surprise' (2.13) – the attempt to leave town on a freighter, the fight against overwhelming odds on the docks.

The theme of betrayal had been established earlier, by her friends' hostile reactions to Buffy's long absence – 'Dead Man's Party' (3.2) –

and her secrecy about Angel's return from Hell – 'Revelations' (3.7) – and by their decision to help Cordelia's campaign for Homecoming Queen – 'Homecoming' (3.5) – and the flirtation between Xander and Willow that starts during 'Homecoming' and reaches its culmination in 'Lover's Walk' (3.8). Gwendolen Post, the disgraced Watcher turned black magician, betrays both her calling and Faith, whose appointed replacement Watcher she has claimed to be, in 'Revelations' (3.7).

In 'Gingerbread' (3.11) Buffy's mother Joyce tries to kill her under the influence of a demon and in 'Helpless' (3.12) Giles obeys the orders of the Watchers' Council and subjects Buffy to a potentially fatal test and is in turn himself betrayed by the Council. In 'Doppelgangland' (3.16), another February sweeps episode, Sunnydale is visited by an alternate world's vampire Willow: in 'Enemies' (3.17) Angel appears to lose his soul again and become the ally of Faith and the Mayor.

Even evil is betrayed – by what was least evil about it. Buffy sacrifices herself to save Angel, giving him her Slayer's blood to save his life from Faith's poison and in her resulting swoon learns, in a dream, from Faith, whom she has earlier fought and put in a coma, that the Mayor has an area of vulnerability – his paternal love for Faith. When he turns into a dragonish demon, Buffy taunts him with the knife with which she stabbed Faith and tricks him into chasing her into Sunnydale High, which Giles and she then blow up.

Season Four

By the time she leaves Sunnydale High, Buffy has grown from being the new girl in town to being the Class Protector who gives her year at Sunnydale High the school's lowest known death rate; at University, in 'The Freshman' (4.1), the parasol that she was given as Class Protector is broken by the cool vampire on campus, Sunday. Buffy has to struggle to find a role, making serious mistakes like sleeping with the sleazy Parker Abrams in 'The Harsh Light of Day' (4.3). She begins to fall for the corn-fed teaching assistant Riley Finn and is impressed by her intense

Psychology teacher Doctor Maggie Walsh; at the same time, she becomes aware of the presence on campus of mysterious commandos.

In 'The Initiative' (4.7) we learn that Riley is the commandos' leader and Maggie Walsh his untrustworthy superior, and that she is engaged in scientific experiments on vampires and demons; after Buffy finds this out at the end of 'Hush' (4.10), she becomes, for a while steadily infatuated with the high-tech demon-fighting of the Initiative and estranged from her real friends.

When Maggie Walsh makes an attempt on Buffy's life in 'The I in Team' (4.12) and is herself butchered by her Frankensteinian creation Adam, the season moves into a new phase, in which the physical opponent is Adam and his attempt to conquer the world for cyborgs that blend machine, human and demon parts. It is significant that Riley, one of Buffy's principal allies, has in fact already undergone treatment with surgery and drugs, secretly intended as a preliminary to making him over into Adam's image. Adam does succeed in altering Forrest, one of Riley's friends, into a monster like himself – 'Primeval' (4.21).

The emotional theme of Season Four is estrangement, estrangement from one's friends and from one's true nature, of which one's friends are part. Adam is the most estranged of all; he has almost no memory of who he was in his earlier life, though he is partially aware of his human past:

> Adam: Scouts honour
> Spike: You were a boy scout?
> Adam: Parts of me ('New Moon Rising' (4.19)).

Forrest's transformation into a monster is an outward sign of his murderous jealousy of Buffy who has come between him and his friend Riley. The chip placed in Spike's head by the Initiative, in 'The Initiative' (4.7), estranges him from his true nature as a predator on humans and sets him, from 'Doomed' (4.11) onwards, as a predator on vampires and demons.

Spike is at this point incapable of loyalty, sometimes supporting the Scoobies out of self-interest, as in 'Doomed', and sometimes betraying them as in 'The Yoko Factor' (4.20) – by exploiting his knowledge of their weaknesses to drive a wedge between them. When he does finally save Giles, Willow and Xander, in 'Primeval' (4.21), after Adam has betrayed him, it is a purely pragmatic decision; challenged by Xander with the suggestion that he has only acted to save himself from being staked, he merely answers 'Did it work?' His alienation is total – hunted by the Initiative and by other demons, with only the Scoobies, whom he hates, to turn to.

When Faith awakes from her coma and briefly exchanges bodies with Buffy, she could not be more estranged from who she is; the bodyswitch episode is even called 'Who Are You?' (4.16). Tara realizes the truth by sensing the unnaturalness of Faith's presence. And yet by this brief total estrangement from her body, Faith rediscovers her true nature as Slayer and her redemption begins, to be continued in various episodes of *Angel*, a show where redemption is a more central theme.

When she is first in Buffy's body, she takes a bath that is clearly a form of perverse love-making, before pulling faces in a mirror and endlessly mockingly repeating what she sees as Buffy's mantra 'Because it's wrong', a phrase she also uses when sexually teasing Spike. She has to be prompted by Willow to kill a vampire in the Bronze; the fact that his victim thanks her starts a process of reconnection to obligation. Seducing Riley does not work out for her either; his love-making leaves her confused and sad. When Riley's fellow-commando Forrest, who dislikes Buffy, calls her 'Killer', Faith claims the title of 'Slayer'; about to board a plane to Mexico in Buffy's body, she goes back to save a church congregation from Adam's vampire – and this time, when she says 'because it's wrong', she means it.

In the two episodes of *Angel* that continue her personal arc, Faith, unable to live with her conscience, tries to drive Angel to destroy her by threatening him, beating Cordelia and torturing Wesley. Able to identify with her, he persuades her that death is too easy a redemption and she chooses the harder path of sustained self-sacrifice, giving herself up to human justice.

The question of following one's true nature arises in the story arcs concerning Oz and Willow. In 'Wild at Heart' (4.5), Oz meets the werewolf (and rock singer) Veruca, who tempts him to her life of wild and murderous abandon, reminding him that the wolf is with him all the time; as the wolf, he kills her to save Willow, but then becomes a threat to Willow himself. Willow explores her nature as a witch, and through this meets Tara. By the time Oz returns with his lycanthropy under control, Willow has made her own decisions about her true nature – 'New Moon Rising' (4.20) – a decision which Faith and Spike understand considerably more rapidly than her friends. It is significant of the liberal atmosphere of the shows that Willow's love affair with Tara is quite specifically not seen as any sort of break with the natural order – needless to say, this is one of the many issues over which the show has been denounced by some Christian believers.

The only way in which Buffy and the others can destroy Adam is by becoming closer than they have ever been, not only bridging the rift Spike has created between them, but literally melding, in 'Primeval' (4.21), into a single warrior with Giles' knowledge, Willow's supernatural abilities, Xander's good-heartedness and Buffy's prowess. Adam's belief that magic is simply a matter of temporary glamours and delusions, welcome influxes of the chaotic ('Superstar' (4.17)) is a misconception – some magics make true things, like the positive force of friendship, more true.

The dreams in 'Restless' (4.22), as well as being an opportunity for the First Slayer to punish them for drawing on her power, brings the four central characters of the show face to face with the dilemmas at the heart of their situations. Willow is confronted with issues around her identity and sexuality; Xander with his failure to find a productive adult role; Giles with the contradiction between his parental relationship with Buffy and his need for self-expression; and Buffy with deep questions about the nature of her Slayer powers. Buffy needs them to keep her human; they need her to keep them alive.

Their dreams, like those Buffy shares with Faith, foreshadow bits of the future. Buffy's death is foreshadowed by her shared dream with Faith in 'Graduation Day Part Two' – counting down from 7-3-0 and the child Willow's book report in 'Restless' – *The Lion, the Witch and the Wardrobe* is after all a story of redemptive sacrifice, followed, it should be noted, by resurrection.[10]

Season Five

Season Five starts with a master of trickery and illusion in Dracula, and is full of illusion thereafter. Not only the characters, but the audience, assume that one or other of the two Xanders in 'The Replacement' (5.3) must be evil, rather than just a representative of different strengths and weaknesses; when both Xanders laughingly reference the parallel episode of *Star Trek* – 'Kill us both, Spock'– it is an acknowledgement that they and we have been misled by a stock trope of popular culture – not every double is a shadow double. Buffy's assumption in 'No Place like Home' (5.5) that Joyce's illness is the result of magic, rather than a physical problem with medical answers, is similarly an illusion – there are some enemies that the Slayer cannot fight.

Love is real, but particular relationships may be delusions; from 'The Replacement' onwards with his almost casual remark that 'She doesn't love me', we are served notice that Buffy's affair with Riley is doomed. Riley's jealous assumption that he needs to be closer to evil for Buffy to love him leads him to brief murderous liaisons with vampire women; the fact that the first of these we see him kill is someone we earlier saw killed as a human makes our feelings considerably more ambivalent.[11] Ironically, his eventual departure from Sunnydale in 'Into the Woods' (5.10) is precipitated by an entirely wrong belief that Buffy has chosen to ignore his ultimatum; she simply arrives at the helicopter landing pad too late to beg him not to go.

Buffy's brief attraction to Ben the intern is based on her assumption that someone charming and apparently good might be a suitable replacement – Ben is in fact the male aspect of her divine enemy Glory. April in 'I Was Made to Love You' (5.15) is noticed as attractive by Xander, Spike and Willow, but she is simply a machine designed for love; it is a long conversation with the dying April that reminds Buffy that she does not need a lover to be complete.

Spike in Season Five is perhaps the most deluded of all; from his sudden awakening from a dream of sex with Buffy in 'Out of My Mind' (5.4), through to his untrustworthy account of his earlier life in 'Fool for Love' (5.7)[12] and his near-demented behaviour in 'Crush' (5.14), when his offer to stake Drusilla to prove his love for Buffy entirely alienates her. Spike's memory of love as a human and his century of obsession with Drusilla confuse him hopelessly about what love is. His fetishistic stealing of Buffy's underwear and sweaters, his persuading Harmony to dress up as Buffy for sex games, his commissioning of the Buffybot – these ensure his rejection, perhaps all the more so because there is a genuine, if perverse, sexual chemistry between them.

And yet, there is a connection between Spike and all three Summers women; Joyce made him cups of tea and his mourning for her is genuine. He endures torture to near-destruction to protect Dawn from Glory, and to protect Buffy from a grief that might kill her were anything to happen to Dawn. When Dawn explores Sunnydale by night, in search of her identity and then in search of ways of resurrecting her mother, he becomes her guardian. When Buffy dies, he weeps; earlier that same night, he says to her 'I'm a monster, but you treated me like a man. And that's. . .' The tailing into silence is one of the most moving moments in one of Whedon's most powerfully upsetting scripts. When Buffy poses as the Buffybot to find out whether Spike has betrayed her, she sees him stripped of his attitudes and his bravado; she does not love him, but she forgives him and kisses him, as a friend. He has made love to her double for days, but instantly knows, and is content with, the real thing.

The answer to illusion and delusion is making fine distinctions, knowing what the truth is. Dawn is not, in literal fact, Buffy's younger sister – she is a superstructure of personality and humanity created by monks as a way to hide a supernatural Key from Glory. But it doesn't matter – she is Buffy's sister in memory and affection; she is the family of Buffy's heart, and, after Joyce's death at the end of 'I Was Made to Love You' (5.15), all the literal family Buffy has left. It is significant that in 'Family' (5.6) Dawn is as quick as Buffy to defend Tara's right to be regarded as part of the extended family of the Scooby gang and protected them from Tara's oppressive birth family. (It is also a significant piece of ambiguity that the question of Tara's true nature is clarified by Spike, who hits her in order to prove her humanity by having it hurt him – a character highly deluded about his own concerns can nonetheless be a truth-teller in other areas.) Dawn is, as the monk tells Buffy, an innocent; the Scoobies embrace their changed memories even after the truth is revealed, as, very precisely, they could not and did not when they discovered Jonathan's entirely selfish deceit in 'Superstar' (4.17).

Story-telling is also trickery. Various of the side issues of the series – the troll in 'Triangle' (5.11), the Buffybot, the link to herself that Glory's mindsuck produces even in Tara – turn out to be desperately relevant to the final conflict, just as the demon Doc turns out to be tragically more to do with Glory's plans than anyone guessed.

Family is a major preoccupation of Season Five and is portrayed as crucial to identity – we have Tara's dysfunctional family based on the practice of deceit as a way of continuing the oppression of women as opposed to the loose family of the heart that the Scoobies have become as they have grown into adults, a family that helps Willow care for Tara after Glory sucks out her sanity. We have the corrupt family of sensuality into which Spike was born as a vampire;[13] his preparedness to kill Drusilla to prove his love for Buffy is a renunciation of Drusilla as his sire as well as his lover.

The relationship between Glory and Ben, originally presented as sister and brother, but later revealed to be divine prisoner and mortal prison, and the fact that Ben has to keep Glory's dress in his locker to change into when changing persona is perhaps a sacrilegious joke at the expense of the Christian doctrine of the incarnation. Gradually they merge – identity and illusion are crucial to the nature of the series villain. Buffy beats Glory back into Ben, and Giles kills him to save the world, just as Ben was prepared to sacrifice the world to remain incarnate in a small corner of Glory.

Buffy's certainty that the monks wrought their illusion well is something on which, at the end she is prepared to gamble her life, guessing that the created sisterhood between her and Dawn is so solidly built that she can be the blood sacrifice which might save the world. Some people have criticized the finale as illogical, but this is only so if you assume that all portrayal of magic has to play by Frazer's rules of similarity and contagion. The sacrifice of innocent blood is charm enough in itself – which innocent blood is almost beside the point. Buffy sacrificed Angel to save the world; she will not kill her sister.

The Prime Slayer tells her that her gift is death, and she chooses to interpret that unselfishly, by dying rather than killing. Everyone has been keen to tell her that the Slayer is a killer, from Dracula to Spike – 'Death is your art. You make it with your hands everyday'; as when everyone from Glory to the Council told her she was powerless, or when Ken and his demons told her she was no-one, or when Angelus told her that she had nothing left, Buffy refuses to be told.

Angel

The first season of *Angel* is the closest thing to a standard anthology series that Whedon and Mutant Enemy have done. A number of the episodes – 'She' (A1.13) for example, or 'I Fall to Pieces' (A1.4) – contribute almost nothing to the story arc save for a sense of the building of a team that is briefly disrupted by Doyle's death in 'Hero'(A1.9) and grows to include both Wesley and Gunn, as well as hangers-on like its rich patron David Nabbit.

Still, the efficient first episode 'City of' (A1.1) introduces new viewers to the vampire with a soul, brings in Doyle, his half-human sidekick, has them rescue Cordelia and lumbers Angel with her as sidekick/reminder of what it is to be human; it also introduces us to Lindsey and the concept of Wolfram and Hart, law firm to the stars of evil. It also establishes the crucial question of temptation – the vampire tycoon Russell offers Angel the good things of LA, the kingdoms of the world in other words, and Angel responds by throwing him out of the window – parodying another of Satan's temptations of Christ with the sardonic 'Can you fly?'

Angel is subjected to various temptations – the Ring of Amara, in 'In the Dark' (A1.4) would allow him to walk in the day and his brief return to humanity in 'I Will Remember You' (A1.7) would have given him not only ice-cream and a heartbeat but also Buffy. He refuses any such soft options – his redemption has to be done the hard way without gimmicks or mere luck. By season end, in 'To Shansu in LA' (A1.22), he thinks that he understands the rules of the game – he resists temptation and fights the good fight and eventually he will be returned to full humanity.

Redemption is clearly an issue in the world of Angel – Doyle earlier refused to involve himself when other Brakken demons were under threat from the Scourge and dies to save Angel, Cordelia and a shipload of half-breed demons like himself. Cordelia and Wesley manage to outgrow her solipsistic vanity and his cowardice to become fully adult. At the point where, in 'Sanctuary' (A1.19), Wesley sides with Angel and Faith against the Watcher's Council mere hours after Faith brutally tortured him, he acquires real moral grandeur. Cordelia's empathic encounter with all the suffering of Los Angeles in 'To Shansu in LA' (A1.22) crystallizes her commitment to others rather than self. Faith surrenders herself to justice on potentially capital charges in order to save Angel from Kate Lockley's murderous spite.

And yet, in Season Two, Angel is tempted closer and closer to his demonic side. Part of the issue is that we find out even more about his past – we knew about the murder of his original family, the whirlwind of murder that was his time with Darla, but now we are forced to see, for example, his driving of Drusilla to mental collapse before turning her. We also discover that he returned to his vampiric family for a while after the return of his soul[14] and that at least one earlier attempt in the 1950s to do good ended in complicity with evil – 'Are You Now or Have You Ever Been?' (A2.2).

More importantly, he has failed to come entirely to terms with old relationships. Members of the evil law firm Wolfram and Hart invest considerable energy in raising Darla from Hell or non-existence and regard their failure to destroy Cordelia and Wesley as no more than an annoyance, rightly perceiving that the answer to killing or suborning Angel lies in his longstanding commitment to her. Angel suffers from the delusion that redemption is simply a matter of saving enough lives to pay off the karmic debt created during his years as Angelus, and staying humane while he does it. The reappearance in his life of Darla and Drusilla makes it clear that things are more complicated than that, not least because of the intense romanticism of his relationship with Darla, who echoes his worst fears by saying: 'No matter how good a boy you are, God doesn't want you – but I still do.'

He tries, while Darla is human and dying, to persuade her to accept mortality and repentance; he succeeds, because of his preparedness to die to buy her a new chance, only to have her re-turned to vampire-hood by Drusilla, the mad creature they made together. In the face of this failure, he quarrels with Cordelia, Wesley and Gunn, severing his links, through Cordelia's visions, with his redemption and the Powers That Be. He claims that he is protecting his employees from danger, but later, in 'There's No Place like Plrtz Glrb' (A2.22), he admits that he was frightened that they would see his true demonic face and reject him. When a far worse demon is revealed under alien suns, he learns to control it, and even Fred, the demented woman physicist who has no past with him at all, can see that there is more to him than the beast.

He allows Darla and Drusilla to take a terrible revenge on the lawyers who have manipulated them; he uses the utmost cruelty in an attempt to destroy Darla and Drusilla; he despairs and has sex with Darla in an attempt to lose his soul again. Once before when he despaired, in 'Amends'(3.10), the Powers intervened, preventing his suicide through sunlight with a Christmas snowstorm; now his return to his true path is rewarded by his being able to enter Kate Locksley's apartment uninvited (breaking the normal rules of his vampiric condition) to save her from suicide.

Yet he does manage to help someone redeem themselves – and it is Lindsey, not Darla. In 'Dead End' (A2.18), Lindsey finally accepts that others pay the cost of his damnation – a replacement hand belonged to a former colleague condemned to Wolfram and Hart's organ bank. It is not just that his schoolboyish rivalry with (crush on?) Angel helps him find and free those mutilated prisoners who are still viable; it is that from Angel's humiliating mockery of him and Lilah in 'Blood Money'(A2.12), he learns how to ensure that he can never go back – he ridicules his superiors and Lilah with endless references to his 'Evil Hand' as he strokes Nathan's bald pate and gooses Lilah.

As long ago as 'Lie to Me'(2.7), Cordelia delivered an impassioned defence of Marie Antoinette – 'It took a lot of effort to look that good' – and portrayed the revolution in terms of 'let's lose some heads.' A mere three years later, she finds herself – in 'There's No Place like Plrtz Glrb' (A2.22) – an enlightened monarch in a sequinned bikini, freeing slaves and pre-emptively banning polyester, saving the entire human population of a demon dimension by personally beheading its High Priest Silas, and abdicating in favour of the one being, the sweet, brave, dim Groosalug, whose mixed heredity means he might bring peace.

The resonance of her actions with an earlier vain selfish Cordelia is a joke that makes us take seriously the extent of her sacrifice – she renounces love and power and glamour in favour of her duty, life-threatening visions and the uncertainties of everyday life in demon-haunted LA. Only Buffy and Angel themselves have made greater sacrifices. Her time as slave and puppet princess has sufficiently crude parallels with her life as starlet – an insolent director calls her 'Princess'; he, her mistress and Silas all tell her to be silent – that we can assume Hollywood is over for her.

Like *Buffy*, *Angel* is an ensemble series; the last four episodes – the Pylea arc – settle important matters for all of the group. Wesley, in spite of the carping of his father, discovers that he is a leader; where once he told Angel 'I am your faithful servant', now he is the general who is prepared if neccessary to send the warrior Angel to death or damnation, the employer for whom a repentant Angel comes to work. Gunn makes his decision – his loyalties are ultimately with this group rather than with his street friends.

And the Host, the new character who graduated from throwaway joke (a demon who foretells the future of those who sing karaoke in his bar) to source of magical advice to loose affiliates of the team, learns that he really does not have a home to go back to, thank Heavens! The high camp of his manner and diva-centred vocal stylings are interestingly opened out in this segment: Pylea is a world without music – the Host always had this unnameable thing in his head. Given the very precise parallel of this to a standard trope of lesbian, gay and trans coming out narratives, and the fact that in 1920s slang, 'musical' meant gay, it is all the more inventive that the Host is not necessarily coded as gay in sexual preference as opposed to style. Like family in *Buffy*, home in *Angel* is where the heart is – people come to LA to accept exile. And with a merry cry of 'There's no place like. . .', Angel strides into the Hyperion Hotel to find Willow waiting for him with bad news.

The Other Scoobies

The last point that needs making speculatively about these two series is that much of their subject matter reflects the working conditions of the people who create them. As various essays in this collection argue, the show has intensely democratic values in its portrayal of heroism and super-powers – Buffy regards herself as accountable both ethically and to her friends and Angel learns to humble himself to a subordinate role and redemption as a daily task. Leadership is a skill; the role of leader at times devolves to Giles or even, in 'The Weight of the World' (5.21) to Willow. Shows that might have been the preserve of an auteur in the old manner are instead a liberal nursery of opportunity and talent – many of the writers now direct and produce as well.

Joss Whedon's personal preoccupations and his genius are clearly dominant, but in a first among equals way. Descriptions of the writing methods of the *Buffy* and *Angel* teams sound unusually collective in the circumstances – Whedon devises the overall story arc, often some time in advance, and the others pitch for story slots within that arc, negotiating as a team the ways in which suggested stories would fit into the big picture. Various writers have cornered particular sorts of script – Marti Noxon is good on tear-jerkers, Jane Espenson at farce, Tim Minear at the darker side of Angel. Whedon always contributes, but rarely shares credits; a Whedon-credited and directed script is always something of an event. On *Angel*, indeed, he yielded leadership to David Greenwalt – his suggestions as to how the Host's cousin Numfar should perform his appalling Dance of Joy led to his casting in the role.

As director, Whedon's gift seems to be for the suggestion that actors have to find their own truth. Asked by George Herzberg how to play Adam in Season Four, he suggested that Herzberg 'find the stillness'. One of the most effective aspects of Herzberg's flawed but impressive performance is just that sense that every time Adam says anything, he pauses to invent it for the first time, and then to consider its implications.

Grand plans have a habit of being disrupted – the decision of Seth Green to leave the show made for some rapid rejigging of Season Four and the crystallization of what might have been rather nebulous plans to explore Willow's sexuality. Some elements in the arc result from chemistry, 'like the romance between Cordelia and Xander. Their arguments kept getting more and more intense until we realized that they needed to be together. We just didn't realize that we started writing them as a couple in episode two', as Joss Whedon explained in an on-line interview. What is impressive about the shows' use of foreshadowing and echoing across the years is that much of it has in the nature of things to have been largely an opportunist improvization and yet never fails to have emotional and metaphysical resonance.

My remarks earlier about Buffy's quintessential obstinacy apply in large measure to Whedon and the rest of his team – they have constantly stretched the limits of what is possible in popular television, both in terms of what can technically be done – the dialogue-less 'Hush' (4.10) – and what can be shown – Whedon is on record as having told the WB network that the kiss between Willow and Tara in 'The Body' (5.16) was simply not negotiable.

'The Body' is, as is remarked in various of the essays in this volume, one of the most extraordinary hours of television ever seen. What needs pointing out about it here is that it takes the extraordinary risk of being a homage to the memory of Whedon's own dead mother, who died of the same causes as Joyce; in interviews, he has remarked on how incidents like Willow's clothes crisis derive from actual lived experience. Whedon's mother, a sixties radical who became a brilliant teacher, is one of the great unsung presences of his shows – when Dawn talks about 'negative space', about defining an object by where it is not rather than where it is, she is perhaps talking as much about Whedon's own loss as about his characters'. It is further remarkable that so flashy, operatic, witty and inventive a writer should be so entirely prepared to portray emotional truth as much through silence, stillness and reticence as his normal palette and to share so intensely personal envisioned series with other talents. The ultimately adult nature of these teenage shows derives from this completeness of emotional range.

Notes

1. In, for example, *The Encyclopaedia of Fantasy,* ed John Clute and John Grant, (1997) many of whose other entries, notably that on 'pariah elites', are relevant to close readings of *Buffy* and *Angel*.

2. Joss Whedon has been selective in which bits of vampire mythology he has chosen to use. His vampires explode when killed, taking clothes etc. with them and preventing unsightly corpses that our heroine would have to remove. They are stronger than in life, invisible to mirrors but not cameras and vulnerable to wooden stakes, decapitation, sunlight and fire; only those victims whom the vampire forces to drink his or her blood at the moment of death from draining become vampires themselves. In the first two series, it is clearer that the vampire that results from a siring is not the person they previously were than is the case later on – to what extent does a loosely conceived of soul trump memory and identity? The tendency to spare Harmony, whom they never even liked when she was alive, and the sending of the vampire version of Willow back to her own world, raises interesting moral questions.

3. At the point of writing, between seasons, it is interesting to speculate on where this is going. Whedon has always refused the tragic in spite of the fact that Buffy cannot escape her role as Slayer except through death. There is a useful distinction to be made between the tragic hero who dies, and the one who transcends; Heracles, particularly in his incarnation as saviour in Alexandrian cultic religion, burns off his human aspect to become progressively divine. So far, Buffy's drinking of Dracula's blood in 'Buffy vs. Dracula' (5.1) is one of the few things in Season Five to have no pay-off – Dracula's 'flashy gypsy tricks' include the ability to reintegrate after destruction. Events among the shadow doubles – Darla's return and re-vamping, Cordelia's reinvention as expected liberator, Faith's self-relegation to passivity – seem to foreshadow greater changes at the centre. My guess is that Buffy will return, not as anything so crude as a vampire, but as something far more uncanny – that in the long-term the dynamic between her and her vampire suitors will become a deal more strange. And the almost classic encounter at the start of 'The Gift' may prove the last time she actually slays a vampire.

4. There is no inconsistency between Spike's participation in Darla's raid on the gypsy camp in 'Darla' and his later ignorance of Angel's curse; quite simply, Darla would never dream of sharing important information with Angel's unruly children with whom she has been landed.

5. It is interesting to note that both Julie Benz (Darla) and Charisma Carpenter (Cordelia) auditioned for the role of Buffy, given that both Darla and Cordelia are in some sense shadow doubles of Buffy and, in *Angel*, of each other. Cordelia is the person Buffy was before her powers; Darla the rival Angel killed for her who perpetually casts a shadow on her relationship with him. Cordelia is Angel's self-chosen link to humanity and, after Doyle's death, his link to the Powers That Be as well; Darla is his link to his demonic past. It is not a coincidence that Cordelia in 'Darla' (A2.7) deceives an informant by referring to Darla as 'My older, like *way* older, like four hundred *years* older, blonde sister, Darla. No last name.'

It is also interesting, given the comparatively minor use of Cordelia as a character in the first season, that her status as season regular can be seen as banking Charisma Carpenter for later use.

6. The film *Buffy the Vampire Slayer* was Joss Whedon's first screenplay to sell and he had comparatively little artistic control over the film itself. Kristy Swanson's portrayal of Buffy was harder, more brittle and less sympathetic than Sarah Michelle Gellar's, though she worked hard at some of the martial arts training scenes. The essential plot – Buffy is called, is trained by her first watcher Merrick, kills the master vampire Lothos, at the cost of burning down the school gym with a lot of vampires inside it, and the death of Merrick, who kills himself rather than be turned – remains understood, though neither Lothos nor Merrick's have ever been referred to explicitly in the show; an officially sanctioned comic book *The Origin* retains most elements of the screenplay and is, paradoxically, now more canonical about Buffy's back story than the film.

7. Joss Whedon discusses this point at length in the commentary to this episode on the DVDs of Season One of *Buffy*; a useful discussion of slasher movies and their crude moralism is 'Men Women and Chainsaws' by Carol Clover (Princeton University Press, 1993).

8. At the episode's end, Chanterelle/Lily takes over the waitressing job

and the name 'Anne', under which she reappears, in the second series of *Angel*, running a hostel for the homeless that is not a demonic scam.

9. My thanks to Farah Mendlesohn for helping me clarify my thoughts about Season One.

10. My thanks to Tanja Kinkel for this and other points.

11. Sandy was killed and presumably sired by the vampire Willow in 'Doppelgangland' (3.16); she next turns up, entirely without comment, drinking in Willie's Bar in 'Family' (5.6) almost two whole seasons later. Perhaps only a show so aware of its fan base could possibly get away with continuity points that subtle.

12. Setting aside the question of whether he tells Buffy everything we see – does anyone believe he told her about his bad poetry? – there is the simple fact that the parallel episode of *Angel* ('Darla' (2.7)) throws a slightly different light on his siring of Drusilla of which he may never have been aware. Drusilla was sulking at her neglect by her 'parents'; Darla regarded Spike as 'the first drooling idiot' that came along at the right moment. Given her desire to be 'punished' and Angel's mockery of Spike's vanilla sexual tastes, it is not entirely clear that Spike's love for her was actually consummated until the night of his killing of the Chinese Slayer.

13. Is there any significance in the fact that William stays to be seduced and killed by Drusilla instead of hurrying home to look after his mother, whereas the Chinese Slayer he kills dies talking of her mother?

14. There had always been a contradiction between versions of Angel's past – he mentioned, in 'Angel' (1.7), that the last time he had seen Darla, she had been wearing a kimono, which never entirely meshed with the Romanian location of his killing of the Gypsy girl and cursing. Some similar contradictions could never be resolved – Spike's reference to Angel as 'My sire, my Yoda' ('School Hard' (2.3), when in fact Spike was sired by Drusilla, being a case in point; others generate plot by being solved. The truth is that Angel simply lied to Buffy about aspects of his past.

This technique, known as 'retrospective continuity' is more common in comics than in television, but in *Buffy* and *Angel* has allowed for some neat evolution of character and of the handling of tropes.

entropy as demon

buffy in southern california

boyd tonkin

'A day as bright and colourful as the night was black and eerie. Students pour in before first bell, talking, laughing. They could be from anywhere in America, but for the extremity of their dress and the esoteric mania of their slang. This is definitely So Cal'

> Joss Whedon, shooting script for 'Welcome to the Hellmouth' (1.1)[1]

'Through the centre, winding from left to right, was a long hill street and down it, spilling into the middle foreground, came the mob carrying baseball bats and torches. For the faces of its members, he was using the innumerable sketches he had made of the people who come to California to die; the cultists of all sorts, economic as well as religious, the wave, aeroplane, funeral and preview watchers, all those poor devils who can only be stirred by the promise of miracles and then only to violence'

> Nathanael West, *The Day of the Locust*, 1939[2]

I

Rupert Giles, ironically nostalgic for the grey skies of his English home, pretends to find the endless sunshine of Southern California terribly boring. For once, appearances deceive the watchful Librarian. Through much of the last century, screenwriters, novelists and critics have relished an exemplary contrast between the relentless glare of the weather and the deep darkness and perpetual turbulence of the region's reputed moral climate.

Here, as nowhere else on the planet, twentieth-century culture indulged its taste for didactic dualism. In 'So Cal' shines the blinding light that hides sinister secrets. The blessed landscape is a playground that doubles as a killing-field, the golden home of laid-back hedonism and deranged 'esoteric mania' alike. This phoney paradise (and paradise for phoneys) may mutate, at any moment, into a sudden inferno. Bertolt Brecht, dismayed by his joyless Hollywood exile, recalled Shelley's comparison of Hell with London, and decided that, on balance, 'it must be/ Still more like Los Angeles'.[3]

Buffy the Vampire Slayer unfolds in a somewhere that pretends to be nowhere (which is what 'Utopia' originally means). Sunnydale stands, as Joss Whedon has remarked, somewhere close to Santa Barbara and it shows.

The scripts' allusive and sophisticated blend of teen soap and Gothic fantasia gives a fresh, and quite distinctive, twist to a strain of Southern Californian suburban noir that has flourished at least since the 1930s. The disillusioned studio hack Nathanael West was dreaming and writing of the incineration of LA in 1937 (also, as it happens, when the action of Roman Polanski's film *Chinatown* takes place). Buffy's followers will need no reminding that, in that year, The Master's blocked eruption into the sunshine of human society almost did for So Cal once and for all.

Forget it, Jake; it's Vampiretown

Angel, the spin-off series, draws rather more explicitly on the cultural mythology of Los Angeles, and its expression in landmarks of hard-boiled crime fiction and film. One can easily imagine Raymond Chandler's Philip Marlowe, Walter Mosley's Easy Rawlins or James Ellroy's Lieutenant Dudley Smith tussling with the supernaturally crooked, blood-sucking lawyers of Wolfram and Hart. Indeed, Ellroy even begins his acclaimed sequence of LA thrillers (in *The Big Nowhere*) with a teasingly vampiric touch, when a corpse turns out to bear mystifying teeth-marks 'too large for a human mouth biting straight down'.[4] In a later LA novel, *White Jazz*, the showbiz floozie Gilda manages to wrap a disparate set of Californian nightmares into a single package when she works on a movie called 'Attack of the Atomic Vampires'. As the Librarian himself has said, 'this world is older than any of you know, and contrary to popular mythology, it did not begin as a paradise' – 'The Harvest' (1.2).

Once in charge of Angel Investigations, our tormented vampire-with-a-soul may have to tramp those mean sewers rather than the sunbaked streets, but his lineage as a private dick is strongly signposted. His rivals boast comparable pedigrees: the ruthless zombie cops in 'The Thin Dead Line' (A2.14) bring to mind the moody precinct warriors of Joseph Wambaugh's LAPD thrillers on a particularly bad day. Earlier in that series, Angel drops into the Hyperion Hotel for the flagrant 1950s pastiche of 'Are You Now or Have You Ever Been?' (A2.2). Here, the persecuting demons of paranoia remind us that Chandler, Ellroy, Mosley and their fellow princes of LA noir grapple not just with high-society crooks and sleazy cops but also with the subterranean powers of Joseph McCarthy and the House Unamerican Activities Committee. 'They feed me their worst, and I kinda serve it right back to them,' chortles the paranoia demon, Thesulac.

Indeed, aspects of the two *Angel* series can sometimes recall a sort of underground theme-park of Californian hard-boiled style. Readers of Thomas Pynchon will recall that, when the novelist wrote his own satirical fantasia on the restless spirits of California in *Vineland*, he actually created a Noir Centre in lower Hollywood, where one could purchase furniture from the Lounge Good Buy, perfume and cosmetics at the Mall Tease Flacon and designer water at Bubble Indemnity.[5] Angel has yet to slide that far into regional burlesque.

Yet I would argue that the blander, brighter locales of *Buffy* itself make it more evocative because of more indirect use of the idio-syncrasies of nature and culture in Southern California. Over time, Buffy and her Scooby Gang confront and overcome most of their significant secrets. Yet the question of where they, precisely, stand in Sunnydale often stays tantalisingly below the surface. The commercial and demographic imperative to be all things to all teens (at least in the US) means that the series often can't, in the most literal sense, tell us where it's coming from. Joss Whedon and his fellow-writers often stress the role of demons and monsters as embodiments of psychic states, or even intellectual tendencies. (He has, for instance, spoken of Angel as a version of the recovering alcoholic.) But why should these fancy beasts of the unconscious not possess an unconscious of their own as costumed markers of a distinctive, and distinctively dangerous, time and place?

II

Buffy rings the changes on Southern California's bad dreams. Its range of reference (virtually the entire corpus of Gothic narrative, plus the broad Far Western edge of contemporary youth culture) surpasses any models or forerunners. And, in two specific areas, it adds new resources to the rich local repertoire of myth and metaphor. These concern the shifting nature of danger and disaster on the Pacific coast: first, as a hotspot of environmental tumult and calamity; and second, as a focus for human mischief contrived by creatures at either extreme of the social scale.

A frequent commonplace of So Cal literature portrays the place as a climatic (and geophysical) wolf in sheep's clothing. The landscape looks and feels young, benign, innocent. In truth, the earth below, the skies above and the seas beyond secrete their ancient and imperishable powers of flood, fire, storm and (most notoriously) earthquake. 'Easterners commonly complain,' writes that expert watcher of So Cal's inner demons, Joan Didion, 'that the days and weeks slip by relentlessly, numbingly bland. That is quite misleading. In fact, the climate is characterised by infrequent and violent extremes.'[6] Sudden calamities strike the coast and hinterland, some predictable (tellingly, the fire-raising Santa Ana winds blow in the weeks around Halloween) but many apparently random, and all the more fearful as a result: 'Los Angeles weather is the weather of catastrophe, of apocalypse.'[7] In the wake of the San Francisco earthquake and fire of 1906, one potential event spread from California to enter global myth: the idea of the Big One, a forever-imminent displacement of the San Andreas fault that will send the urban Far West to its long-awaited and (in some accounts) long-deserved perdition.

Buffy's adopted town, of course, has its own original fault and its own memories and dreams of catastrophe. The thin membrane of the 'Boca del Infierno', the unstable portal between the human and demonic worlds that lies beneath the library at Sunnydale High, transforms a geological fact into the premise of fantastic drama. What anthropologists would call the liminal status of Sunnydale and its residents shifts the tectonic status quo into an endlessly resonant metaphor.

Sunnydale remembers, endures or fears its own one-off catastrophes. In the show's prehistory, The Master's attempt to regain the surface of the earth was accompanied by a severe earthquake that flattened half the town. This was not quite the Big One, of course: the Master's plan misfired, with the senior vampire ignominiously stuck, since 'opening dimensional portals is a tricky business' ('The Harvest' (1.2)). Yet the very idea of the Harvest when all Hell really will break loose and 'come to town' preserves the concept of a very rare, but somehow inevitable, terminal event.

Earthquakes are not the only endemic terrors of Los Angeles and the surrounding counties which *Buffy* re-locates onto the supernatural plane. Giles remarks that the Harvest 'comes once in a century'. A conscientious Watcher and Slayer can reasonably plan, if not for its exact timing or location, then at least for its overall incidence. Do Californian engineers watch *Buffy*? If so, all this will sound spookily familiar to them.

For the creation of populous So Cal as an island of abundance in an unstable semi-desert ecology depends entirely on a series of calculations about the frequency of catastrophic events. The mighty dams and irrigation networks devised by William Mulholland, that Godfather (or Master) of the interwar Californian boom, rested on the assumption of an extreme flood once every century. This 'hundred-year event' might end the bliss of sunny suburban dales not in a 'harvest', but an inundation. And yet this ominous meteorological hypothesis, on which much of So Cal hopefully stands, came to pass not once but twice within the single decade after 1955.[8]

Mike Davis, the cultural historian of Southern California whose work opens the portal between places on the map and places in the mind, introduces us to the chilling notion of 'disaster deficit'. Geological probability suggests that the area has suffered fewer natural calamities than it should have done over the past century. 'Recent research on past climatic change and seismic activity,' Davis reports, 'has transformed the question "why so many recent disasters?" into the truly unnerving question, "why so few?" Put another way, twentieth-century Los Angeles has been capitalised on sheer gambler's luck'.[9]

Buffy energetically makes up that deficit. Its regular commuter traffic of monsters and demons surges through the thin crust of the new suburbs to bring mayhem and threaten annihilation. Some of these entities clearly harbour ambitions to be, or at least to provoke, the Big One. Acathla, notably, tried to swallow the entire world with one demonic breath but was buried 'where neither man nor demon would be wont to look. Unless, of course, they're putting up low-rent housing' ('Becoming Part 1' (2.21)).

Yet, on reflection, *Buffy*'s bestiary of the underworld is memorable less for its heavyweight apocalyptic talent than for its capacity to generate interminable, medium-level annoyance. As the week-by-week, season-by-season rhythm of the television series demands, those demons just keep on breaking through. And plenty of them seem more vandalistic than strictly millenarian: the face-chewing Gavrok spiders, say, or the Hellhounds with their grungy antipathy to formal wear. Yes, the ground beneath the Slayer's feet can still shake in traditional fashion. And when it does, awful events will certainly impend, as in 'Doomed' (4.11).

All the same, the prevailing business at Sunnydale High and, later, Sunnydale University is a form of reactive crisis management. Davis, whose work reads uncannily well as a sort of real-world translation of the supernatural disturbances in *Buffy*, has pointed out that constant, low-intensity disruption is replacing fears of a final tremor in Californian life. The Northridge earthquake outside Los Angeles in 1994, combined with a rising incidence of extreme weather events, helped replace terror of a single Big One with expectation of recurrent Middling Ones.

Fire, flood and drought (abetted, in 2001, by the purely human disaster of power-cuts) now induce rumbling paranoia rather than once-for-all fits of panic. And one new peril has arisen as rampant urbanization stretches the 'wild edge' of Southern California to encircle and confine the local wildlife. Towns very like Sunnydale may, for the first time in the history of settlement, find themselves plagued by attacks on humans from coyotes and mountain lions. The 'freak' event has become a semi-regular occurrence, as legendary monsters stalk the affluent tracts. Unexpected daily demons now shadow the suburban dream.

In *Buffy*, primal creatures such as the reluctant werewolf Oz, or the hyena folk who snack on Principal Flutie in 'The Pack' (1.6), often prompt discussions about the Beast in Man and the animal passions that beat within civilized breasts. Yet, remarkably, wealthy communities in the Sunnydale mould have, during the 1990s, faced actual danger to life and limb from real cougars, real bears, real packs of feral coyotes. To the horror of residents and authorities, carnivorous predators on suburban streets transgress 'the essentially imaginary boundary between the human and the wild'.[10] This being So Cal, there is now a support and therapy group for survivors of mountain-lion attacks. Fancifully witty as they always are, the writers' team for *Buffy* might hesitate before they ever made that up.

In the mid-1990s, the Hispanic population of the state thrilled, half in earnest, half in jest, to the urban myth of the vampire of Chupacabra. This fearsome being allegedly drained dogs and goats of every drop of blood in short order. First 'described' in Puerto Rico, the goat-sucker appeared 'just like the devil four or five feet tall with red eyes and a hideous forked tongue'. In Latino suburbs around LA, 'some people locked themselves in their houses and refused to send their children to school' while many others chuckled and cheerfully embroidered the rumour.[11] As a plotline, it seems tailor-made for *Buffy* except that *The X-Files* managed to purloin it first.

III

Threats to suburban well-being can take human form as well, of course. Here, the demonology of *Buffy* comes closer to the murky mainstream of Californian noir. In social terms, the danger emanates both from below and from above. From below, it has periodically taken the form of gang warfare: a staple of Southern Californian reality since the 1940s, and of wider legend since the 1970s, when the Crips and Bloods of South Central Los Angeles first won national notoriety. In fact, the first postwar gangs of LA and its environs often wreaked their small-time havoc in high schools. Their fights and rackets accompanied the stresses of local class and racial conflict. One white-supremacist group of the 1950s, active around the time that California's schools desegregated, actually called itself the Spook-hunters.[12]

Inevitably, Spike and his testosterone-fuelled vampire mates often strut their stuff in gang-like guises. "Three bad-ass gang types hang out on a deserted corner,' runs David Greenwalt's shooting script for 'Angel' (1.7). 'You wouldn't want to meet any of them on a dark street or a sunny one'.[13] The school and street gangs of above-ground LA became a trigger for national panic only when their Black and Latino variants grew conspicuously larger and tougher than the rest. In general, *Buffy* refuses to encode its infernal crews with a clear racial identity, a sign of its writers' self-aware approach to the real-world reverberations of caricature in genre art.

After surveying 138 depictions of the destruction of Los Angeles in film and fiction since 1908, Mike Davis concluded that 'white fear of the dark races lies at the heart of such visions (with the sardonic critique of cults and fringe culture coming in a distant second)'.[14] Among these apocalyptic works, 'monsters' or 'alien hordes' did away with LA on 20 occasions; only earthquakes (with 28) and nuclear warfare (49) managed a higher score. In contrast, a pretty average assassin's fraternity in *Buffy*, such as the Order of Taraka, will look like a model of multicultural inclusiveness. Its deadly ranks welcome all sorts of human and demonic malefactors – 'What's My Line Parts 1 and 2' (2.9 and 2.10) – even the aesthetically-challenged Mr Pfister, who is made up entirely of maggots.

Yet the most exhilarating *Buffy* scripts sometimes confront genre cliches and typologies face on, rather than tiptoeing around them. And the ethnic marking of a demonic troublemaker becomes exuberantly in-your-face (even over-the-top) in the figure of the African-American vampire hoodlum, Mr Trick in 'Faith, Hope and Trick' (3.3). This undead homeboy, come straight outta Hell and Compton to organize the 'Slayerfest', rather labours the obvious when he points out that Buffy's textbook 'white flight' neighbourhood is 'not a haven for the brothers, strictly the Caucasian persuasion in the Dale but you gotta stand up and salute their death rate'. Indeed you have. Funnily enough, the most homicidal community in Southern California turns out to be not Compton, Watts or any other infamous inner-city wilderness, but the classic (if decayed) 'bungalow suburb' of Pomona. In this ruined idyll, 'since 1970 nearly 1 per cent of the population has been murdered'.[15]

Yet the greatest menace to society always comes from creatures a lot further up the scale of human (and demonic) privilege. Mr Trick eventually goes to work for Richard Wilkins III, Mayor of Sunnydale for 100 years and the superbly depraved heir to a vast literary and cinematic canon of corrupt officials in the state of California. The Mayor, indeed, has a goal for his municipal villainy that rather puts the traditional West Coast pursuit of bribes, land and girls in the shade, ascension to the status of a pure demon.

Warner Brothers, the network which until April 2001 owned *Buffy*, illustrated the mischievous way in which the show's creators connect dark fantasy to daylight reality when they pulled transmission of the Mayor's big moment in 'Graduation Day Part 2' (3.22). Ostensibly, the postponement came about because the episode's scenes of wholesale destruction on a high-school campus chimed uneasily with fears of classroom carnage perpetrated by rifle-toting, Goth-clad teens. Fans, however, quickly spotted a WB publicity stunt. They asked, reasonably enough, how many elected officials had recently metamorphosed into 60-foot demon serpents during high-school ceremonials.

The incident reminds us that, though *Buffy* can indeed be read in the light of an underlying social truth, it is also a clever and knowing enough enterprise to be able to mock (in this case, preemptively) its own more pedestrian analysts. The Mayor (who is also, incidentally, an avatar of 'Richard III') does not act alone in his century-long devotion to the powers of Hell. Running allusions to a malign conspiracy of local notables, including Bob the police chief and, inevitably, Principal Snyder, draw on every confidential tale of skullduggery in high places to have emerged from LA and its hinterland since Philip Marlowe first trod its streets.

And one customary tactic of all such plotters is to blame every dark deed on the disorganised crime of the nearest underclass. 'I'll need to say something for the media,' pleads Sheriff Bob after a vampire raid on the Parent-Teacher Evening. 'Usual Story? Gang-related, PCP?' in 'School Hard' (2.3).

After the Mayor's transfiguration, and the blitzing of Sunnydale High, the motif of élite conspiracy moves to the sinister Initiative. This demon-hunting, federally-funded programme turns out to be promoting its own, much more infernal agenda. Its crack team of tooled-up law-enforcers gradually emerge as champion law-breakers in hi-tech disguise. Professor Maggie Walsh's Frankenstein-flavoured creation of the monster 'Adam', and his projected hybrid army of 'demonoids', are scheduled to fight a final battle between the powers of sunshine and of night: 'the war that no one can win' in 'Who are you?' (4.16). Well-funded, lavishly equipped, secretive and ruthless, the Initiative has affinities of style and method with the technology-driven 'wars' on gangs and drugs that helped undermine the social peace of Southern California in the 1980s and early 1990s. Bankrolled by populist politicians, and often led by an out-of-control Los Angeles Police Department, these initiatives sailed under minatory acronyms such as HAMMER and GRATS. They licensed an explosive mixture of condign violence, street harassment, provocation and entrapment (for example, by sending undercover 'drug dealers' into schools). Predictably, they also hastened LA's most recent dress rehearsal for a purely human Armageddon: the pandemic rioting and looting that followed the LAPD assault on Rodney King in May 1992.

Since the 1950s, the Department has pioneered the research and application of high-tech policing methods in pursuit of 'pathbreaking substitutions of technological capital for patrol manpower'.[16] Senior officers fashioned their force not as sweaty neighbourhood beat-pounders, but as remote and well-armed avengers: as Marines, in fact (a term also used to describe the Initiative's soldiers). As for the street-level targets of their hardware and hubris, the war on drugs came to mean that 'every non-Anglo teenager in Southern California is now a prisoner of gang paranoia and associated demonology'.[17]

Demonology, indeed.

IV

Buffy, as I have argued, hangs out with the undead, struggles against her demons and endures a multiply haunted adolescence in a some-where that purports to be nowhere. In addition to an encyclopaedic repertoire of allusion to fantasy and horror genres, *Buffy* draws more covertly on local sources, notably, the physical and social threats to peace and prosperity that lurk on the shadow-side of the Southern Californian dream. *Buffy* taps into the rich vein of anxiety which imagines this balmy civilization as not merely cosmetic, but positively fraudulent. Built on lies or evasions about its safety and permanence, this lotus-eating bliss must periodically fray to reveal the darker continuities beneath. 'No other place,' admonishes Marc Reisner, historian of California's perennial water wars, 'has put as many people where they probably have no business being'.[18]

Its superficial bounty, in other words, stems from a fundamental act of trespass. In *Buffy*, the recurrent challenges to the pursuit of happiness posed by monsters, demons and vampires mimic this So Cal predicament. A surface mood of blithe optimism is tempered by constant, worried vigilance. To adapt the old Austro-Hungarian quip, the current situation in mythical Sunnydale as much as in its real, opulent but water-deficient neighbour, Santa Barbara can often be desperate but not serious.

Interestingly, Buffy herself makes this prevailing temper explicit when she grasps that the Vahrall demons represent a clear and present danger to the future of the planet: 'I said "end of the world," and you're all like, pooh pooh. Southern California pooh pooh' –

'Doomed' (4.11). Here, Giles has to remind the blasé, seen-it-all-before Scooby Gang that Armageddon will probably entail more than a little local nuisance: 'Hell itself flows into our lives like a sea of fire'. It's a striking image, as that 'sea of fire' has sometimes taken more than a metaphorical shape around those parts. At Halloween 1993, a sudden forest conflagration swept by the Santa Ana winds made short work of the ocean-front millionaire mansions of Malibu. One witness to this high tide of flame anticipated the peculiar climate and language of the Buffyverse very exactly. 'This is Hell, dude,' he told the *Los Angeles Times*. 'I'm expecting to see Satan come out any time now'.[19]

In some respects, *Buffy* breaks away from the Gothic tradition with which it so deliriously plays. It masks, or allegorizes, few of its abiding themes. To take the most glaring example: vampires can hardly function as merely an erotic, Freudian 'return of the repressed' in a context that foregrounds sexual desire in such an endearingly matter-of-fact way. Unlike many of its models, the series has very little to hide. As Giles says on one occasion, 'I believe the subtext here is rapidly becoming text' ('Ted' (2.11)). Rather, the fantastic machinery of *Buffy* works so well because the hard truths that may be swiftly said, about sex, power, parents, identity, community still have to be imagined with a force and depth that more realistic popular art will seldom match.

The show does all that, and more. But one can still suggest that it contains one semi-occluded terrain of hints, nuances and even disguises. This area belongs, precisely, to Southern California: to the specific somewhere that must be translated into a generic nowhere for the series to stake its claim as a national, now international, cult success. In time, even the strong local signal of Valley Girl slang, with its 'esoteric mania', begins to sound like, so much the routine argot of trend-hopping teens in the US and beyond. Yet traces of a peculiar place, with a peculiar physical and social geography, do rupture the surface. Like the demons themselves, they may burst unbidden through the flimsy portal of the Boca del Infierno.

'This is definitely So Cal,' as Joss Whedon wrote: forever the land of uprooted incomers, who in the case of *Buffy* include Celtic vampires, who might once have fed in Anne Rice's New Orleans, and the ancient, malignant 'Old Ones' blown in from H.P. Lovecraft's *New England*. 'In spite of all the healthful sunshine and ocean breezes,' wrote Louis Adamic (the social critic, and a real Slavic immigrant to Southern California), 'it is a bad place full of old, dying people, who were born of old, tired pioneer parents, victims of America full of curious, wild and poisonous growths, decadent religious cults and fake science, a jungle.'[20]

Even the wilfully eclectic modes of supernatural style in *Buffy* can be seen as a So Cal trademark just as the region's vernacular architecture may famously shunt Spanish Mission next to Scots Baronial next to Bauhaus Streamlined, lot by lot and cheek by jowl. Kevin Starr, state librarian of California and its *de facto* official historian, stresses the state's hunger for a recreated past rather than its flight from the old world. 'Let others speak of California, Los Angeles especially, as the erasure of memory,' he recently wrote. Just as characteristic is 'the persistence of memory on this far American shore, the way California hungered for history and orthodoxy along with a sense of new beginnings.'[21]

You can, of course, hunger for ancient heterodoxy as well: the Goth cult among schoolkids caught on in So Cal earlier than anywhere else. In summer 1997, police arrested many teenage Goths for drug offences at night in the Disneyworld park at Anaheim. 'It's a great way to get out of the house,' a young friend of the fanged told the *LA Times*.[22]

Buffy flies, I would maintain, the double flag of Southern California: on the one hand, a far-reaching cultural eclecticism and, on the other, a stubborn bedrock of sheer natural wildness and terror. 'Gingerbread' (3.11), written by series co-producer Jane Espenson, deftly grafts the German Gothic figures of Hansel and Gretel onto an up-to-the-minute scare about child abuse and ritual magic. Driven to paranoid hysteria by the demon who has adopted these eerie children as his guise, Joyce Summers and other Sunnydale moms found Mothers Opposed to the Occult. Their ill-fated campaign emulates the moral panics that have swept large tracts of affluent suburbia over the past decade, especially, perhaps, the long-running McMartin Preschool case in Southern California, when day-care centres stood accused of mass 'satanic' rituals. At the McMartin trial, 'children testified about molester-teachers who flew around on broomsticks, and other manifestations of the evil one.'[23]

Yet underneath the 'Gingerbread' witch-hunt, with its mingled flavour of borrowed folklore and headline news, Jane Espenson envisaged another force, an inchoate, primeval demon of chaos. Below social morality and collective paranoia, nature itself seethes in a distinctly So Cal way with a blind urge towards breakdown and mayhem. 'The world is full of disorder,' Espenson has said. 'Human beings are constantly trying to bring it into some semblance of order, and the world fights back. Disorder became demonised, as if it were an actual entity against which we struggle. Entropy as demon. I think that's why so many of our demons have that function. They just want to get in and mess things up.'[24] 'The world fights back': it's a pretty serviceable motto for anyone who watches *Buffy*, or who lives in Southern California.

Notes

1. *Buffy the Vampire Slayer, Script Book: Season One, Volume One* (New York, 2000), p.9.
2. *The Collected Works of Nathanael West* (London, 1969), p.153.
3. Bertolt Brecht, 'On thinking about Hell', in *Poems 1913–1956*, ed. John Willett and Ralph Manheim (London, 1994), p.367.
4. James Ellroy, *The Big Nowhere* (London, 1990), p.9.
5. Thomas Pynchon, *Vineland* (London, 1990), p.326.
6. Joan Didion, 'Los Angeles Notebook' in *Slouching Towards Bethlehem* (London, 1993), p.219.
7. Ibid, p.221.

8. Marc Reisner, *Cadillac Desert: The American West and its disappearing water* (London, 2001), p.358.

9. Mike Davis, *Ecology of Fear: Los Angeles and the imagination of disaster* (London, 1999), p.37.

10. Ibid, p.208.

11. Ibid, p.271.

12. Mike Davis, *City of Quartz: Excavating the future in Los Angeles* (New York, 1992), p.293.

13. *Buffy the Vampire Slayer, Script Book: Season One, Volume Two* (New York, 2000), p.6.

14. Mike Davis, *Ecology of Fear*, p.281.

15. Ibid, p.398.

16. Mike Davis, *City of Quartz*, p.251.

17. Ibid, p.284.

18 Marc Reisner, *Cadillac Desert*, p.333.

19. Quoted in Mike Davis, *Ecology of Fear*, p.127.

20. Quoted in Mike Davis, *City of Quartz*, p.36.

21. Kevin Starr, 'The Musso and Frank Grill in Hollywood', in William E Leuchtenberg (ed), *American Place: Encounters with history* (New York, 2001), p.291.

22. Quoted in Richard Davenport-Hines, *Gothic: Four hundred years of excess, horror, evil and ruin* (London, 1998), p.355.

23. Mike Davis, *Ecology of Fear*, p.386.

24. Jane Espenson, interviewed in Christopher Golden, Stephen R Bissette and Thomas E Sniegoski, *Buffy the Vampire Slayer: The monster book* (New York, 2000), p.39.

vampire dialectics

knowledge, institutions and labour

brian wall and michael zryd

Buffy and *Angel* can be, and often are, consumed as if the supernatural elements were merely intensified teen love traumas or noir menaces. But as the insightfully laconic Oz suggests, 'a radical interpretation of the text' – 'Doppelgangland' (3.16) – is not only possible but necessary. These shows, seemingly based in fantasy, both strive to understand the real and to offer suggestions for change. We are asked to care about the inequalities of power in Sunnydale High and Sunnydale University, about the machinations of the evil Mayor, about the insidious military-industrial complex served by Maggie Walsh, about the corrupt law firm Wolfram and Hart, because they reflect our lived experience in the late industrial world.

Ultimately, these characters and institutions possess mythic force because they mirror reality, not because they contradict it. This is a world in which knowledge is power and all too often the wrong people are in control of both. Both shows suggest a radical utopian alternative: a non-alienated way of working together, of bringing various sorts of experience, knowledge, talent and ability together without exploitation and for the common good.

Regimes of knowledge in *Buffy* and *Angel*

The theme of knowledge takes a number of different forms in *Buffy* and *Angel*. First, educational institutions (high school and university) are the primary settings for *Buffy*, bringing characters together to a home base. In the first three seasons of *Buffy*, the gang converges in the Sunnydale High School library; in the fourth season, now ex-librarian Rupert Giles's apartment becomes the *de facto* meeting place for the collective, before shifting to the Magic Box, Giles's foray into small business. In both shows, schools, libraries, archives and laboratories function as crucial sites wherein the ideological conflicts dramatized in *Buffy* and *Angel* play out.

Second, in both shows, the characters consistently conduct research by consulting both the *arcana* of dusty tomes and computer/internet data. The 'hard knowledge' of books is associated with tradition (including pre-capitalist medieval and ancient texts) and with older British male characters like Giles and Wesley, originally from the UK-based Watcher's Council. This hard knowledge exists alongside the 'soft knowledge' of computers, which is associated with modernity and with young American female characters like Willow, Cordelia and Miss Calendar. Both hard and soft knowledge are valued by the collective, although they often seem to be in conflict, with 'hard' tradition usually resisting 'soft' modernity. But both hard and soft knowledge can take negative form when used by institutions, eg, the Watcher's Council, the Mayor's bureaucracy, the Initiative's laboratory and Wolfram & Hart's law office.

Third, knowledge is the product of labour and, unlike much else in the shows, is not 'magical.' That is, knowledge results from *work*, from the research and collective experience of the characters. When Willow innocently asks Giles in Season One of *Buffy*, 'How is it you always know this stuff? You always know what's going on. I never know what's going on.' Giles looks up from his book and responds, 'Well, you weren't here from midnight until six researching it.' (1.07)

Indeed, this intellectual labour – and pleasure seems necessary to endorse another form of labour and pleasure: the violence meted out to forces of evil. The collectives on both shows first engage in research through a variety of methods (both ancient texts and computer/internet) and in a variety of social spaces, including the on-the-street research of the film noir/detective genre referenced in *Angel,* often demonstrating a subversive knowledge of the institutions they contest. *Via* research, the violence they subsequently enact on their enemies – another form of labour – is 'earned'.

Institutional knowledge and categories of villainy and heroism

Villainy in *Buffy* and *Angel* is consistently associated with hierarchical institutions that, over the five years of the show's evolving allegorical universe, take on more and more explicitly modern and covert institutional configurations. In the first season, the Master and his short-lived Anointed One are *Buffy's* villains, controlling a troupe of vampires who slavishly worship and sacrifice themselves to the Master's authority. Confined to torch-lit underground caverns, the Master is associated with ancient, pre-modern power, hierarchical, even archeological in its mise-en-scène.

In the second season, Spike and Drusilla appear, aligned briefly with a newly evil Angelus (Angel's pure vampire side). Spike is the only arch-villain to survive a season and become a major recurring character, significant for the fact that his villainy is more anarchic than institutional: his ascendance is self-announced with his arbitrary assassination of the Anointed One: 'From now on, we're gonna have a little less ritual and a little more fun around here' – 'School Hard' (2.3). Meanwhile, minor villains like Principal Snyder, who abuses his institutional authority at Sunnydale High School, and the intimations of corruption in the upper levels of the Sunnydale municipal hierarchy eventually point to a new institutionally-installed villain for Season Three: the Mayor. (Notably, the Mayor, although he is given a proper name, Richard Wilkins, is like the Master in being addressed mainly by his institutional title).

The Mayor's eventual defeat coincides with the destruction of the high school itself, suggesting the higher stakes and increasingly anarchic politics of the show. Not coincidentally, broadcast of two episodes of *Buffy* in Season Three were delayed as they coincided with real-life high school violence (especially the Columbine school massacre in 1999).

In *Buffy*'s fourth season, the institutional quality of villainy is even more pointed, and achieves much greater scale and modern substance in the Initiative, significantly housed under the University, the next stage after high school in 'knowledge production.' A condensation of amoral science and technology (figured by Professor Walsh) and the government-military-industrial complex, the Initiative concocts a Frankenstein monster in the figure of Adam. On *Angel*, whose first season coincided with the appearance of the Initiative on *Buffy*, the main villain continues to be an institution, Wolfram & Hart, the 'law' firm with demonic senior partners who seek to organize and protect the otherwise presupposed villainy of urban space in Los Angeles (and Hollywood).

If, in the story-world of both shows, villainy is constantly associated with institutions, evil is expressed more deeply through the way that institutions reduce human being to cogs in the machine, reduce human beings to instruments that further their goals. The villains in *Buffy* and *Angel* have totalizing and apocalyptic goals, especially nihilism, the desire for nothingness.

In the second season of *Buffy*, when Angel-turned-Angelus seeks literally to plunge the human world into hell, he is ultimately resisted by Spike who, while evil, nonetheless is enough of a hedonist to enjoy the pleasures of the human sphere (sex, drugs and rock 'n 'roll). Angelus is a wholly negative force seeking the annihilation of human and demon worlds alike.

On the second season of *Angel*, soul-restored Angel is manipulated by Wolfram & Hart, through his guilt and obsession with Darla, to the point of non-demonic nihilism: he abandons the collective (firing

Wesley, Cordelia and Gunn) and attempts suicidally to destroy Wolfram & Hart. Before his subsequent epiphany – a realization that to regain his 'path', he must accept the humble necessity of small 'good works' – he sought the totalizing moral solutions of revenge and obliteration (of Wolfram & Hart) and redemption (of Darla).

Adam is another villain who embodies a critique of institutional knowledge, and demonstrates *Buffy* and *Angel*'s condensation of the way that questions of knowledge and questions of good and evil are interrelated. Although created by an institution, Adam extends the Initiative's inherently destructive logic to such an extreme that he destroys the institution itself – produced by vivisection, he applies reductiveness to everything. Yet there are things he cannot understand: muttering 'Interesting', he is disassembled by the *uber*Buffy *gestalt*, who tells him 'You can never understand the source of our power' – 'Primeval' (4.21).

Interestingly, Adam's clarity and almost zen-like sense of self make him invulnerable, when in 'Superstar' (4.17), the entire show's reality, including its credits, is reconfigured to make a minor character, Jonathan, suddenly the star and dominant character . . . Jonathan's magic, by playing with knowledge/reality, splits him between a (false) all-powerful 'good' self and a counterbalancing, and equally powerful evil demon-doppelganger: in the universe of *Buffy* and *Angel*, epistemological categories are inextricably tied to moral and ethical ones.

Morally ambivalent characters – those positioned between the good (but fallible) collective and the villains – combine a provocative mixture of ethics and anarchy. As mentioned above, the only villains who have survived on the show are those with more allegiance to chaos than to institutional or totalizing evil. Spike and Harmony are given a shot at redemption and rehabilitation, whereas those characters aligned to institutions are, more often than not, those who have literally – sold their souls. Rigid order is associated with instrumental rationality. Drusilla is the most chaotic character, figured as both insane and guided by her 'gift' of prophesy and premonition. She disappears from the show until Wolfram & Hart's attempt to harness her power backfires upon the room of lawyers massacred by her and Darla.

Darla, Faith and Lindsey, meanwhile, appear as villains periodically troubled by ethical doubts. Too lacking in social responsibility to be (thus far) included in the collective, they nonetheless wrestle with the consequences of their actions when faced with clear personal dilemmas. Crucially, these character's self-involved motivations make them subject to manipulation by villainous institutions. Darla's anger at (and masochistic love for) Angel motivate her manipulations of him at Wolfram & Hart's behest. Faith's emotional insecurity – a consequence of childhood neglect and institutional abuse at the hand of her Watchers – leads her to work for both the Mayor and Wolfram & Hart. Her apotheosis follows yet another gesture of suicidal nihilism: she fights Angel so that he will be forced to kill her to put her out of her ethical misery.

Lindsey's lower-class roots motivate his interpellation by Wolfram & Hart – who are clever enough to harness the imagination and risk-taking ferocity that his ethical ambivalence and class-based self-loathing generate. His final rejection of them occurs only when he comes face-to-face with those people who have been literally harvested for body parts on his behalf – a commodified version of the Adam narrative – as part of his quest for promotion on the corporate ladder. That Lindsey learns that he personally knows the man whose hand he 'purchases' through his services to Wolfram & Hart, and that he is forced to kill him to put him out of his misery, underlines how the episode foregrounds the usually invisible costs of corporate perks. Like a Nike sales rep forced to oversee the child labourer who manufactures sneakers in Malaysia, Lindsey can only understand ethical consequences in personal terms, as the so-called 'invisible hand of the market' is given a human dimension, becoming the 'evil hand.' He is more motivated by individualism than ethics – he could never, for instance, work in a collective – but his individualism distinguishes him from the dull conformity of other

Wolfram & Hart employees, as his farewell 'evil hand' speech suggests.

The positive representation of chaotic anti-institutional and anti-totalizing logic is also expressed in relation to the heroic, 'good' characters. Crucially, none of them are figured as paragons of morality, as *Buffy* and *Angel* prefer to push conflicts into ethical domains rather than overarching moralistic combat. Although the shows clearly differentiate between 'good guys' and 'bad guys,' following its genre tradition of action melodrama, its heroes are not crusaders inhabiting a moral high ground. Their 'missions' are remarkably passive and reactive: the *Buffy* gang patrols for vampires and demons but does not have a grand plan to eradicate evil. The *Angel* crew must await visions sent to Doyle and then Cordelia by the Powers That Be; indeed, when Angel goes on the offensive against Wolfram & Hart, or thinks he can defeat them utterly, he falls into the destructive nihilism which threatens the collective and their capacity to do any 'good.'

In short, heroism is not defined as a grand quest to eliminate evil, but rather an existential determination to fight it, 'to help the helpless,' as the Angel detective agency motto proclaims. Thus, although *Buffy/Angel* imagines a utopian collective of non-alienated labour, it does not, in its narrative universe, presume to imagine a moral utopia itself – a failure which notably mimics modernity itself. Both shows have increasingly represented their narrative universes as chaotic, mixed worlds in which human and demon coexist in uneasy tension and ethical choices must continuously be renegotiated.

Heroism and the powers of 'good' are consistently presented in non-monumental and anti-hierarchical forms. The mysterious Powers That Be – represented on *Angel* by Greco-Roman oracular servants – are unpredictable, non-moralizing authorities who function as chaotic guards against evil forces and whose ambiguous and ambivalent grace is as cruel as it is poetic – eg, the snowfall which prevents Angel's self-immolation in the sun in 'Amends' (3.10).

Although the self-conscious and even reflexive use of irony, sarcasm, and word-play on *Buffy* and *Angel* are attributable to the genre of teen comedy-drama, the use of irony and bathos function on another level to contrast with the way forces of evil on both shows are given stuffy, arrogant, monumental and institutionalized form. This 'serious irony' distinguishes *Buffy/Angel* from both the high seriousness of such allegorical science fiction television as *Star Trek* and *The X-Files* and from camp melodrama like *Xena: Warrior Princess*.

Knowledge and authority

On *Buffy,* the loose collective of friends (Buffy, Willow, Xander), lovers (Oz, Tara), and ex-enemies (Spike, Riley, Anya, Angel/Angelus, even Cordelia) centres on Buffy and Giles, the benign, fallible, struggling adult who ethically and emotionally wrestles with his own dark side, 'Ripper'. The collective (self-ironically named the Scooby Gang) has no leader, although Buffy and Giles generally function as such. Their authority, however, becomes increasingly non-institutional. Giles's authority is based on his knowledge and experience rather than his hierarchical position. His authority in the collective comes from his learned knowledge, reasoned judgement and emotional maturity. Meanwhile his British sense of cultural superiority and occasional bouts of self-righteous anger – and those moments in the first few seasons when he exerted his executive authority as Buffy's Watcher – are consistently undercut.

Buffy, as the anointed Slayer, is the reason for the group's existence and indeed is often turned to by the collective for leadership. However, she constantly consults with the collective and is most vulnerable when she isolates herself from the group, dramatized most explicitly when Spike helps Adam by spreading dissension in the group; they defeat Adam by uniting in a magical enhancement of the collective.

Buffy's vocation as 'the Chosen One' is a form of embodied knowledge, with a power that was never sought, merely bequeathed.

She is positioned as an instinctual leader, but as one who knows that she serves her calling more than she controls it. Her Slayer intuition, moreover, connects critical thinking to an ethical base that distinguishes her from the two other Slayers featured in the shows.

Kendra is a by-the-book Slayer whose regimented training by the Watchers' Council (she even follows the Slayer's Handbook) functions as more of a limitation than a strength. But the doomed unselfish Kendra's ethical integrity is unquestioned, unlike Faith, who functions as an anarchic force whose lack of emotional and ethical centre leads her to be, as mentioned above, the pawn of institutional forces.

Buffy's relation to authority remains questioning and critical. She challenges all of the authority figures in the show (including Giles), and her defiance of self-important villains is one of the show's deepest pleasures. Buffy's anti-authoritarian instinct is most fully dramatized in relation to the Initiative. While temporarily made a deputy of the Initiative (the one time, after her break with the Council of Watchers, that she is ever harnessed to an institution), she challenges the instructions and logic of Professor Walsh, leading to Walsh's attempt to kill her (although Walsh is also no doubt motivated by sexual jealousy given the incestuous tones of Walsh's mother-love for favourite-son Riley).

Buffy's critical way of thinking about the fascistic and military-structured Initiative also facilitates Riley's transformation from chemically-enhanced All-American soldier boy to self-described 'anarchist' by the end of Season Four of *Buffy*. Riley's 'anarchism' is, of course, hardly rigorous and instead reflects a shorthand alternative to institutional logic, just as anti-corporate protestors in Seattle, Prague and Quebec City self-identify as 'anarchist,' as if it was the only position free from corporate taint.

The Initiative that Riley rejects is a non-demonic institutional villain that, unlike the Mayor who attempts to become a demon, attempts to harness demons to institutional ends. Although it resembles Wolfram & Hart in this respect, its leadership seems more neutral than the law firm's malevolent senior partners. The Initiative survives in modified form after Adam's destruction, as a shadowy para-military group that re-recruits Riley for anti-demon combat.

Frames of knowledge and the allegory of the supernatural

The idea that *Buffy* and *Angel* are allegories of contemporary society gets off the ground by proposing the existence of the supernatural, and with it, non-rational entities like souls, Powers That Be, and indeed vampires. Of course, such categories are easily understood as remnants of quasi-religious pre-Enlightenment mythology functioning ideologically to reinstate metaphysical categories: a regressive return to magical thinking.

But unlike moralistic shows like fellow-WB drama *Seventh Heaven*, *Buffy* and *Angel* are not religious programmes, despite their surface trappings; indeed, institutional religion is as suspect as any other institution on the show. Not only does the supernatural function as a subversive allegory symbolizing social and political Powers That Be, ie, institutions and logics of hierarchical, governmental and corporate power, but the very lack of mythological coherence on the shows points to a diverse and mixed universe in which multiple and shifting regimes of knowledge are aligned with salutarily multiple and shifting ethical domains.

Buffy's title, 'the Vampire Slayer,' could be seen to propose a simplistic moral universe: Buffy should kill all vampires, because they are, by definition, evil. But the show in fact requires the continuing existence of vampires to drive its increasingly complex critical universe. Moreover, Angel, the vampire-with-a-soul, immediately complicates the moral universe, a human-demon and good/evil mulatto who signals the shows' heterogeneous universe. Even more striking is Spike's evolution from villain to tragic hero. Without the benefit of Angel's gypsy-imposed soul, Spike, motivated by his erotic love for Buffy, has *cultivated* a soul, suggesting a materialist rather than metaphysical conception of human ethics: his goodness is built, not given. Burdened with a computer chip that prevents him from harming humans, a pre-programmed ethical imperative to do no harm, Spike embodies how human 'excess' finds itself *in* the monster. The more we know about the nature of the universe, the more grey its complexities become – take as an example, the show's shift from seeing vampires as purely demonic to an increasing acknowledgement that, say, Vampire Willow or Harmony also *are* the person they were before.

Buffy and *Angel* are shows about the ethical consequences of knowledge; they also portray a split even more fundamental than that between good and evil – the split between those who know about the supernatural existence of demons and underground forces in the world and those who do not – or choose not to – have such knowledge. This conflict over knowledge evolves gradually over the first five years of the *Buffy/Angel* universe and produces a split between the public and private status of knowledge of the supernatural.

This evolution, of course, parallels the evolution noted above of villains increasing in public power, from the underground ancient Master to a massive (but still underground) government-military organization of the Initiative. Those who know about the 'real' existence of supernatural forces are distinguished from those who are caught in the conventional, rationalist sense of reality-people who usually figure as victims, whether targeted by, or caught in the crossfire of, supernatural/structural forces. *Buffy* and *Angel* invert conventional rationalist belief, requiring enlightened characters to believe in the existence of structural forces beyond their control (Powers That Be), characters crucially infused with an ethical and moral and, we argue, critical political understanding. Unenlightened characters are depicted as not only ignorant but often as existing in *denial* of the supernatural: those who survive supernatural attack usually try to 'explain it away.'

Buffy and *Angel*'s foregrounding of *disavowal* of a reality that literally attacks and allegorically threatens all unenlightened characters dramatizes a critical politics. Disavowal – the way in which we can 'know very well but all the same ignore' a truth – points to the poverty and danger of unselfconscious ideological surrender in the shows' larger allegory of capitalist knowledge production: the way capitalism perpetuates itself by inviting disavowal of its negative consequences.

The first five years of *Buffy* and *Angel* have witnessed a gradual evolution in terms of *public* and *private* knowledge. The supernatural is increasingly naturalized in the public sphere of both shows – more secondary characters and extras are exposed to supernatural reality – but this exposure is accompanied by an increasing sophistication in characters' abilities to disavow – or even more pointedly, not care about – the supernatural forces that affect reality.

In the first season, the pilot episode features an attack by vampires at the Bronze which is explained away as a fight between rival gangs. Buffy's mother, Joyce, does not learn that Buffy is the Slayer until well into Season Two. Indeed, earlier in that season, in 'Bad Eggs' (2.12), she and many other Sunnydale residents are brainwashed into serving a demon, but 'wake up' with no knowledge of what happened.

By the third season of Buffy, however, references to the special nature of Sunnydale (a suburb situated over the Hellmouth) creep into the show more and more. First, there are gradual intimations that officials at institutions like the high school, police and Mayor's office are aware of the supernatural (and are manipulating it for their own purposes). Second, ordinary students note the extraordinary number of deaths at Sunnydale High School and Buffy is awarded – 'The Prom' (3.20) – the 'Class Protector' award for keeping the death rate at the school at its lowest point ever. Finally, at the end of Season Three, all of the graduating students are mobilized into an army to help defeat the Mayor who, after a century of corrupt misuse of executive authority, has his self-aggrandizement literalized with metamorphosis into a giant snake-demon. The demon threatens all of the students and they are, however temporarily, brought into the collective to fight for their survival, leaving the school destroyed in its wake.

This destruction is appropriate for the major shift that occurs in Season Four of *Buffy* (and the first season of *Angel*), as the status of public and private knowledge of supernatural/structural forces takes a quantum jump in sophistication. On *Buffy*, the setting shifts from high school to the university, an ostensible leap as a site of critical knowledge. The arch-villain becomes the Initiative, a move that reveals a knowledge of the supernatural at the military and governmental institutional level. (This is intimated in 'Out of Mind, Out of Sight' (1.11) which shows a government school for magic assassins.)

The Initiative, embodying instrumental reason, tries to understand the supernatural by literally dissecting demons and harnessing their power for military reasons. This approach is presented as a fundamentally flawed form of knowledge, one that both creates Adam as the logical extension of its logic and cannot distinguish between the increasingly subtle moral and ethical distinctions among the demons that inhabit the world. Season Four is the most articulate depiction of institutional knowledge structures and parallels a contrasting crisis in the collective as they are gradually socially dispersed (Buffy and Willow in university, Xander and Giles unemployed), entering a more adult world – which nonetheless culminates in 'Primeval' (4.21) a powerful fantasy of a magic collective circle defeating a seemingly invincible nuclear-powered military demon machine.

On *Angel,* the shift in setting to Los Angeles opens up the demon world to a much broader allegorical existence. In suburban Sunnydale, the demon world is marginalized to spaces like underground sewers, abandoned buildings, industrial sites and back alleys, foregrounding the contrast between the ostensibly bright normality of the American suburban paradigm and the dark forces which exist at its margins or underground – like *Twin Peaks*, undergirding its normality, indeed, dialectically at one with it.

In urban Los Angeles, the demon world is much more integrated; even though it still exists in the same marginal spaces as in Sunnydale (alleys, abandoned buildings), those spaces are far more integral to the city, especially to the *film noir* imagery that *Angel* mobilizes in its depiction of Los Angeles. Moreover, special social sites enter the mix: abandoned buildings where half-human demons flee Neo-Nazi purebloods; fight clubs where the *haute bourgeoisie* enjoy the demon world in the same way that dominant culture consumes marginal sub-cultures for entertainment, and of course, the law firm of Wolfram & Hart, which protects the evil demon world from public scrutiny. Gunn's black 'ghetto' community, forgotten by the larger social world, is threatened by vampire gangs and later policed by zombie cops resuscitated by an over-zealous precinct captain.

In this Los Angeles, there are characters like Anne, the head of the youth shelter who has a world-weary knowledge of the supernatural and 'has been around.' Indeed, her character first appeared as Chanterelle, a deluded vampire wannabe in 'Lie To Me' (2.7) and later reappeared as Lily, a runaway imprisoned with Buffy in a factory-like hell. She and Buffy escape this hell, an important episode in which Buffy reaffirms her Slayer duties (after attempting to drop out as a runaway teen), her reclamation of ethical duty underscored visually when she fights her captors with a hammer and sickle. These icons of socialist political struggle (the tools of the industrial and agricultural proletariat) are flashed every week when Buffy poses with them in the final image of the *Buffy* credit sequence from Seasons Three to Five.

Despite the explicit political reference in this *Buffy* episode, the underground world of demons is allegorized in directly socio-political terms on *Angel,* standing in for social issues: poverty, homelessness, sexual violence and class and racial conflict. Moreover, in the Los Angeles of *Angel,* the demon world itself is far more differentiated, demonstrating a polymorphous perversity and range of coexisting evil/good/benign moral qualities, resisting a totalizing logic. The lone demon bar in Sunnydale habituated by vampires and demons in *Buffy* is extended to an entire network of sites in *Angel,* most prominently the karaoke bar, all of which form a kind of underground world, usually figured in the mise-en-scène as lower-class, down-and-out, a world of fringe bars, sewers, industrial parks, back alleys or all measure of abandoned structures.

While *Buffy* and *Angel* differentiates between those humans who have critical knowledge of supernatural/structural forces and those who do not, it presents several complex options for what characters might *do* with critical knowledge. Those 'in the know' fall into roughly three categories (with many characters shifting among them), epistemological categories that are, again, aligned with ethical categories.

First, there are those (the two collectives on the two shows) who fight evil. They understand or come to understand the reality of supernatural/structural forces and seek to fight forces devoted to domination and power.

Second, there are those who come to critical understanding and are largely neutral in relation to the supernatural/structural forces. Many within this group are simply trying to survive: Gunn's black, ghetto-bound community fighting off parasitic vampires, or Anne as youth shelter organizer, all understand the nature of the supernatural (and the ideology its structural forces represent) – they stare it in the face daily – but can do little but fend it off.

Third, there are those who understand the existence of the demon world and work cynically and self-interestedly to profit from it. Wolfram & Hart are the master manipulators of this category, a firm of lawyers that takes a potentially progressive system (Law and its potential for critical knowledge) and manipulates it through instrumental logic to the ends of profit and power. The obscurantist priests who rule the demon dimension of Pylea in the last four episodes of *Angel* Season Two are explicitly affiliated to Wolfram and Hart, whose name appears on their sacred books as embossed images of the three animals that make up the name.

The Initiative also represents this third form of public understanding of the demon world: in the name of fighting demons, they seek to profit from their knowledge of them in the secular world, hitching their wagon to the underground forces disavowed or unknown to the public. Like Oliver North, they seek institutional power under cover of 'national security'. To the Initiative, the Scooby Gang can only be characterized as 'civilian insurrectionists'. The military is less an overt tool of the state than a corporate entity like Wolfram and Hart and is threatened by a new collective configuration of labour, more mobile, less bound by hierarchy and tradition, as represented by the Scooby Gang.

Another example which dramatizes the power of the reality/ supernatural inversion which founds *Buffy/Angel* is 'The Body' (5.16) in which Buffy's mother, Joyce, is mourned. Jacques Lacan distinguishes between two kinds of death, Symbolic and Real; this episode presents, finally, after the multitude of Symbolic deaths that populate the rest of the show, a death that is Real. Joyce's death is by natural causes, a death that 'happens' as opposed to being involved in some symbolic economy of good vs. evil, a death that resists easy incorporation into the Symbolic texture that characterizes the show. This inversion is reflected in the visual and especially aural style of the episode.

Buffy and *Angel* generally follow contemporary television drama codes of composition, editing and sound, largely derived from classical Hollywood cinema. This episode, though moored in the Real, uses stylistic elements of realism (long takes, dead time, and especially silence) that, in comparison to the regular style of the show, become defamiliarized in order to echo the dislocated and unmoored subjectivity of its mourning protagonists. The almost total lack of supernatural elements in the episode (save a sole vampire attack at the episode's end) also marks this episode's difference.

In understanding the importance of denial and disavowal to *Buffy* and *Angel*, it is useful to compare them to *The X-Files*, which also posits the existence of an ideological supernatural underground, but to radically different effect. In *The X-Files*, the supernatural is posited as both conspiracy and as scientifically possible. All of the unnatural phenomena are explicable through some pseudo-scientific paranormal and/or alien power, often bio-technological; indeed the crucial drive of the show is *explanation* itself, trying either to make the phenomena in question conform to known scientific law or to conform to the grand conspiracy which grounds the show's self-conscious Mythology. Both science and conspiracy, however, demand consistency and relative coherence; hence the show's increasingly paranoid and hermetic attempts, as the Mythology expands over many seasons, to create a unified theory of alien invasion are increasingly more contorted than convincing. Mulder and Scully assume that if they can just gather enough evidence, and bring the villains to justice, then the conspiracy will be exposed. Evidence is consistently destroyed or removed by the forces of conspiracy, suggesting that the secret knowledge inherent to conspiracy must continually be *repressed*.

No such repression of secret knowledge is necessary on *Buffy* or *Angel*. Evidence of the supernatural – the hidden forces and systems of economy and ideology – is often in plain sight, but is denied, disavowed or simply conveniently ignored by the ordinary citizens of Sunnydale and Los Angeles. The supernatural does not have to be proven; rather, once one comes to critical consciousness of it, it is taken for granted. The 'truth' of the supernatural is all around the characters but little effort is made, or needed, to suppress it because false consciousness is the default condition of knowledge. Wolfram and Hart, for example, not only rely on false consciousness, it is a condition of possibility for their power.

Slavoj Zizek notes that the functioning of ideological apparatuses today depends upon the cynicism of 'enlightened' subjects – ie, we all 'know' that the state, corporations, and institutions are self-interested, an acceptance that results in our own passivity, masquerading as (cynical) reason. However, in comparison to *The X-Files*, the construction of the supernatural as a knowledge system potentially available to anyone who wants to see beyond the external world's appearances pitches *Buffy* and *Angel* at the level of allegory and fantasy, permitting a far more flexible imaginative fictional universe which can constantly reinvent itself capriciously. *Buffy* and *Angel* stage the conditions for cynical reason, but also stage a utopian conception of resistance through collective struggle.

Labour

We have been discussing knowledge and knowledge production in these shows as always being interested, as participating in a critique of certain forms of institutional power. Knowledge is central to the new economy, and thus we must now turn our attention to the economic dimension. A consideration of labour is central to any economic analysis, and reading the work of the Scooby Gang and Angel Investigations as *labour* — even a utopian depiction of non-alienated labour — will allow a more profound appreciation of the allegorical dimensions of the shows.

Their frequent flirtations with apocalyptic scenarios expose these conflicts, contradicting the ideological smugness of neo-conservative discourses of the 'end of history', for which Francis Fukuyama must stand as the most well-known advocate. Fredric Jameson writes that

> It seems to be easier for us today to imagine the thoroughgoing deterioration of the earth and of nature than the breakdown of late capitalism; perhaps that is due to some weakness in our imaginations. ('The Antinomies of Postmodernism' 50)

It may also be easier to accept the reality of vampires and demons. This might be one way of relating what in film and television has seemed to be a generalized *fin du millennium* angst with a more concrete experience of culture and the economy – indeed, without such an explanation it becomes difficult to account for the popularity of films such as *Armageddon* (1998).

Buffy and *Angel* both stage the dialectical unfolding of late capitalism and propose – tentatively, and in a qualified manner to be sure – what might follow our current mode of production by presenting it in the context of a complex and compressed allegorical narrative of its own, figuring it if not as a total breakdown of late capital, then at least as a decisively collectivized mutation. *Buffy* and *Angel* subversively argue that the supernatural – vampires, ghosts and demons – more accurately reflect the logic of the economy, challenging its presumption of rationality, puncturing the arrogance of its domination: which is to say that money is magic again, as the logic of production has been superseded by the magic of monetarism and the stock market.

For unfolding out of *Buffy*/*Angel*'s critique of institutional affiliations and knowledge production is a parallel narrative that entails a virtual cataloguing of possible labour relationships. Consider the narrative of Buffy's relationship to Giles, her 'Watcher.' At once such a title seems tinged with values of supervision and hierarchy – as if the Slayer, the Chosen One, were little more than a resentful worker on the assembly line.

Indeed, we have already evoked the Council of Watchers as a representation of a corporate board of directors, opposed to yet dialectically consonant with the law firm of Wolfram & Hart in *Angel*. The Council's time has passed as we shall see, depending as it does for its authority on an outmoded, specifically British institutional culture. Yet the role of Watcher is first enacted in a context far removed from the shadowy multinational boardroom of the Council, as Giles and Buffy meet and affirm their relationship in Sunnydale High School where he is the librarian. Within a couple of seasons Giles is fired by the Watchers, cut loose from this institution; when, in 'Checkpoint'

(5.12) he is reinstated, it is on his and Buffy's terms as freelancers, with the Council's leadership reduced to advisory and funding status.

While high school as an institution is subjected to frequent critiques as a repressive institution both intellectually and socially, Giles's relationship with Buffy at first evokes a master/apprentice relationship enacted in a manner that will set the stage for a representation of non-alienated intellectual labour, as the show proposes an alternative to this non-alienated relationship to labour and knowledge. For the representation of Giles as intellectual worker depends on a pre-existing fantasy – a cultural imaginary and almost a parody – of what research as labour might entail.

Giles is coded as the cultured product of Oxbridge, for which the archive of canonical literature that he manages stands in. It is Giles's role as a fantasy-figure of non-alienated labour that necessitates the texture of his representation – his 'mystique', his prestige and social function – rather than his representation that inspires the fantasy. Giles's figuration as a non-alienated worker is not created by the show – rather, it is what the show exists to represent.

Giles's initial status in the show is distinct in that he models a non-alienated intellectual labour seemingly independent of traditional conceptions of work: he often works nights, unfettered by the clock time of the 9 to 5; his home, like the archive he oversees, fascinates with its plethora of antique books, weapons and fetishes, distinct from the commodification that obtains elsewhere in Sunnydale. Giles's home replicates the library, but shorn of its pernicious institutional affiliations – though retaining its fascination and authority – and transplanted to where it promises the possibility of an integration of labour and its other free from institutional and corporate determinants by virtue of its entry into the private sphere. At home, Giles's labour belongs to him, and thus escapes the alienating logic of the institutional workplace. Money and wages are of less import than the cultural and symbolic authority that accrues to him through these objects and his labour; and, particularly, his relationship with Buffy activates fantasies of a return to older, more libidinally satisfying forms of labour organization like the guild.

The authenticity of his relationship with Buffy — based as it seems to be on a mutual trust and respect — also includes an idealization of the teacher/student relationship and draws the opposition between Giles's and institutional forms of knowledge and labour — like the tedium and inauthenticity of high school — into sharper relief. In comparison to the nightmarish exemplification of instrumental reason that Adam embodies at university, the show takes pains to provide Giles with a mediating role. Both *Buffy* and Buffy know knowledge to be always interested, so the Giles/Buffy teacher/student relationship is consistently set at odds with institutionally validated forms of knowledge production. What Giles takes with him from library to home, what gets exchanged between Buffy and Giles, is precisely an *attitude* towards labour.

So from guild master to teacher — yet this cannot be the end of Giles's evolution. The show gives us yet a further transformation of Giles that would seem to oppose this one we have been following. Giles, in Season Five, becomes a small businessman, owning and operating the Magic Box, a store which often provides Buffy and the gang with the tools necessary to defeat their foes. Whatever fantasy of non-alienated labour Giles's previous work serves to inspire seems undone at a stroke here and replaced by a reactionary fantasy that finds its fullest realization in bourgeois self-employment. It is as if our desires as viewers, as alienated workers in our own right, had been anticipated, evoked and then managed. It is precisely in this sense that Giles's treat to himself after his spell of unemployment — a red BMW — affirms his ownership of the shop as an important culmination, a realization of a rather less than utopian desire.

Dialectically, however, Giles's transformation can be understood as a reflection of another transformation in the economic logic of capitalism that we have been tracing. The 'evolution' of Giles's role from guild master to small businessman evokes in miniature another, broader narrative: the history of capitalism itself. Specifically, Giles's coding as *British* points to a larger historical narrative of economic transformation suggested by Giovanni Arrighi. Arrighi, seeking to trace the relationship between capital and the nation state, describes four historical centres of capital – Genoa, Holland, Britain and the United States – that, over the last 700 years, have displayed the same logic of development, one characterized by breaks and reconstitutions rather than steady expansion:

> Long periods of crisis, restructuring and reorganization, in short, of discontinuous change, have been far more typical of the history of the capitalist world-economy than those brief moments of generalized expansion along a definite developmental path like the one that occurred in the 1950s and 1960s. In the past, these long periods of discontinuous change ended in a reconstitution of the capitalist world-economy on new and enlarged foundations.

It is difficult to avoid interpreting Giles's disturbing transformation from a non-alienated knowledge worker into a prosperous burgher in light of Arrighi's description, with the Magic Box as a materialization of the American phase of this uncanny break. Both Britain – Giles's home – and the United States – his current residence – figure in the history that Arrighi details and it is precisely in the fractious logic of his transformation that we find the conditions that have brought it about.

In light of Arrighi's narrative, we can see some of the trans-formations of the *Buffy* and *Angel* series narrative as symptomatic of larger developments in capitalism, especially changes in the mobility of labour. Giles has been a member of a global organization known as the Watchers, whose mandate involves keeping track of the Slayer. But the Watchers are inflexible, bound by a petrified, vertically integrated hierarchy and bureaucracy, organized around a strict division of labour and specialization that can only be abhorrent to the humanist Giles and the individualist Buffy.

However, the ideologies of humanism and individualism that seem to be affirmed here are themselves pretexts for another conflict to whose presence Giles's role as small businessman should alert us: the conflict between the corporation – whose structure the Watchers' Council reproduces – and small business. Even the Scooby Gang itself cannot hope to remain immune, as their own participation, both in Buffy's job and in the running of the shop, suggests at once a collective alternative to the stifling bureaucracy and alienation perpetuated by corporate culture and a reproduction of the logic that Arrighi describes, where Fordism must make way for 'small-batch craft production, carried out in small and medium-sized business units coordinated by market-like processes of exchange'. Which is to say: as soon as Giles opts for the Magic Box, the Gang's collectivity gets recoded in terms of capital's reconstitution. Angel Investigations too, despite its social justice agenda and collective constitution, accords to the same logic: it is the small business in conflict with the oppressive corporate machinations of Wolfram & Hart.

If these institutions – the Magic Box, the Scooby Gang and Angel Investigations – set some of the parameters that govern the expansion of capital and the organization of labour, then we need to square the circle by looking at how *Buffy* and *Angel* figure consumption. To do this we can usefully turn to the villain of Season Five, Glory, who is from the beginning coded as a super-consumer. In her luxury apartment, surrounded by all of the trappings of conspicuous consumption – 'Gods don't travel light' – and served by supernatural attendants that also occasionally function as her personal shoppers, Glory the evil god gives a deadly inflection to the old saw, 'the customer is always right,' as the customer here is virtually omnipotent, possessing the desire and need to consume the sanity of random victims and ultimately all dimensions of existence. Similarly, Anya embraces capital with a demonic zeal that evokes ridicule from the other characters, reaffirming *Buffy/Angel*'s self-conscious and deeply critical stance towards capital and consumerism.

Conclusion

To distinguish history from mere repetition of the perpetual fashionable present of a postmodern media culture – this is the task for materialist criticism. For Walter Benjamin in *The Arcades Project* hell is this perpetual present, where the new is only the ever-same, where new styles and new models of consumer goods – and new forms of cultural production – all serve to reproduce the underlying static logic of capital. We must think of our pleasure in the new as implying our own possible destruction as part of what others consume.

For Benjamin the new technologies of modernism have a potentially critical vocation too, and one opposed to this more conservative pleasure. To read any work of popular culture as merely symptomatic is, as Benjamin argues, to reproduce and reaffirm the logic of its production. Thus Buffy and Angel's encounters with the uncanny are taken on their own obviously symbolic terms: this demon stands in for racism and intolerance; that vampire represents the 'excess' of adolescent sexuality.

Yet Buffy and Angel's skirmishes with supernatural creatures are battles with the very logic of modernity that Benjamin identifies. What is the deeper logic at work here? The show anticipates and participates in such an allegorical coding – such is one of the sources of its pleasure – but also offers itself up for another kind of reading, for which these bourgeois teen allegories are only the manifest content. While the pleasures offered by these allegories remain the property of Benjamin's satanic sadist, *Buffy/Angel* offers too a more complex and unsettling set of pleasures that often stands in direct opposition to those persistent bourgeois teen allegories and the opportunities for identification that they provide.

Scandalously in our current moment of history, *Buffy* and *Angel* propose a pleasure grounded in the collective, critical of, yet dependent on institutions; invested in labour, yet a labour that is intellectual as well as libidinally gratifying, performed and embodied rather than alienating.

Bibliography

Arrighi, Giovanni, *The Long Twentieth Century: Money, Power, and the Origins of Our Times* (London, 1994).

Baudrillard, Jean, *The Mirror of Production*, trans. Mark Poster (St. Louis, 1975).

Benjamin, Walter, *The Arcades Project*, ed. Rolf Tiedemann, trans. Howard Eiland and Kevin McLaughlin (Cambridge, Mass., 1999).

Benjamin, Walter, 'The Work of Art in the Age of Mechanical Reproduction.' *Illuminations*, ed. Hannah Arendt, trans. Harry Zohn (New York, 1968). p 217–52.

Jameson, Fredric, 'The Antinomies of Postmodernism' in *The Cultural Turn: Selected Writings on the Postmodern, 1983–1998* (London, 1998). p 50–72.

Jameson, Fredric 'Metacommentary.' in *The Ideologies of Theory: Essays 1971–1986* Vol. 1 (Minneapolis, 1988). p 3–16.

Zizek, Slavoj *Enjoy Your Symptom!: Jacques Lacan in Hollywood and Out* (New York, 1992).

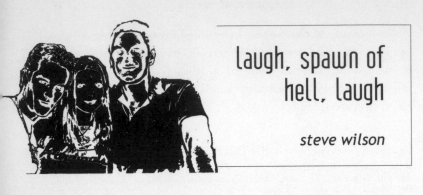

laugh, spawn of hell, laugh

steve wilson

When Buffy and her friends laugh in the face of danger, the face of danger laughs back. No wonder Dracula barely lasted an episode ('Buffy vs. Dracula' (5.1)):

> Xander: You know what? You're not so big. One round of old-fashioned fisticuffs, you'd fold like a bitty baby.
>
> (Dracula scowls.)
>
> Xander: Okay, let's do it. And no poofing. Come on, puffy shirt. Pucker on up, 'cause you can kiss your pale ass —
>
> Dracula: Silence.
>
> Xander: Yes master. (Shakes head) No, that's not —
>
> Dracula: You will be my emissary, my eyes and ears in daylight.
>
> Xander: Your emissary?
>
> Dracula: Serve me well. You will be rewarded. I will make you an immortal. A child of darkness that feeds on life itself . . . on blood.
>
> Xander: (In Dracula's accent) 'Blood?' (Switching to Woody Allen homage that will only intensify as the episode progresses) Yes! Yes! I will serve you, your excellent spookiness.

(Dracula frowns.)

Xander: Or master. I'll just stick with master.

Dracula: You are strange and off-putting. Go now.

Xander: But master, how can I find – (Sees Dracula is
  gone) Brilliant. What an exit! Guy's a genius!
  (Giggles insanely and walks off)

Despite this momentary victory for evil, the Count, in all his Bram
Stoker seriousness, never really stood a chance on a show whose very
name is a nudge in the ribs of the old school horror he epitomizes.
Surviving *Buffy the Vampire Slayer* requires a sense of humour, for villain
and viewer alike.

Without its jokes, jokes finessed just so, *Buffy* would be little more
than your average teen melodrama action horror hybrid. And a silly
one at that. Improving on the 1992 film, which was torn somewhere
between *Heathers* and *Abbott and Costello Meet Frankenstein* (and nowhere
near as good as either) in its blunt spoofery of high school and horror
movies, the television version treats young adulthood seriously. That
is, if you can call using monsters to symbolize growing pains serious.
Plenty of shows have dealt with adolescent sexual angst, but *Buffy*
may be the only one to do so by pitting its protagonist against a giant
reproductive blob monster that breeds mind-controlling egg hatchlings
in the school basement ('Bad Eggs' (2.12)). Addressing its characters'
internal demons through external ones is a conceit that would seem
a lot more heavy-handed if the writers didn't soften the blow with
comic relief.

Whether the metaphors that dress the theme of every episode are
clever – Riley becomes a vampire bite addict ('Out of the Woods'
(5.10)); Dawn lives the ultimate adolescent nightmare on learning
she's really a 'negative space' fashioned in the body of a pre-teenager
('Blood Ties' (5.13)) – or completely obvious – an unpopular student
is ignored so thoroughly she turns invisible ('Out of Mind, Out of
Sight' (1.11)); hexed beer drains college students of intelligence –
'Beer Bad' (4.5) – a heavy dose of silliness is just the distraction to

keep *Buffy* from devolving into an after-school special with fangs. When
– in 'Ted' (2.11) – Buffy doesn't like Joyce's new boyfriend (and not
just because he turns out to be an evil wife-napping robot), sarcasm
alleviates the didacticism of Angel's advice:

> Buffy: I don't need some new guy in my life.
> Angel: Well maybe your mom does.
> Buffy: Well, sure, if you're gonna use wisdom.

When Buffy takes on the Judge, a demon summoned by her
enemies to end the world (ground zero: Sunnydale Mall), in
'Innocence' (2.13), she's really dealing with an apocalypse in her
personal life: Angel has turned into an abusive asshole. That a
mystical curse ripped away his soul after they had sex is a whole
other thicket of allegory to roam; we're too busy laughing to mull
over the implications:

> Judge: You're a fool. No weapon forged can stop me.
> Buffy: That was then. (Raises a rocket launcher to her
>   shoulder) This is now.
> Judge: (Looking confused) What's that do? (Is blasted
>   to smithereens)

Humour, which can disarm the most stubborn cynicism, similarly
freshens up an old saw inevitable in genre entertainment. A vicious
attack in the woods doesn't turn Oz into a werewolf, he's changed by
a bite from his lycanthropic young nephew ('Just got his grownup
teeth in. Does not like to be tickled') – 'Phases' (2.14). The quiet
kid's ventriloquist doll in 'The Puppet Show' (1.9) isn't a projection
of his twisted psyche, it's a cursed demon hunter who's trying to help,
even though he's about as charming as Don Rickles. ('You call those
jokes? My jockey shorts are made out of better material. And they're
edible.')

After the Master delivers a familiar-sounding arch-villain speech
about how an earthquake racking Sunnydale is 'A sign! We are in the

final days! My time has come! Glory! GLORY!' he makes a very California inquiry into its Richter scale status: 'Whadaya think? 5.1?' ('Prophecy Girl' (1.12)). Spike, on the other hand, dispenses with evil mastermind blather altogether upon destroying the Anointed One and establishing himself (for a time) as the baddest vamp in town: 'From now on, we're gonna have a little less ritual and a little more fun around here.' (Turns to Drusilla) 'Let's see what's on TV.' ('School Hard' (2.3))

In later episodes, we learn more of Spike's taste in the tube as he watches *Passions* with Giles and Joyce and shouts in frustration at the characters of *Dawson's Creek*. Far from lessening the horror, these comedic twists actually enhance it; Buffy's foes are menacing not because they're capable of destroying the world (what competent villain isn't?), but because they're able to get in the last word. The Mayor leaves Buffy and Angel speechless when he chastises, 'What kind of a life can you offer her? I don't see a lot of Sunday picnics in the offing. I see skulking in the shadows' ('Choices' (3.19)). Angel's evil incarnation delivers one of his most powerful digs to Buffy after they've had sex but before she realises he's lost his soul: 'You got a lot to learn about men, kiddo. Although I guess you proved that last night' ('Innocence' (2.14)).

With so many monsters running around, sometimes it's the interactions of human beings that require a suspension of disbelief in Sunnydale. Laughs fill this need by helping potential melodrama go down more smoothly. That Willow can still be neurotically witty on discovering Xander and Cordelia's secret tryst, ('Innocence' (2.14)) makes her even more sympathetic, raising her anguish high above standard high school soap opera yappity-yap:

> I knew it! I knew it! Well, not 'knew it' in the sense of having the slightest idea, but I knew there was something I didn't know. It's against all laws of God and Man! It's Cordelia! Remember? The 'We Hate Cordelia' club? Of which you are the treasurer . . .'

And Jonathan's heart-wrenching (especially in the context of his recent suicide attempt) presentation to Buffy of a goofy, umbrella-shaped Class Protector award at the prom ('The Prom' (3.20)) could easily descend into sappiness without a straight-faced aside to balance things out:

> Whenever there was a problem or something creepy happened, you seemed to show up and stop it. Most of the people here have been saved by you, or helped by you at one time or another. We're proud to say that the Class of '99 has the lowest mortality rate of any graduating class in Sunnydale history.' (Earnest applause and cheers from the crowd.) 'And we know at least part of that is because of you . . .

The show's flippancy is flexible enough to handle more serious matters as well; just the right touch of the tragi-comic both relieves and deepens the solemnity of Joyce's death in 'The Body' (5.16):

> Anya, crying: I don't understand how this all happens. How we go through this. I mean, I knew her, and then she's, there's just a body, and I don't understand why she just can't get back in it and not be dead anymore. It's stupid. It's mortal and stupid. And, and Xander's crying and not talking, and, and I was having fruit punch, and I thought, well, Joyce will never have any more fruit punch ever, and she'll never have eggs, or yawn or brush her hair, not ever, and no one will explain to me why.

Buffy wouldn't work without its sense of humour, but what makes its sense of humour work isn't easy to quantify. The show's particular brand of comicality can't really be labelled as verbal, slapstick, satirical or dark because it's all of the above and then some. As any number of works from Shakespeare to *The Simpsons* prove, the best comedies never rely too much on one type of whimsy, and *Buffy*'s fanciful premise gives it the creative leeway to take that truism to the limit. Time-honoured buffoonery:

> Xander: Boy, what a long day.
> Willow: But you skipped three classes.
> Xander: And boy did they fly by.

alongside modern world-weary disaffection:

> Cordelia: You saw Death.
> Willow: Did it have an hourglass?
> Xander: Ooo, if he asks you to play chess, don't even do it. The guy's, like, a wiz. ('Killed By Death' (2.18))

smell-it-a-mile-away sight gags:—

> Buffy, as Kendra picks up her crossbow: 'Be careful with that.'
> Kendra: 'Don't worry, I'm an expert with all weapons.' (Accidentally shoots out lamp.) ('What's My Line Part 2' (2.10))

beside head-scratching non-sequiturs:

> Willow: Well, don't you have some ambition?
> Oz: Oh, yeah! Yeah. E-flat, diminished ninth.

literary allusions: Xander: 'Yikes! The quality of mercy is not Buffy'— butting up against more contemporary riffs — Cordelia: 'Willow! Nice dress! Good to know you've seen the softer side of Sears.'; classic puns — Buffy, pulling the warlock Ethan Rayne out of a crate: 'Look, a box full of farm-fresh chicken'—; bad puns — Buffy: 'I know Faith isn't gonna be on the cover of Sanity Fair' — and still-worse puns — Buffy, to a demon that thrives on disease: 'You make me sick' — sharing air time with more cerebral word antics:

> Xander: And speaking of love.

> Willow: We were talking about the reanimation of dead
>   tissue.
> Xander: Do I deconstruct your segues? ('Some
>   Assembly Required' (2.2))

An episode may contain influences as far-reaching as bawdy Greek farce to brainy post-modern theatre in a steady flow of absurdity that switches from low-brow to high-brow at the drop of a stake. Take most any zinger from the show and it's not hard to connect the dots to a wide range of familiar material: the nonsensical stylings of Groucho Marx – Oz: 'That's great, Larry, you've really mastered the single entendre' – the epigrammatic wit of Oscar Wilde – Cordelia: 'Tact is just not saying true stuff' – the absurdist self-deprecation of Woody Allen – Xander: 'Well, this is new territory for me. I mean, my valentines are usually met with heartfelt restraining orders' – the biting observation of Jerry Seinfeld – Cordelia: 'You expect me to wear this? It smells like grandpa breath'– the understatement of Bob Newhart – Oz, on awakening naked in the woods after a forgotten night of hunting as a werewolf: 'Huh'– the bawdy nervousness of Bob Hope:

> Faith: (Seducing Xander) You up for it?
> Xander: Oh, I'm up. I'm suddenly very up. It's just,
>   I've never been up with people before.
> Faith: Just relax. Take your pants off.
> Xander: Those two concepts are antithetical. ('The
>   Zeppo' (3.13))

There's as much Shakespeare as there is *Three's Company* in the air when Spike, wearing a 'blood moustache' from his daily mug of type O, leans over the couch on which Anya is napping to pick up some books and finds himself pummelled by Xander, who has naturally assumed the vampire is feasting on his girlfriend's neck. This sort of mixup has served comedy writers well for ages. Or take the male rape of Coach Marin by a pack of swim team members transformed into fish men –

Buffy, looking on: 'Those boys really love their coach.' Is this bit of burlesque more Aristophanes or Farrelly Brothers? Since it takes place off camera, maybe neither.

Granted, the way humour evolves and hybridizes as it's passed along from generation to generation, an enterprizing scholar of mirth could trace any joke's lineage to any source in this way. Still, the writers of *Buffy* have occasionally hinted that they're aware of some of their influences, however reflexively they may use them. It's no accident that Scott invites Buffy to a Buster Keaton film festival or Xander, on spilling a tray of drinks at the Bronze, waves away ironic applause from the crowd with a Borchst Belt-ish 'Thank you! Thank you. We're here through Saturday. Enjoy the veal.' Both Keaton and the stand-up comic tradition came out of Vaudeville, that vast umbrella of hilarity that shaded so many comedy traditions before they spread to movies and television. At times, the characters may as well be carrying seltzer bottles for all their Vaudevillian schtick:

> Willow: What kind of punch did you make?
> Buffy: Lemonade. I made it fresh and everything.
> Willow, trying a glass: How much sugar did you use?
> Buffy: Sugar?
> Willow: (Face blanching) It's very good. ('School Hard' (2.3))

> Xander, on seeing a dissected demon spawn: Can I just say 'Gyughhh!'
> Buffy: I see your 'Gyughhh!' and raise you a 'Nyaghhh!'

> Buffy: . . . Oh, the one that nearly bit me mentioned something about kissing toast. He lived for kissing toast.
> Giles: You mean 'Kakistos?'
> Buffy: Maybe it was taquitos. Maybe he lived for taquitos. What?
> Giles: Kakistos.

Buffy: Is that bad?

Giles: 'Kakistos' is Greek. It means the worst of the worst.

Buffy: I'm gonna talk to Faith, see if 'khaki trousers' rings –

Giles: Kakistos. ('Faith, Hope and Trick' (3.3))

Too often when a Vaudevillian standard crops up on television or movies these days, it feels more like a respectful homage than an organic part of the story. That's because pies in the face and slips on banana peels rarely happen in real life. With a premise that removes it a few steps from reality, *Buffy* has the creative leeway to pull off, say, Giles getting shot by a tranquilizer gun ('It's alright! Bloody priceless.' Proceeds to wobble and fall) without feeling forced. By the same illogic, vampires usually endure the best pratfalls on the show since their very existence is even more fanciful than the trips and spills they take. Passing out after an evening of drinking and griping about Angel (playing drunk being another hallowed Vaudeville tradition), Spike wakes up the next morning to find a shaft of light has ignited his outstretched hand. Screaming and tripping madly about, he douses the flame with his booze which causes him even more pain before finally jumping into the shade of his tinted car and grumbling, 'This is just too much.' ('Lover's Walk' (3.8))

Other times, when it makes the ongoing battle between human perspective and the laws of the universe fodder for laughs, the show attains the Buster Keaton ideal of physical comedy (and by extension, that of his present-day heir, Jackie Chan). In 'Bewitched, Bothered and Bewildered' (2.16), Xander centres a card catalog in the opening of the library's double doors to stave off an assault of love-charmed women; the 'doh!' moment comes seconds later when one of the doors opens outward, not inward as he had assumed, and Buffy walks around the barrier with nary a glance. Fortunately, the Keatonian universe always comes back on the side of the protagonist in the end. Marching toward Willow's evil doppelganger during a face-off at the Bronze

('Doppelgangland' (3.16)), Buffy deftly picks up a pool cue and, without looking or breaking stride, whacks it against the head of an oncoming vamp, simultaneously knocking out the creature and splintering the wood into a handy stake.

Some of the best visual jokes on *Buffy* take an opposite tack, finding folly in the most routine of human movements, our non-zany but still ridiculous social manners and mores. In 'Becoming Part Two' (2.22), the camera lingers with palpable awkwardness on Spike and Joyce as they sit in the living room together, trying to think of something to say to each other until Buffy returns. Nothing comes to either of them, so they sit some more. Appearing on *Angel* ('In the Dark' (A1.3)), the spinoff that deploys *Buffy*'s humour in a darker setting, Spike imports this particular brand of visual behavioural gag while watching from a rooftop as Angel rescues then talks to a grateful woman:

> Spike, extrapolating the out-of-earshot dialogue:
> (high voice) 'How can I thank you, you mysterious, black-clad hunk of a night thing?'
> (low voice) 'No need, little lady, your tears of gratitude are enough for me. You see, I was once a badass vampire, but love and a pesky curse defanged me. Now I'm just a big, fluffy puppy with bad teeth.'
> (Rachel steps closer to Angel, and Angel steps back warding her off with his hands.)
> Spike: (low voice) 'No, not the hair! Never the hair!'
> (high voice) 'But there must be someway I can show my appreciation.'
> (low voice) 'No, helping those in need's my job, and working up a load of sexual tension, and prancing away like a magnificent poof is truly thanks enough!'
> (high voice) 'I understand. I have a nephew who is gay, so . . .'
> (low voice) 'Say no more. Evil's still afoot! And I'm

almost out of that Nancy-boy hair-gel that I like so
much. Quickly, to the Angel-mobile, away!'

You wouldn't think recycling 100-year-old-material (give or take a
few millennia) in a cartoonish context satisfied *Buffy*'s hallowed duty
as a teen melodrama for the MTV generation. That's where the
contemporizing comes in. The ancient prop gag lifts from pop culture
when demonic grey pincers erupt *Alien*-like from the belly of a teddy
bear backpack; the ethnic joke picks a safe, politically correct target
(Xander to Giles: 'You Brits are such drama queens'); and the dusty
screwball tradition of 1930s movies finds eager new adherents:

> Xander: Sorry I snapped at you before.
> Cordelia: Well, I'm reeling from that new experience.
> Xander: I was crazed. I wasn't thinking.
> Cordelia: I know. You were too busy rushing off to die
>   for your beloved Buffy. You'd never die for me.
> Xander: No, I might die from you. Does that get me
>   any points?
> Cordelia: No.
> Xander: Come on, can't we just kiss and make up?
> Cordelia: I don't wanna make up. But I'm okay with
>   the other part.

Buffy works the same alchemy with more recent humour, rediscovering
the fun in already-tired clichés like Schwarzenegger-esque 1980s
action movie puns (Buffy: 'Hey Pat.' Hurls shovel into Pat's eyes. 'Made
you look') and pop culture deconstruction patter from independent
films of the 1990s:

> Trick: I like Marmaduke.
> Mayor: Eww! He's always on the furniture. Unsanitary.
> Trick: Nobody can tell Marmaduke what to do. That's
>   my kinda dog.

However, of any comedic sensibility to emerge in recent times, contemporary irony reigns supreme on the show. A very twenty-first-century ironic self-awareness infuses every episode of *Buffy*. The show's writers are fond of making punchlines out of editing techniques, as when Buffy asks Tucker why he's trained Hellhounds to descend on the Prom and he replies mysteriously, 'I have my reasons.' Cut to a three-second scene of Tucker asking a girl to the dance and getting rejected. They're not above using those techniques to prank viewers: in 'Lover's Walk' (3.8) the show goofs on its penchant for killing off major characters by following a shot of Cordelia at death's door with a funeral scene. Only after the camera pans tortuously from the mourners to the street, where Buffy and Willow happen to be walking by as they discuss Cordelia's recovery in the hospital, do we realise we've been had. However devilish it may be to tease an audience this way, the show has paid its karmic debt many times over by thoroughly mocking nearly every aspect of itself.

When it's not lampooning the clichés it embraces (Angel at a goth club/cult: 'These people don't know anything about vampires. What they are, how they live, how they dress.' A goth kid dressed just like Angel comes down the stairs and gives him a once-over before moving on), *Buffy* tweaks its own idiosyncrasies. 'Passion' (2.17) acknowledges the unlikely convenience of the library's perpetual emptiness when Jonathan and a friend make the mistake of using it during a Scooby Gang meeting:

> Xander: Excuse me, but have you ever heard of knocking?
> Jonathan: We're supposed to get some books. On Stalin.
> Xander: Does this look like a Barnes & Noble?
> Giles: This is a school library, Xander.
> Xander: Since when?

Irony saturates so much of today's culture, it usually feels empty and hollow on screens big and small (*Being John Malkovich*, *It's Garry Shandling's Show*, etc), often stifling true emotion and relevance. Yet many of *Buffy*'s most poignant episodes are drenched in the stuff. 'The Zeppo' (3.12) for instance uses deconstruction, self-parody and the same wise-ass post-modern treatment Tom Stoppard gave *Hamlet* in *Rosencrantz and Guildenstern Are Dead* to take Xander on a moving and hilarious rite of passage.

In the first scenes, Xander feels uncool and useless; Buffy wants him 'fray-adjacent' as she tries to stop a group of demons from opening the Hellmouth and unleashing unspeakable evil. A tiff with Cordelia hints that his identity crisis reaches existential heights; a normal person, he has no place in a world of super heroes and monsters:

> Xander: Why is it that I've come face-to-face with vampires, demons, the most hideous creatures Hell ever spit out, and I'm still afraid of a little bully like Jack O'Toole?
>
> Cordelia: Because, unlike all those creatures that you've come face-to-face with, Jack actually noticed you were there.

As Xander reluctantly embarks on a comic quest to defeat a pack of just-raised juvenile delinquent zombies (Dickie, poking his rotted head through the ground of his gravesite: 'Dudes!'), save Sunnydale High from a bomb and lose his virginity in the course of an evening, the earth-shattering threat Buffy faces quickly gets shoved into the narrative's background. After a while, this increasingly cookie-cutter menace only even comes up when Xander pops in on other Scooby Gang members, who mope with exaggerated doom and gloom while preparing to face it. By the time Xander interrupts Buffy and Angel in an extra-cheesy moment of melodrama, it's clear that the hellmouth sub-sub-plot is intentional parody:

> Buffy: (The Buffy / Angel romance theme playing in the background) I can't watch you die again.
>
> Angel: I love you.

Buffy: I love you.

Angel: Nothing can change that. Not even death.

Buffy: Don't talk to me like that! You may be ready to go, but I am not ready to lose you. Okay, this is my fight, and if you won't do it my way, then you're. . .

Xander: (Clearing his throat, cutting off the music.) Hey. I've got this, um . . . There's this, uh . . . It's probably a bad time.

(As Xander walks away, Buffy turns back to Angel, and their theme song starts playing again.)

In the same way that Stoppard's Rosencrantz and Guildenstern jump in and out of familiar scenes from Shakespeare's well-known tragedy, Xander is essentially travelling through what amounts to a separate Buffy episode, and a trite one at that. In the pomo tradition, the very structure of 'The Zeppo' reflects the character's dilemma: Xander is such a misfit, he can't even find a place in the first story, so he makes himself the hero of his own. And while he gains no profound insight into the nature of existence (even after accidentally knocking off his zombie informant's head during questioning), he grows up a little and finds his place in Buffy's world by the end.

Whether it dresses a gag in intellectual tweeds or moronic clown shoes, *Buffy*'s breezy versatility with a full spectrum of comedy would alone earn its place in the annals of jocosity. But the show has made its mark with a distinctive new archetype to call its own – really weird dialogue. To the casual viewer, the characters speak in the normal, if incredibly clever, way of most television casts, each filling a certain role to produce dependable punchlines. Buffy is a traditional smart mouth, the proverbial wise guy:

Buffy: Hey, Ken, wanna see my impression of Gandhi?

(Clubs and crushes Ken's skull)

Lily: Gandhi?

Buffy: Well, you know, if he was really pissed off.
('Anne' (3.1))

Willow's sarcasm, on the other hand, is of a friendlier nature: 'Buffy,
I too know the love of a taciturn man.' Xander vacillates between
goofball (excitedly following a gathering crowd at the Bronze: 'What's
going on, is there a funny thing?') and wag ('It's Rodney Manson,
he's God's gift to the Bell Curve. What he lacks in smarts he makes
up for in lack of smarts'), while Cordelia stays dependably rapier sharp
('Look, Buffy, you may be hot stuff when it comes to demonology or
whatever, but when it comes to dating, I'm the Slayer.'). Giles's wit is
so dry, it sometimes leaves you guessing:

Bedouin Wizard: My debt to you has been repaid in
    full. Do not call on me again. (Disappears)
Willow: His debt to you is repaid? What did you do?
Giles: I introduced him to his wife. ('Enemies' (3.17)

There's no such uncertainty with Oz's equally subtle quips; you always
know he's joking, no matter how unflappable his delivery:

Xander: Yep. Vampires are real. A lot of them live in
    Sunnydale. Willow will fill you in.
Willow: I know it's hard to accept at first.
Oz: Actually, it explains a lot. ('Surprise' (2.12))

Angel tends toward dark-tinged turns of phrase when he's evil
(presenting a severed heart to Drusilla: 'I knew you'd like it, I found
it in a quaint little shop girl'), while the Mayor prefers to pepper his
threats with a David Letterman-inspired use of folksy colloquialisms
('I don't suppose I could sell your soul, huh? It'd really help my game.
I'm just funnin"). Spike tops them both when he's feeling aphoristic:
'I may be love's bitch, but at least I'm man enough to admit it.'

Scratching under the surface of this banter turns up something
deeper than mere cleverness. Writers of any self-respecting teen show
or movie routinely lace their lines with the latest slang, possibly even

coining a few new phrases or words in the process so long as it sounds like the way teens speak. *Buffy*'s writers have apparently never felt this obligation. Their dialogue is only loosely based on the reality of how anyone of any age communicates. 'Clever wordplay' doesn't begin to describe the phraseology on a show that makes every episode a love-in with the English language:

> Xander: Sit here Buff, demilitarize the zone between me and Cordelia.
> Cordelia: Yeah, and delouse him while you're at it.

> Oz, asking Xander for the next ingredient in a spell they're preparing:
> Toad me.

> Xander: No, but it's different now. It's more a verbal nonverbal. He speaks volumes with his eyes.

Like reverse engineers hell-bent on uncovering the heart of a machine, the writers routinely dismantle parts of speech and jury-rig them back together however they please. In the free-for-all grammar-implosion of a typical episode, adjectives make themselves verbs, (Buffy: 'Gee, can you vague that up for me?'), verbs force themselves on nouns (Giles: 'This leaves me flummoxed.' Buffy: 'What's the flum?'), nouns cling desperately to their turf (Buffy: 'I'm sorry, I've been crankiness all day'), participles mutate with prepositions (Xander: 'They were in the ugly way looking') which pop culture (Buffy: 'I'm the one getting Single White Femaled here') and consumer culture (Willow: 'He's a super-maxi jerk for doing it right before the prom') fill in the remaining cracks. Familiar phrases and expressions don't fare much better, either willfully mangling (Cordelia: 'Well, you've really mastered the art of positive giving up') or openly scrutinizing themselves (Giles: 'Buffy, can I have a word?' Buffy: 'You can have a whole sentence even'). To further confuse matters, Buffy and pals speak to each other in a slangy shorthand, tossing unnecessary words overboard until their utterances are stripped down to the limits of sense and reason: Xander: 'We were expecting a boy, and here you are in a girl way.'

> Buffy: So we're cool?
> Willow: Way! That's why, with the party, 'cause we're all glad you're back.

> Buffy: Raise your hand if 'ew!'

This isn't the blather of kids who can't speak well, it's an honest reflection of the way our increasingly odd and perplexing world eludes easy expression. By pushing language to do what it's not supposed to, these lines capture the sensations and images of modern life that Webster's hasn't caught up with yet.

At the same time, *Buffy* also takes delight in the formal, literary side of speech:

> Buffy: Make not with the long faces.
> Xander: My intent is pure. Revenge, pure as the driven snow.

Some of this verbiage comes directly from books (Snyder tells Xander that everything from his mouth is 'an airborne toxic event,' a reference to Don DeLillo's *White Noise*); most of the time, though, it merely sounds like it. After Cordelia tries to arrange dinner with Wesley because 'I have an English paper to write and you're English,' Xander scoffs: 'And on the day the words "flimsy excuse" were redefined, we stood in awe and watched.'

The high and the low, the broad and the obscure, they all come together like a Rube Goldberg machine on *Buffy*, each part playing off another in a dizzying interplay of wit and whoopee. Or, as Spike once put it, 'wackiness ensues.'

> Xander: (Reading *On the Road*) Everything in life is foreign territory. Kerouac. He's my teacher. The open road is my school.

Buffy: Making the open dumpster your cafeteria?

Xander: Go ahead, mock me.

Oz: I think she just did.

Xander: We Bohemian anti-establishment types have always been persecuted.

Oz: Well, sure. You're all so weird.

Willow: I think it's neat, you doing the backpack-trail-mix-happy-wanderer thing.

Xander: I'm aware it scores kinda high on the hokey-meter, but I think it will be good for me. You know, help me to find myself.

Cordelia: And help us to lose you. Everyone's a winner.

Xander: Well, look who just popped open a fresh can of venom. Hey, did you hear about Willow getting into Oxnard?

Willow: Oxford.

Xander: Oxford. And MIT and Yale and every other college on the face of the planet. As in, your face I rub it.

Cordelia: Oxford? Whoopee! Four years in tea-bag central. Sounds thrilling. And MIT is a Clearasil ad with housing. And Yale is a dumping ground for those who didn't get into Harvard.

Willow: I got into Harvard.

Xander: Any clue on what college you might be attending so we can start calculating minimum safe distance?

Cordelia: None of your business. Certainly nowhere near you losers!

Buffy: Okay you guys, don't forget to breathe between insults.

Cordelia: I'm sorry Buffy. This conversation is reserved for people who actually have a future. (Leaves)

Oz: An angry young woman.

Willow: Oh Buffy, she was just being Cordelia, only
more so. Don't pay any attention to her.

Xander: She's definitely got a chip going.

Willow: Maybe if you didn't goad her so much?

Xander: I can't help it. It's my nature.

Willow: Maybe you need a better nature. ('Choices'
(3.19))

Most fans would agree that a high point of *Buffy* was the Season Two
finale, 'Becoming Part 2' (2.22). It's a powerful story in which the
slayer loses a friend and nearly loses another, gets suspended from
school, 'outs' herself to Joyce (replace the word 'slayer' with 'gay'
and you'll find quite a subtext in that exchange), runs away from home,
evades a police warrant for her arrest and sends Angel to Hell moments
after realizing he's regained his soul. The intensity is operatic; the
question is why. This is a show about imaginary creatures and
teenagers, after all. In truth, 'Becoming Part 2' might be little more
than the sum of its parts if Spike weren't chewing up scene after scene,
equating people to 'Happy Meals with legs' and finally finding
something to talk about in the living room with Joyce:

Joyce: Have we met?

Spike: You hit me with an axe one time. Remember?
'Get the hell away from my daughter!'

Joyce: Oh.

Without the levity of his presence, the rhythm of emotion, suspense
and action would lose its potency. The episode demonstrates how,
through comedy, *Buffy* lives up to the potential of fantasy and science
fiction. Since it's not tethered to reality, this much-maligned art form
is primed to explore it. Unfortunately, the earnestness and hokiness
of works like *The Lord of the Rings* and franchises like *Star Trek* often get
in the way of the important messages and themes they contain. The
average reader or viewer has difficulty accepting that tales of a hairy-

footed hobbit or an overweight, toupee-wearing starship captain contain any value beyond nerdish entertainment. And for good reason.

Buffy reaches greater depths of feeling and insight than most books, shows or movies of the genre because it isn't afraid to laugh. The show's fantasy element gives it the room to explore life and death, love and hate and other heady matters, but it's the jokes that hook and reel the audience. A little ho-ho and ha-ha and even the most credulous viewer is looking past the fright masks, not quite suspending disbelief, but willing to be entertained, moved, perhaps edified and, above all, to refrain from dwelling too long on the absurdity inherent in watching a show about a vampire slayer with the dubious name of Buffy.

it wasn't our world anymore – they made it theirs

reading space and place

karen sayer

What is space? How can we 'read' space and place? What does this mean in the context of watching TV series like *Buffy the Vampire Slayer* and *Angel*? The best way to begin is perhaps to think of a moment in *Buffy*, a moment when Xander is running – something he frequently does – running from place to place, space to space, searching for meaning. In 'Restless' (4.22), the last episode of Season Four, Buffy and her friends dream. They have beaten the season's resident enemy, a reworked Frankenstein's monster, and now they're sleeping it off. What we see as a result is an unreal world, a world of portents made up of their lives, their hopes and fears. Each is represented as being crucial to Buffy; they see their roles in relation to the Slayer, as well as their desires.

While Xander dreams he moves from scene to scene, each scene set within the sets of *Buffy*. Though apparently unrelated, what becomes clear is that the experiences he moves between in his dream are linked, linked by their setting. While on the one hand he moves around the Sunnydale we are familiar with on screen, and this movement seems chaotic, he simultaneously moves between sets that are actually connected. The faster he moves between these spaces the more we see that there is an alternative map at work here, not the broadcast Sunnydale map, but the studio map. As he dreams, so the show reveals its hidden spaces, the backstage spaces we are not normally meant to see. Xander's dream therefore unmasks and deconstructs the show's space.

Space is more than just setting, however, be that setting 'real' or 'imaginary', it is also about the way the show is constructed. In 'The Body' (5.16) for example, the spaces we see seem enlarged, the corridors seem impossibly long, Buffy's house seems to have grown. What's happening is that we're watching in real time; normally we never see a character walk down a whole corridor, we cut between spaces/sets, even when they're running. This time, we see them walk, the ordinariness of their walking simply feels odd compared to the way in which the show is normally edited, it has the effect of expanding the spaces the characters inhabit, and of making their actions, their feelings, everyday actions and feelings. This separates Joyce's death from all the other deaths on the show, it intensifies the experience so that her death is 'real'.

In approaching the spaces of TV series like *Buffy the Vampire Slayer* and *Angel* it is important to understand them *as* series, ie as fluid texts that exist in space and time. Structurally, each episode belongs in a relationship with each other episode, across and between series, not just within them — crossover episodes make deliberate use of this relationship, but it affects every broadcast. So, though we tend to think of an episode as a continuous and perfect whole, it has a number of origins and remains subject to (dis)continuities. Indeed, in 'fat' popular texts like *Buffy* and *Angel* a comfortable recognition of the extra-textual relationships is built into the mode of address.

This is why, as Rhonda Wilcox has noted, *Buffy* relies on its teen audience being well versed in contemporary TV and film in order that they may identify with the younger protagonists. Buffy actually apologises to Giles at one point in 'I, Robot' (1.8) for a 'pop culture reference' when she says 'My spider sense is tingling'; in 'The

Pack'(1.6) she rounds on Giles with 'I can't believe that you of all people would Scully me.' Questions of intertextuality are consequently crucial in understanding the spaces of programmes like *Buffy* and *Angel*.

The actual, broadcast space of both series is explicitly intercut with products, sold via advertising, placed between acts. Each 'act' is so constructed as to allow this to take place. Even in the UK, where *Buffy* airs on the (non-commercial) BBC, or on video, where the advertising is erased, you will still find commonplace commodities embedded in the shows – the most obvious product to be seen in *Buffy* is the ubiquitous Apple.

When considering the value of such a placement, companies like Apple read shows like *Buffy* and *Angel* with a commercial eye to the audience's demographic and though *Buffy* and *Angel* are aimed at different groups – viz. *Buffy*'s audience is meant to be younger than *Angel*'s, as indicated via the (age of) the protagonists, language and content, and the hours (8pm and 9pm) at which they are originally broadcast in the US – both shows are broadly 'young'. They are aimed at the 'youth' market.

Insertion of commercial objects into the fictional and broadcast space of any show has a number of effects. Aside from helping sell Apple, the products we see belong to an actual time and a genuine place (late twentieth/early twenty-first century California, USA) and so link the fictional setting (in this case Sunnydale/*Angel*'s LA) to that place.

In this way *Buffy* and *Angel* are illusory, they create the illusion, as any realist text would, that they encompass, represent and belong to the real world. Both series and audiences belong to wider cultural and commercial contexts, of which they make use, which shape their form and mode of address and which give the shows truth-seeming authenticity.

When we look at the 'space' of a TV show we therefore need to be aware that its construction is not simply a question of aesthetics, of plot, genre and character; TV shows are made in studios, on location, with material objects, by flesh and blood people. However, we should be equally wary of simply spotting its locations and matching them to 'real' places. 'Place' has become subject to widespread scrutiny, not simply as a location or territory, but as a phenomenon that 'is inseparable from the consciousness of people who occupy it':

> 'Places are fusions of human and natural orders and are significant centres of our immediate experiences of the world. They are defined less by unique locations, landscapes and communities than by the focusing of experiences and intentions onto particular settings.'

Here, places are products of discourse, hence human geographers argue that 'space' is about power, while places are multiple, contingent and plural.

For Doreen Massey, for example, all places are 'always already hybrid.' No place has ever had a single rooted identity; every community has always been characterized by diversity — of class, age, race or sex and so on — and by the links between it and the rest of the world. In one sense or another, most apparently distinct, bounded communities are 'meeting places' and this has always been the case.

There are always multiple routes through any one place, through which each individual or group has to make up their own map. Traditionally we don't see this, because this hybridity is traditionally denied by those who (a) wish to see a place, especially a place called home, as providing 'stability, oneness and security' and (b) those who associate the concept of place 'with stasis and nostalgia, and with an enclosed security.'

Place, whether fictional or real, is always imagined. As David Herbert argues in respect to literature, imaginative texts may allude to topography, 'but few are pre-occupied with place . . . imaginative literature goes well beyond area, landscape and environment and touches upon topics such as quality of life, social class divisions, women in society and sources of inequality; all of these are relevant to . . .

meanings of place.' So, in reading *Buffy* and *Angel* it is the shows' use of imaginative space that is key: the subjective qualities of the world constructed in the show and the audience's access to that world.

The Imaginative Spaces of *Buffy* and *Angel*

Buffy and *Angel* clearly differ in their use of imaginative space. First of all, *Buffy* is set in Sunnydale, a completely fictional location to be found somewhere on the coast of southern California, while *Angel* is set in Los Angeles. As a real city, LA lends *Angel* additional authenticity and weight. Secondly, where Sunnydale is apparently characterized by open bright suburban pleasantness, the LA of *Angel* is darker, more urban, erotically claustrophobic and explicitly seedy. However, both shows co-opt places beyond their ordinary demesne, so that their imaginative space actually extends to the world and world history, most notably Spike's nineteenth-century London, Angelus' eighteenth-century Ireland, China (the Boxer Rebellion) and New York (a subway in 1977).

In the case of Angel/Angelus, Spike, Drusilla and Darla's back history, both shows in fact share the same space, if sometimes seen from different points of view. For example, re the Boxer Rebellion, we hear Spike's story of his first Slayer kill in 'Fool for Love' (5.7). At the end of his fight all four vampires meet up and leave at Angelus' request: he's bored. Spike is full of himself, Drusilla proud, Darla compliant. There is no reason for the audience to doubt the scene, unless they doubt that Spike is a reliable witness. The scene is then reprised in *Angel* 'Darla' (A2.7), and seen from Darla's point of view it seems to end differently, though the setting and action are the same. The characters move through the same space, in the same way, with the same words, but this time the audience knows what Spike does not: that Angelus has already been cursed and so has his soul.

Earlier, he has begged Darla to take him back and he has backed away from a kill (of a missionary, his wife and baby). As they leave this time, Angel seems sickened by the violence that surrounds them, Darla is suspicious, the others oblivious due to Spike's triumph. The ensemble of lighting, setting and scale, theme and mode of address directs the audience's access to each scene. To become aware of each show's imaginative space, the subjective qualities of the places constructed, we therefore need to be sensitive to their use of language, the impact of convention, their methods of narration and motifs.

In its iconography — described by Annette Kuhn as a genre's 'dominant visual facts, motifs or symbols' — *Angel* predominantly draws on references to the hard-boiled conventions of film noir. It's this that makes it different to *Buffy*. The rain-soaked streets and low lighting do not represent the 'real' LA, 'real' crimes or 'real' detection, rather they reflect a stylistic attempt to present thematic ambiguities around good/evil, corruption, social disintegration and disillusion in an imagined LA.

Meanwhile, *Buffy*'s visual feel and mode of address are drawn from a mix of action, horror and soap better suited to themes of teen angst. Take for instance the Initiative's deep underground bunker in the fourth series; overwhelmingly *Bond*-like and built for destruction, which can stand equally for the operation of covert government structures and adult power.

Of course, as series the shows tend to be structured the same way. Because of the shows' use of teasers, for instance, both *Buffy* and *Angel*'s audiences typically enter Sunnydale and LA in darkness or conflict. If that entry is in daylight they normally find themselves in the middle of a relaxed spell — friends talking, brief romantic interlude, office gossip — which suddenly cuts to a more intense night scene for suspense. Even without a cut to violence, any happy moment in the teaser will inevitably be framed by the shows' credits, which recycle predominantly dark scenes overlain by sudden energetic bursts of action. In terms of consumption, this keeps the audience involved, waiting for and wanting more.

However, beyond this, light always contrasts with dark, mapping out the territories of good vs. evil in both shows. In *Angel*'s credits this contrast frames the principals: Angel in white, Cordelia in green, Doyle then Wesley in yellow/gold, Gunn in red. The colours suggest the key attributes of each character – Angel's essential innocence, Cordelia's naïveté, Doyle/Wesley's cowardice and comic timing, Gunn's obsession with death – but the visual fact of light/dark continues to be used, and used much more heavily than in *Buffy*, borrowed, again, from film noir. Finally, *Angel* as a more 'grown up' show makes explicit play of rapid cuts from night to day and of almost stroboscopic cutting to represent the vision headaches of Doyle and Cordelia, thereby drawing attention to the show's artificiality, breaking the realist mode, while simultaneously gesturing towards 'time passes'.

Though well-versed in the conventions of genre TV, on the whole *Angel* is therefore more cinematic than *Buffy* and more willing to draw on those recent experiments that allude to the fact of cinematography for its effects. In 'Are You Now or Have You Ever Been?' (A2.2), for instance a photograph of a hotel is used to draw the audience into a 'flashback'. As Wesley studies it, so the picture becomes animated and resolves into a new scene. This adopts some of the compressed conventions of time-scale used in film noir and highlights the constructed nature of the episode itself. Meanwhile, as Angel moves through the hotel his centrality as protagonist is used to link 'past' with 'present', each intercut with the other. This draws attention to Angel's longevity and the biological fixity of his body, in contrast to his psychological or emotional development – possibly the inverse of what most teenagers experience as growth. It is only in Season Five that *Buffy* has opted for this more experimental approach – for example, the use of dislocating cuts to represent Glory's wobbly sanity, inter-dimensional instability and fluid identity.

Aside from the editing, during any one episode design details, like the uncanniness of some of the fretwork at Sunnydale High – which looks like mouths or lips – contribute to the connotations or available meanings connected with any one site. The organization of space on screen, exterior shots of key buildings and subsequent sight of their interiors, tells the audience something about the characters that live/work in them, their wider relevance to the community they belong to, and the relationships the protagonists live — Xander's decision to take charge of his life in *Buffy* Season Five is signalled by his move from a dank cluttered basement to an airy second-floor flat. They may also add to the inter-textual connotations that that character builds upon — in Season One of *Angel*, his office resembles all other private-eye offices in film, while his personal space is dark, tomb-like and tasteful.

Shots are carefully delineated in the scripts to reflect the audience's or a character's point of view, to reveal and hide information. New settings, like the hotel in *Angel*, which becomes the second season's primary base of operations, are added to each neighbourhood as the plot demands. This enlargement of the fictive map is noticed parodically by Riley in 'Buffy vs. Dracula' (5.1) when he wonders why he has never come across a large castle in Sunnydale before, (it's introduced simply to house Dracula on a visit to the Slayer — presumably, like all the other ways in which Dracula differs from the show's standard vampire mythology — ability to transform into beasts or suddenly appear — it can be dismissed, as Spike does those traits, as 'flashy gypsy tricks').

Sunnydale's zoo, museum and college are only mentioned when it becomes necessary to take the protagonists out of school and/or bring in fresh foes — hyenas at the zoo, mummy girl at the museum, Adam under the college. Once introduced, however, these new locations add to the overall scale and feel of the place as cultured and well to do. In both series the viewing audience is therefore moved between and around these sites as required; and, as the imaginative map gains detail and becomes clear, so a sense of place is gradually built up. Between audience and screen, the specific apparatus used by each shows helps direct the audience's experience of Sunnydale and LA. What the audience is given in a sense is a spatial script.

As each series has evolved, their audiences have come to know the spaces the characters inhabit, the social conventions of the place and local relationships based on age, class, race, sex and species. We learn very quickly in *Buffy* that the school library, for example, is the oldest building on campus. This building is representative of what might be called Sunnydale's 'polite' bourgeois society, its values and its norms. Libraries, like museums, are not simply neutral buildings/rooms in which books/artefacts are housed, but are in and of themselves invested with cultural authority. The Sunnydale High library's age alone guarantees its cultural capital. This is equally suggested through its colonialist design, which echoes Carnegie's social imperative, and holdings that comprise most obviously ancient leather-bound tomes. As in a 'real' museum its 'spatial organisation . . . and the installation of selected pieces within specific sites contribute to the meanings of the artworks and shape the experiences of diverse museum visitors.' This association of the Sunnydale High library with authority is also suggested by the noticeable absence of most of the high school's students. When two students do turn up to look for some textbooks in 'Passion' (2.17), Xander's initial reaction is hostile, he has forgotten that this is a public space that his peers might want to use. Meanwhile that authority is reinforced by Giles, the school librarian who though a repository of occult knowledge was previously a curator of the British Museum. Each setting carries its own connotations and is productive of its own meanings, derived from the 'real' world as well as the show; each setting can therefore be treated as a highly complex text in its own right. Beyond questions of extra- and inter-textuality, this in itself opens both shows up to multiple readings as their audiences work to negotiate their way through.

Home

Neither the homes nor the meanings they produce in *Buffy* and *Angel* are necessarily conventional, yet the treatment of home lies at the heart of an overriding thematic concern with, as Susan Own suggests, 'friendship as family', the maintenance and loss of community. At the same time, *Buffy*'s dialogue and use of 'social monsters' clearly relates to a generation divide, so that teenagers and adults fail to communicate because adults fail to understand the realities of teen life. As Wilcox puts it 'the horror of becoming a vampire often correlates with the dread of becoming an adult.' Bringing these two points together, what I want to suggest is that as the shows have progressed, it is not simply adulthood that is questioned, but the (masculine) individualism of becoming grown-up in contrast to the (feminine) companionship of youth.

In *Buffy* adults and adult figures fail to connect. Though the 'old ones' work as a community of sorts, it is one grounded explicitly in patriarchal dominance, abuse and submission, one that seems to write large the realities of family life from a teen point of view. The next generation of vampires, Spike and Drusilla, though apparently devoted to each other and more equal, subsequently struggle and fail to form and re-form their own 'family'. Indeed, as the show progresses the audience learns that that family has already been shattered, firstly by Angelus having been cursed and secondly by Darla's death at the beginning of Season One. In the end even Drusilla and Spike split up and by Season Five, though Darla has been reborn, Drusilla cannot bring them all back together again.

This inadequacy might be expected of monsters, but the human adults fair just as badly, if not worse. Joyce's attempts to find a new man not only result in her having a relationship with a Stepford husband, as it were, but also a plea, after she has invited Dracula into her home, that she finds it hard to meet men. Just as she starts dating again in Season Five, she dies. Giles forms one steady relationship with Miss Calendar in Season Two, but just as love is beginning to blossom she is killed. Though Joyce and Giles have a fling in 'Band Candy' (3.6), this is in a regressed state as teens and they cannot maintain the attachment once they've 'grown up'. What is perhaps worse is that none of the adults in the show seem to have any ordinary, everyday friends – Joyce is befriended by the overbearing Pat – in 'Dead Man's Party' (3.2) – but Pat is promptly killed by zombies.

This is in direct contrast to the relationships built up by the young protagonists, the Scoobies. Their friendship is founded on a set of common experiences, in part against a common set of enemies, but also a common set of expectations, a shared culture and references. Moreover, as each gang member ages and develops so they work to take their friends with them. This is tested almost to destruction during Season Four and wins out in that season's finale. In 'Fool For Love' (5.7), Spike – now living alone – makes it clear that Buffy's will to live resides in her family and friends, and that if they're taken away she could be killed; this remains a threat as the series progresses and gradually friends and (biological) family are taken from her.

In 'Family' (5.6), Tara is rejected by her (biological) family and replaces them with the family of Buffy, Dawn, Willow, Xander, Anya – and peripherally Spike – while Riley's absence at this point foreshadows his departure from the show. This moment is also important because until this point Tara has felt that she is an outsider, not one of the gang; sitting on the margins, she is all too aware of the centre's location and wants desperately to belong. One of the first to affirm support for Tara is Dawn, whose own status in the group is questionable – apparently Buffy's sister, she is by this point known to Buffy and Giles to be an artefactual person created to hide a mystical Key. Dawn's action reaffirms Buffy's decision that the important relationships are those of the heart, and that Dawn is her sister, because she just *is*.

When Tara is subsequently driven mad by Glory – 'Tough Love' (5.19) – her friends rally round as her only protectors. The fact that in the end she does belong, even when she needs to be actually cared for and fed, shows that though the group is tested and proven to be strong, it is not immutable, passive or fixed. The Scoobies' fluidity and therefore their strength is highlighted when, though he has been absent since the middle of Season Four, in the middle of Season Five Xander wistfully remembers Oz's companionship as another man who'd get his jokes. Incidentally pointing up the strong female bias of the Scoobies in this series, this also reminds us that this Scooby gang, unlike its cartoon namesake, is yielding, shifting and adaptable. This is why though Dawn — introduced in Season Five as Buffy's sister, when the audience knows full well that she doesn't have one — is discovered not even to be human, the gang is able to take her in not just as an innocent to be protected but for her own sake.

In *Buffy* friendship is key and in the first three seasons it is the school library that frames the friends' actions and thereby emphasizes their strength. In the conversion of public into private we see the malleability of architecture, its ability to adapt and shift from one use to another. People remake places to their own liking; buildings are not as fixed as we might think. In the case of the library, its structure (which should mark it out as separate from the world because what it houses is timeless and universal) is used against the grain. This is why Xander has forgotten that other students might want to come in. The library is treated by the Scoobies as a sanctuary. It provides them with a protective, even cloistered, space that they can defend. Though it sits over the Hellmouth and is subject to repeated incursions, it is the most secure place that the Scoobies can go to. During the day its fanlights allow the sun to stream in, while at night its yellow lamps, mahogany desks, circular door-panes, layered hexagonal patterns, offer a womb-like homely kind of comfort and warmth. It is because of this that despite all previous assaults — principally directed at the library as symbol of authority and in one case largely off screen — the Mayor's entry to taunt them in 'Graduation Day Part One' (3.21) is still shocking. This moment foreshadows the library's ultimate penetration, his and its final destruction. Even then, in 'New Moon Rising' (4.19), Riley turns to it as a safe haven, while in 'Out of My Mind' (5.4) Willow suggests that he has run there again because it feels nostalgically 'homey'.

After the library has been blown up, the friends search for a new 'home'. In parallel to the emphasis on friendship as family, the characters continue to make and remake their own space. Their friendship and its sanctuaries stand in contrast to the status of their 'real' families and 'real' homes, which are consistently threatened or destroyed and normally fail in the face of repeated attack. In 'Bewitched, Bothered and Bewildered' (2.16), when Xander runs to Buffy and her mother's home with Cordelia for protection, all the girls/women who have fallen in love with him break in and attack — even Buffy's mom, Joyce, joins in. In 'Ted' (2.11) Joyce's new Stepford man beats Buffy up in her own room. In 'Bad Eggs' (2.12), in which we see the mother/child relationship represented as inherently parasitic, again Buffy is attacked in her room — this time by an egg-dwelling spider-like critter. When Angel goes bad, he abuses his invitation to both Buffy's and Willow's homes in order to drive Buffy mad. His preferred mode of operation is to kill his victim's family and friends before finally turning on them individualized and alone, in effect, making them grow up.

In Season Four, once Buffy goes to college, her home is abruptly taken from her as her mom converts her old room for storage. Though materially her home withstands these incursions, it never works as a safe haven, a place to which she can run and hide. In Season Five, it isn't secure enough to hide Dawn and needs to be protected with spells provided by Tara and Willow.

In the earlier seasons we therefore see the instabilities of growing up and of being the child of a lone parent written into domestic space. In Season Five this is emphasized by Joyce's death. But, Buffy's dorm, her new home at college, is equally unstable. In fact, the stress placed on the Scoobies' friendship is emphasized in Season Four by the failure to find them a real base/home. They colonize Giles's flat, but also cycle through Buffy's room, her old home and Xander's basement. Xander has such a poor relationship with his own family that he sleeps in the garden on holidays and, though we see no actual violence, we hear and therefore imagine why he wants to get out. It is only once the Scoobies' crisis is resolved at the end of the season that they can settle again.

At this point, Giles becomes steadily more dissatisfied with both the loss of identity he has suffered in losing his old job (when the library is blown up) and the loss of his own individual space in the Scoobies' use of his condo. In buying the magic shop he initially finds (if unwittingly) a new sense of purpose. Then, pointing up the group's investment in the project as well as his new-found skill as a carpenter, Xander helps in its refurbishment. Subsequently, in reflection of the Scoobies' recovered strength, it is finally adopted as their new centre of operations/home. Private space therefore consistently gives way to public space in *Buffy*. In other words, public space is remade by the group, and though never truly secure, it is always more secure than any individual's 'real' home. Just as the biological family, reliant as it is on detached, particularized adults, is unstable and insufficient, so the biological family home is represented as a site of conflict and pain, rather than nostalgia or comfort.

In counterpoint to this argument, vampires regularly trespass in the public space of the Bronze, using the night-club as a handy feeding ground on the wrong side of town. As such it's a convenient allegorical site for a variety of conventional 'just say no' messages. But, as they are able to ignore these attacks, the teenage protagonists continue to meet here to work up their own social maps beyond adult sight. They still feel at 'home'. Again in opposition to what's been presented so far and, as noted, the library is ironically located directly over the Hellmouth from which/through which monsters emerge throughout the first three seasons, suggesting that you can never be sure that you know what is lying beneath a respectable suburban surface, a common enough theme in American fiction.

Indeed, to take a more psychoanalytic stance, if the library is 'home' then it is also womb, in which case the Hellmouth is its vagina/cervix. Given that in the first season the Master is initially trapped in there –

'like a cork in a bottle' – this adds to his initially foetal-like unborn (as much as undead) status. Alternatively, his Nosferatu-like appearance – Nosferatu being notably linear, rigid and erect – provides a more penetrative reading. Or, perhaps the library is representative of the conscious/ego, while the Hellmouth is unconscious/id, the Master the embodiment of that which is repressed and uncannily returns. However, seeking out this reading simply highlights the inherent ambiguities of space.

The library is patently not a 'home' yet it becomes one because it is used as such: home as function not simply as place. To paraphrase Xander misquoting Robert Frost in 'Pangs' (4.8): 'Home is where they need to take you in when you need to go there.' This function works in part because of and is reinforced by the increasingly female bias of the Scoobies, which by Season Five is central to the construction of the group. Over the course of the show, it is primarily the men (Angel, Oz, Riley and to some extent Spike) who have left, suggesting a higher degree of activity on their part. Though Angel and Riley move away and join new communities (Angel Investigations and Special Ops), there is a sense in which they have reluctantly grown up and left home. Oz fails in his relationship with Willow and leaves town, Spike fails to become truly human, but both are driven off to act out lonely, individual lives.

The one woman to have left, Cordelia, is represented as consistently ambitious with an almost excessive masculine drive, only later learning to value friendship once she joins Angel in LA. Giles and Xander, the only men to remain are, in direct contrast, passive, uncompetitive, settled. The community of friends, then, the Scooby gang itself, like home and family, is coded feminine, in opposition to the fractured, driven, individualized and consequently masculine world of vampires and adults. However, this community, far from being natural and static, is always at risk and in flux. Community/friendship as family has to be worked and fought for, as Season Four and Season Five, which rests on the statement 'they get to you through your family', both show.

A similar balance can be found in *Angel*, though, because the relationships are already adult, more is at risk for the friendships made and the communities formed. Here the protagonists have more baggage, and friendship/communal 'home' becomes a place for the discovery of one's self. As something of an outsider, for instance, we don't get to see Wesley's place until he has acquired a girl (whom he soon loses). But he nonetheless belongs to Angel Investigations, a group which continues to persist once he, Gunn and Cordelia are fired, and until Angel returns to the fold. Wesley is initially brought in from the cold as a 'lone/rogue demon hunter', an identity that he constructs for himself having failed as a Watcher, but which he never lives out alone. Wesley can only grow, find strength and self-belief in friendship as family, and it is only paradoxically by walking in Angel's shoes for a day that he finally discovers his self-esteem. In Season One Angel uses the basement of his LA office as his home. Once this is destroyed, he uses the hotel as both home and office in Season Two. It is in these ostensibly public spaces that much of the ensemble work takes place and here that Angel Investigations takes form. Failed private homes in *Angel* include Cordelia's first place, Doyle's apartment and Gunn's underground hide. These locations represent the characters, map out their emotional condition and relationships with the rest of the team.

A key story in *Angel* Season One is therefore 'Rm w/a Vu' (A1.5). Cordelia's fight to make her new and suspiciously cheap flat her own by expelling the original occupants' ghosts – or rather ridding the flat of the mother and moving in with the son. The acquisition is a rite of passage and through it she too rediscovers herself – 'I'm not some little cry Buffy . . . I'm the nastiest girl in Sunnydale.' In the same episode Doyle rejects such a journey and it's made clear that only those who feel that they deserve to be punished live in squalor. Potentially this is a conservative message, particularly as Doyle's sense of self subsequently crystallizes as literal self-sacrifice; on this occasion it might have been better to 'grow up' much sooner.

In both series, this idea of 'home' is constructed against the spaces that the shows' Others inhabit. The secure spaces of each programme help determine alienation as they lie opposite the deep chilling world of the night. It is in part because of this that both home and family become especially problematic in *Angel* and help emphasize the tensions around Angel himself as the vampire with a soul. Angel perpetually inhabits dark spaces. In *Angel,* though his office basement and hotel room are both annexed to the group's 'home' and though some of his homes are well furnished, these spaces in and of themselves are quite barren. Yes, he is a vampire and needs to avoid sunlight, yet the rooms he occupies seem chosen more for aesthetic effect than necessity – after all, he works close to the light all day long. His 'homes' if they can be called such, are a reflection of his own darkness, demonic aspect and self-loathing. As already noted, Doyle observes in 'Rm w/a Vu' sometimes people deliberately live in ways and places which don't get their expectations up.

In *Angel* Season Two Gunn's hideout works the same way. By living in the same places as vampires, Gunn risks death, which he does want, and becoming one of them, which he may not know that he wants. Both men seek redemption, both live on the margins. As this becomes clear, so Angel descends into this darkness, becoming steadily more and more alienated from the group, so that he finally fires Gunn, Wesley and Cordelia. This is prompted by Darla's return. She is his lover and 'sire'. As she haunts him, so Angel descends into and starts to explore his deepest dreams and worst desires, alone, drawn on by memories of his old vampire 'family' – Drusilla, Spike, Angelus, Darla. In fighting this battle, he increasingly works alone, and in the end, in 'Epiphany' (A2.16) discovers that what he really needs to fight evil is company. He therefore seeks to return to his friends and must work to regain their trust. Again, in friendship there is strength, but it must be valued and fought for.

In *Angel* of course the city the characters inhabit is 'real' – some of it known or knowable to audiences, other elements redrawn. The fixity of location – as signalled by the continued existence of the hotel, as well as LA – is important in reinforcing the values of the show, and this fixity in itself is reinforced by the stability of Angel's body. As noted earlier, though on a road to redemption physiologically he remains unchanged. At the same time, though people and society shift around him, what he learns to hold dear apparently remains constant and, thereby, universal. The values he represents are typified in his transformation into a knight in 'Judgement'(A2.1). Here the Powers That Be – themselves apparently timeless, as well as all-knowing – rewrite downtown LA into the site of a ritualized medieval joust. Like Doyle and Gunn he is prepared to sacrifice himself for the greater good.

That Angel's values might be awry, or misplaced, is suggested by the fact that he is there at all. He has killed when he should have helped and he has had to take on a battle that is not his own. He wins, the episode plays with the idea of the convergence of ancient and modern evil, but the battle itself is absurd. His values, meanwhile, are paralleled by the fixed values of the city itself, vested in certain kinds of property (such as the hotel), exploitation and conceit. The city's corporate architecture stands implacable and proud against his assaults. In 'Reprise' (A2.15), on descending to Hell, what he learns is that as an individual he can do nothing, he learns that he has been tilting at windmills.

In *Angel* the search for home and family can be read fundamentally as the search for a lost feminine, womb-like space of rebirth. Contextually, in the search for home there is the desire for a lost territory, an idealization of the family relationship that binds us to the home and of the home itself as 'Woman/Mother/Lover'. 'Home' has become a place that we tend to look back to as having come from, and is therefore generally constructed through the lens of nostalgia and the search for vanished perfection. Though it does not literally have to be a domestic space, it has come primarily to be associated with maternal imagery, and it is that imagery that normally makes it 'comfortable'. *Angel* and *Buffy* use these images. Yet the most protective spaces in both *Buffy* and *Angel* seem to be found in what are traditionally much more masculine domains: the school library, a shop, an office and a hotel. In both shows the preference for companionship over individualism, even in adulthood, remakes these spaces into sanctuaries, and therefore overturns the usual opposition of public and private, so that public and private are subverted and transgressed or transformed.

The last and narrow house?

> Much it concerns a man, forsooth, how a few sticks
> are slanted over him or under him, and what colors
> are daubed upon his box. It would signify somewhat,
> if, in any earnest sense, *he* slanted them and daubed
> it; but the spirit having departed out of the tenant,
> it is of a piece with constructing his own coffin, —
> the architecture of the grave, and 'carpenter,' is but
> another name for 'coffin-maker.' One man says, in
> his despair or indifference to life, take up a handful
> of the earth at your feet, and paint your house that
> color. Is he thinking of his last and narrow house?
> Henry David Thoreau, *Walden* (1854) p. 31

The maternal imagery that remains in the continued association of 'home' with 'family', whether that home be 'public' or 'private', sits alongside the womb-like grave, the dark, dank underground spaces that in *Buffy* and *Angel* keep spawning monsters. As Thoreau suggests, the architecture of the grave and the architecture of the home can be uncomfortably close. Here we meet the wider issue of the establishment of boundaries with respect to the vampires. As Owen observes, vampires are also able to 'lurk' disguised in quite ordinary places, as long as it's dark. Not only is the Master trapped in the Hellmouth, vampires in general cannot cross into a home without invitation – though that invitation might be spoken or written, hence the general invitation written onto the fabric of the school building to those seeking knowledge. Moreover, the fictive spaces of *Buffy* include dreamscapes. The last episode in *Buffy* Season Four is not the finale we might expect, ie the destruction of the Initiative's base, but the journey into dreamtime, in which each friend learns their role within the Slayer's life. Earlier, in 'Nightmares' (1.10) a little boy dreams and traps everyone in his nightmares as he seeks to flee the 'monster' he fears: his coach. The boy's dreams rewrite all the spaces of the series, inside and out. For Buffy herself, dream is often as concrete as reality given that her predictions often come true, while *Angel* incorporates fractured visions for Doyle and then Cordelia. These aspects of the shows' organization of space, and the Slayer's ready transgression of all borders, lend both shows to a psychoanalytic reading, which has not been attempted here. Rather, I have surveyed the shows' organization of space on screen and the meanings produced in and around one particular site: home.

It's odd that Buffy & co rarely inhabit spaces typical of their age-group, (eg the mall or the movie theatre. Both attract large numbers of people, suitable victims of vampiric incursions, one might assume. Instead, teen socializing focuses on the Bronze and, until it's destroyed, high school students hang out in the quad. Occasionally we have a visit to the high street, which still seems to boast independent cafes (The Expresso Pump) and stores, and which can support lavish boutiques and a gallery. There is a mall, a very fine one in fact, but we rarely see it. There is one example of Buffy slaying there ('Innocence' (2.14)) and one episode where she shops there with her mom ('Bad Eggs' (2.12)).

This coupled with the Spanish-style architecture of its older buildings and its 43 churches (perhaps 44), adds to the almost nostalgic sense of Sunnydale as a 'nice' place. It has well-appointed Mediterranean-style condos, such as Giles's place, adapted from multi-

storeys, a mansion, a castle and tidy neighbourhoods like Revello
Drive. Its manufacturing district mostly gone, except for the docks,
the Sunnydale we see is primarily a privileged white neighbourhood
à la Beverly Hills. Its population works and plays in the sun, on the
beach, in playgrounds, on the sports field. It has an ice rink as well as
a museum, a zoo and an ivy league college. This might be adaptive on
the part of its residents, but it also works to heighten the tension
between Sunnydale as perfected community and Sunnydale as access
to Hell.

Like *The StepfordWives,* Sunnydale's imaginative space plays with the
longstanding tradition of revealing the rotten or even vicious under-
belly of (white, Christian, wealthy) suburban USA. Space is a social
construct that is dynamic and unstable, and spatial categories such as
'suburban' and 'urban' have significance in everyday life, constructed
in and through culturally and spatially specific social practices. In
Sunnydale we therefore have what, in Jane Austen's time, might have
been called a division between 'polite' and 'impolite' society.

Bibliography

Brake, L., 'Gendered Space: *The Woman's World*' in *Women: a Cultural Review*,
    Vol. 2, No. 2, 1991

Brand, S., *How Buildings Learn, what happens after they're built* (Phoenix
    Illustrated, London, 1997)

Braun, B., '*The X-Files* and *Buffy the Vampire Slayer*: The Ambiguity of Evil in
    Supernatural Representations', *Journal of Popular Film and Television*, Vol.
    28 Issue 2, Summer 2000

Duncan, C. and Wallach, A., 'The Universal Survey Museum', *Art History*,
    Vol. 3, 1980

Herbert, D., 'Place and Society in Jane Austen's England' in *Geography*, Vol.
    76 part 3, July 1991

Kuhn, A. (ed.), *Alien Zone II: The Spaces of Science Fiction Cinema* (Verso, London
    & New York, 1999)

Massey, D., 'Places and Their Pasts', *History Workshop Journal*, No. 39, Spring
    1995

Massey, D., *Space, Place and Gender* (Polity, Cambridge, 1994)

McTavish, L., 'Shopping in the Museum? Consumer Spaces and the Redefinition of the Louvre' in *Cultural Studies*, Vol. 12, No 2, April 1998

Owen, S.A., '*Buffy the Vampire Slayer*: Vampires, Postmodernity and Postfeminism', *Journal of Popular Film and Television*, Vol. 27, Issue 2, Summer 1999

Rose, G., *Feminism and Geography, the limits of geographical knowledge* (Polity, Cambridge, 1993)

Van Slyck, A.A., *Free to All: Carnegie Libraries and American Culture 1890–1920* (Uni Chicago Press, Chicago, 1995)

Weissberg, L., 'Gothic Spaces' in V. Sage & A. Lloyd Smith (eds) *Modern Gothic, A Reader* (MUP, Manchester, 1996)

Wilcox, R.V., 'There will never be a 'very special' *Buffy*; *Buffy* and the monsters of teen life' in *Journal of Popular Film & Television*, Vol. 27 Issue 2, Summer 1992

Websites

http://www.apple.com/hotnews/features/starringapple.html

http://www.macobserver.com/news/00/january/000119/applespnsorsangel.shtml

http://cbs.marketwatch.com/archive/20000114/news/current/rebecca.htx

http://www.newstimes.com/archive2000/mar25/tvd.htm

http://www.wirednews.com/news/culture/0,1284,15919,00.html

http://www.wirednews.com/news/topstories/0,1287,16046,00.html

Film

The Truman Show

what you are, what's to come

feminisms, citizenship and the divine

zoe-jane playden

Eve am I, great Adam's wife,
I killed Jesus long ago . . .

Irish lament

Theoretically there would be no such thing as woman.
She would not exist.

Luce Irigaray, *Speculum of the Other Woman*

Invitation

'As a woman, I have no country. As a woman I want no country. As a woman my country is the whole world.' This famous declaration is Virginia Woolf's, championing women's rights both to education and entry into the professions, in a seminal feminist manifesto, important aspects of which are reflected in *Buffy the Vampire Slayer*.[1] Buffy's particular combination of knowledge and power places her outside the mainstream of super-heroes and leads to particular ideas of learning, of spirituality, and of citizenship, which challenge the dominant discourses of Western patriarchy.

Over the years, the feminist project has been concerned to slay its own vampires, in the form of ideas that, hundreds of years old, have prowled and fed on society's marginalized communities, especially women. My invitation, therefore, is to come on patrol with a select group of Slayers, to join Buffy, the Scoobies and feminist thinkers, and to help in doing the dusting.

Cemeteries and Sunlight

Let me map out the territory you will be working in. On the one hand is a monumental cemetery full of undead white males, the grand narrative of Western thought from Freud back to Plato, which, as Irigaray points out, consistently excludes women, by denying them subjectivity, that is, an existence of their own, in language, thought and imagination. They provide the patriarchy, that is, state-sanctioned patterns of thought and action, which consistently cast out from social identity marginalized groups and individuals, who do not meet their economic or political definitions.

Such works are not only the product of men – the tradition may be typified by works such as Janice Raymond's *The Transsexual Empire* and Germaine Greer's *The Whole Woman*. Both of those female writers provide deterministic, dystopian accounts of woman as having an homogeneous identity which is inescapably constructed by white, capitalist, male heterosexism.

Judged by standards such as Raymond's and Greer's, Buffy is another degrading sexploitation of the patriarchy, a woman who is objectified as a function – 'the Slayer' – and controlled to serve ends which are not her own. She is a constructed woman, a kind of 'cyborg', 'a creature of social reality as well as science fiction': constructed within the terms of the series, as the means for a male élite, the Council, to get their dangerous work done; constructed by the entertainment industry as soft SM porn, disguised as adventure story to legitimize scenes of violence against women; and constructed within media capitalism to provide image-branding and related merchandizing opportunities, whether as tie-in 'Buff-Stuff' or generic halter-neck tops for eleven-year-old girls.

Exposing these ideas to sunlight, though, is the job of a more recent literature. Feminist writing reclaims the agency of marginalized individuals, it recognizes subjectivity as valuable, and it resists the fixity of state-sanctioned patterns of thought and behaviour. Trans theory – the use of the lived experience of inter-sexed and transgendered people to critique contemporary notions of gender and sexuality – provides a further means of exploring liminality, that is, the 'in-between' areas that constitute the physical and intellectual boundaries of society. These ideas, and feminist thought in general, are accessible to everyone, not just women: male writers such as Deleuze and Foucault contribute to feminist thought, which is concerned with the circumstances of all people, just as Giles and Xander are part of the Scoobies, who protect all Sunnydale.

The stakes are, these ideas against those of the patriarchy. Read any further, and you will be involved in an argument that *Buffy* offers not degrading readings of woman in society, but emancipatory ones and that the series is suggestive of a series of feminisms: feminist theory, feminist mythology and lesbian feminist politics.

In Giles's Library: Philosophy

Education and training

My starting point is, that Slayers are both born and made. As Giles tries to tell Buffy in the first episode of the series, 'Welcome to the Hellmouth'(1.1):

> Giles: Into each generation, a Slayer is born. One girl,
>   in all the world, a Chosen One. One born with
>   the . . .
> Buffy: . . . the strength and skill to hunt the vampires,

> to stop the spread of evil, blah, blah. I've heard it,
> okay?

Not only is Buffy born as the Chosen One, however, but also part of Giles's role as her Watcher is to teach her how to slay vampires, as a scene in 'Angel' (1.7) makes clear:

> Buffy (looking at some crossbow bolts): Huh, check
> out these babies; goodbye, stakes, hello, flying
> fatality. What can I shoot?
> Giles: Nothing. The crossbow comes later. You must
> become proficient with the basic tools of combat.
> And let's begin with the quarterstaff. Which, in-
> cidentally, requires countless hours of rigorous
> training. I speak from experience.
> Buffy: Giles, twentieth century. I'm not gonna be
> fighting Friar Tuck.
> Giles: You never know with whom — or what — you
> may be fighting. And these traditions have been
> handed down through the ages. Now, show me good,
> steady progress with the quarterstaff and in due time
> we'll discuss the crossbow. (Buffy demolishes him
> with the quarterstaff)
> Giles (on the floor, breathing hard): Good. Let's move
> on to the crossbow.

The undercutting of Giles's role in controlling Buffy's learning, provides part of the humour of the series and indicates that the means by which Buffy learns to *become* a Slayer, as well as being *born* the Slayer, is a particular one, negotiated between them. The introduction of another Slayer, Kendra, in 'What's My Line Part 2' (2.10) makes this point. Kendra has been trained in what is to be understood as the traditional way:

> Kendra: My parents — they sent me to my Watcher
> when I was very young.

Buffy: How young?

Kendra: I don't remember them actually . . . I've seen
  pictures. But that's how seriously the calling is taken
  by my people. My mother and father gave me to my
  Watcher because they believed they were doing the
  right thing for me – and for the world.

By contrast, Buffy's single-parent mother is unaware that she is the
Slayer, while Giles has made specific decisions not to intervene in
Buffy's learning in the usual way. So, in 'What's My Line Part 2', he
has not objected to her having friends who know that she is the Slayer:

Giles: Kendra. There are a few people – civilians if you
  like – who know Buffy's identity. Willow is one of
  them. And they also spend time together. Socially.

Kendra: And you allow this, sir?

Giles: Well . . .

Kendra: But the Slayer must work in secret. For
  security . . .

Giles: Of course. With Buffy, however, its . . . some
  flexibility is required.

and he has not even bothered to introduce her to the Slayer handbook:

Kendra: I study because it is required. The Slayer
  handbook insists on it.

Willow: There's a Slayer handbook?

Buffy: Handbook? What handbook? How come I don't
  have a handbook?

Giles: After meeting you, Buffy, I was quite sure the
  handbook would be of no use in your case.

The need for Giles to support Buffy's learning in a particular way, is a
continual theme, so that when, in the fifth season, Giles decides to leave
for England, since he believes he is no longer needed by Buffy, she makes
it clear that she still needs his support in 'Buffy vs Dracula' (5.1):

Buffy: You haven't been my Watcher for a while. I haven't been training and I haven't really needed to come to you for help.

Giles: I agree.

Buffy: And then this whole thing with Dracula. It made me face up to some stuff. Ever since we did that spell where we called on the first Slayer, I've been going out a lot. Every night.

Giles: Patrolling.

Buffy: Hunting. That's what Dracula called it, and he was right. He understood my power better than I do. He saw darkness in it. I need to know more, about where I come from, about the other Slayers. Maybe, maybe if I learn to control this thing, I could be stronger and I could be better. But I'm scared. I know it's going to be hard and I can't do it without you. I need your help. I need you to be my Watcher again.

This negotiated learning relationship between Buffy and Giles may be typified as education rather than training. As Peters points out, training is concerned with 'some specifiable type of performance that has to be mastered'. Its focus is on transmission of skills, from an authority to a passive recipient, where the authority knows why the work has to be performed and the recipient simply does it.

Education, though, takes place through 'conversation' rather than 'courses', in which 'lecturing to others is bad form; so is using the remarks of others as springboards for self-display. The point is to create a common world to which all bring their distinctive contributions'. The goal of education is 'transformation', since 'education implies that a man's outlook is transformed by what he knows,' rather than 'transmission' of a set of behaviours. It is clear from what has been said so far, that the relationship between Buffy and Giles is one of education: she doesn't need training in the quarterstaff, but she does need his distinctive contribution of esoteric knowledge and she needs the relationality of friendships to achieve personal growth and transformation.

For Buffy, her role as Slayer is fundamental to her being, as Kendra recognizes ('What's My Line Part 2'):

> Kendra: You talk about slaying like it's a job. It's not.
>   It's who you are.
> Buffy: Did you get that from your handbook?
> Kendra: From you.

Knowing and being

The philosophical concept lying behind the distinctions between education and training, is a division between 'knowing' and 'being' which has been fundamental to Western civilization since Plato. Feminist thinking has taken these two philosophical categories into new areas. Now, a distinction may be made between 'praxis', knowledge developed from lived experience, including that of marginalized groups, and 'the Academy', knowledge hallowed by the patriarchy, which foregrounds objectivity and the unquestionable 'truths' of scientism. Similarly, being is typically seen by patriarchal thought as ranking ideas in strict layers of importance in a Copernican, regulated universe. Feminism though places community and the organization of ideas in webs of relationship in the foreground. Virginia Woolf developed this idea in her utopian notion of a group of women, which:

> would have no honorary treasurer, for it would need
> no funds. It would have no office, no committee, no
> secretary; it would call no meetings; it would hold no
> conferences. If name it must have, it could be called
> the Outsiders' Society.

To contextualize this, most super-heroes are *either* born *or* made. Into the first category fall figures such as Superman, whose powers result from the accident that has placed him on earth, and those, such as Spiderman, whose powers come about as a result of a physical accident like a radioactive spider bite. Their superiority arises from their simple physical being. Into the second category falls figures such as Batman, who teaches himself physical skills and scientific knowledge, and Xena Warrior Princess, who has learned special skills in combat, healing and esoteric knowledge. Their strength comes through knowledge.

For Slayers, though, there is no division between being and knowing: they are born Slayers and simultaneously they learn to slay, they have inherent physical gifts of strength, stamina and recovery from injury and they have to learn to fight effectively so as not to be killed. Their actions reflect both their being in the world and their approach to learning about the world: Kendra is trained; Kendra is mesmerized and killed. Buffy is educated; Buffy survives. By reconciling knowing and being, Buffy falls outside the mainstream of super-heroes, therefore, a position which is underlined in the series by a constant stream of references to popular culture, with the implication that those icons are less real than the (fictional) characters who are referring to them: Power Girl ('Killed by Death' (2.18)); Clark Kent ('Never Kill a Boy on a First Date'(1.5)); Human Torch ('The Witch' (1.3)); Xena Warrior Princess ('Halloween' (2.6)); and, of course, 'the Scoobies' ('What's My Line Part 1' (2.9)).

Plato's world

This distinction between knowing and being, reconciled by Buffy, is fundamental to reading the series' religious symbolism and political significance. It finds its origins in Greek thought. In Plato's world view, that which is best in human life is just a shadow of Ideal Forms which exist out of this world, and are only accessible to those with spiritual intuition. Ordinary people, who simply are, are never going to know transcendence; only philosophers, men who know, can pierce the veil and are therefore the only ones qualified to rule. 'Those who are now called kings and potentates must learn to seek wisdom like true and genuine philosophers, and so political power and intellectual wisdom will be joined in one . . . it is the proper nature of these to keep hold of true wisdom and to lead in the city,' says Plato in *The Republic*, whereas the others must 'leave philosophy alone and follow their leader.'

Knowledge and power

For Plato, knowledge is power, 'most mighty of all powers' and he reserves power by restricting knowledge. Herein lies the political distinction between 'training' and 'education': training is an act of subjugation, education an act of empowerment. When Buffy refuses to acknowledge the power of the Council – 'the council is not welcome here. I have no time for orders' (Graduation Day, Part 1' (3.21) – she is challenging a political philosophy which is more than two thousand years old and championing a feminism which has existed for less than a century.

This challenge is particularly important because the idea of democracy, in Western civilization, consistently refers itself to ancient Greek states, particularly Athens, and to principles propounded by its philosophers, especially Plato, who hated democracy. The challenge provided by Buffy is significant, therefore, both because she combines knowing and being and because she is a woman.

In Athenian society, the model for modern Western democracy, women had no status as citizens: the 'brothers in the city', whether Philosopher-Kings or farmers or shoemakers, were all brothers: spiritual power and political authority were purely patriarchal, with women, at best, having a handmaiden role in religion as a servant of a god – such as the Pythoness who spoke for Apollo at Delphi – in a pantheon which was understood as a patriarchal structure with Zeus as its head.

Other super-heroes consult and take guidance from the male head of society who knows best how to use their special powers of being – Superman talks to the President and Batman to Commissioner

Gordon, for instance. Buffy herself knows best how to use her being, and also knows what assistance she needs to learn more, to live and be more effective. This is demonstrated conclusively in 'Checkpoint' (5.12), where Buffy tells the Council that their claims to have power over her are false, and where she reverses the balance of power by giving them orders, which they must take, including the re-employment of Giles. Unlike other pop-culture heroes, therefore, the character of Buffy the Vampire Slayer is highly suggestive of alternative spiritual values and political relationships.

On Patrol, first shift: Religious Symbolism

Beastly women

In the Western myth of Paradise, there were two trees, one the tree of life (and being) and the other the tree of knowledge of good and evil. The Fall, the expulsion from Paradise, arose from eating one fruit and not the other, an action used by the orthodox Christian church to create the doctrine of Original Sin, and to erect a power system to provide salvation, through the divine agency of Christ. Such salvation was available to all those with souls, which, to the medieval Church, did not necessarily include women: Eve had been created out of Adam's spare rib, in the creation story they preferred, and while she shared his body, did not necessarily share his soul. Rather, like the vampires slayed by Buffy, women had more in common with animals: *habet mulier animum?* – has woman a soul? – was the perplexing debate of the European Middle Ages.

The numinous female

Buffy, however, reaches through this traditional Christian inter-pretation, to alternative viewpoints. Buffy herself dies and is resurrected, and thus becomes a kind of woman-Christ, an idea of the divine feminine which follows the mystical Christian tradition exemplified by Juliana of Norwich. She exemplifies the redemptive potential which is an important theme of the series, and which, arguably, operates for all of its central characters, on different levels. It is a particular idea of redemption, however, and one which, as Buffy's status as 'woman-Christ' hints, belongs to earlier theologies than that of contemporary state-endorsed Christianities. As Elaine Pagels points out, the doctrine of the bodily resurrection of Christ is a political one, which 'legitimizes the authority of certain men who claim to exercise exclusive leadership over the churches as the successors of the apostle Peter.'[2]

Plato's Philosopher-King, with special spiritual intuition, is translated into a Bishop of Rome, divinely ordained by God and legitimized by the apostolic succession instituted by a resurrected Christ. This position reflects a struggle for power in the early Christian church, led by Irenaeus on behalf of the 'orthodox' – literally, 'straight thinking' – Christians, which was won by that group when they gained military support from the converted Emperor Constantine in the fourth century.

It eradicated a different theological and intellectual tradition, that of the Gnostics, who believed that divinity was not transcendent but was immanent, that God was not in heaven but was present in everyone on earth. So, as Pagels explains, in the Gnostic tradition, 'self-knowledge is knowledge of God; the self and the divine are identical'; 'when the disciple attains enlightenment, Jesus no longer serves as his spiritual master: the two have become equal – even identical'. Gnosis, literally 'knowledge', is a particular kind of knowledge: not the 'straight thinking' of mathematics or logic, but self-knowledge and intuitive understanding of others, a discipline of reflection and compassion.

It is this sensibility which informs the spiritual dimension of *Buffy* and of *Angel*. Redemption – not a salvation from a transcendent god, but a here-and-now personal wholeness – is always possible and available, here on earth. This is exemplified by Buffy herself, who, as the Slayer, must face and deal with vampires and demons – powerful symbols for the darkness encountered on any private inward journey. She dies, more than once; she rises from death; she harrows Hell. (In an iconographic reference to an entirely other tradition, she does so with a hammer and a sickle-like axe ('Anne' (3.1)).

This sensibility is true, too, for those that she saves physically, for they are her friends and neighbours, rather than people from whom she is emotionally distant. These people, though, are not reliant on Buffy for anything other than their physical safety: their spiritual journey is their own work and a personal redemptive experience equal to that of Buffy's is accessible to them, as the principal characters demonstrate, through their own particular sensibilities. So, Angel, explicitly, continually seeks atonement and redemption; Giles leaves the orthodoxy of the Council; Oz seeks control of his werewolf side through yogic meditation; Willow develops spiritually through Wicca; Buffy's mother learns financial and emotional independence; Cordelia develops selflessness and responsibility; Xander finds self-respect through craftsmanship; Tara realizes her complete humanity; Spike's evil becomes ambiguous and then turns to a love for Buffy that is at once bawdily profane and entirely selfless and Faith embarks on a journey of self-discovery and ethical reconstruction.

To underline the point that Buffy's death and resurrection are not reserved for her alone, Angel, too, dies and is resurrected, becoming a further 'Christ-analogue', an identity emphasized by the scene in 'City of' (A1.1), evocative of Christ's temptation, when, in the high place represented by the top floor of corporate offices, he refuses worldly authority with his question to Russell Winters, 'Can you fly?'

The gnostic writings that remain, known as the Nag Hammadi Library, point to earlier traditions, in which Eve gave life to Adam, at the bidding of a female godhead. The tractate *On the Origin of the World* tells that:

> After the day of rest, Sophia sent Zoë, her daughter,
> being called Eve, as an instructor in order that she might
> make Adam, who had no soul, arise . . . she said,

'Adam, become alive! Arise up upon the earth!'
Immediately her word became accomplished fact.

Female subjectivity is writ large here, in a Christian account of the
creation myth which transsexualizes the orthodox tradition and
challenges patriarchal political authority, just as other texts replace
the apostle Peter's delegated authority with a primary relationship
between Christ and Mary Magdalene.

Buffy provides an interplay between the redemptive and the
creationary aspects of the sacred female. The re-creation of Angel,
naked like Adam, is brought about by Buffy-Zoë's silent invocation of
him, symbolized by the placing of her Claddagh ring at the place where
she killed him ('Faith, Hope and Trick' (3.3)). Angel-Adam, returned
from Hell, is also Angel-Christ, on an equal footing to Buffy-Christ,
whose death and return to life is emphasized in the same episode by
her mother being told of it. As in the gnostic sensibility, therefore,
the relationship between Buffy and Angel is not only primary but also
equal, so that Angel's redemption is of his own willing as well as of
Buffy's action – as Giles points out, 'there are two kinds of monster.
The first can be redeemed, or more importantly, wants to be
redeemed'('Beauty and the Beasts' (3.4)).

The moon
Baring and Cashford point out that the gnostic tradition draws on
earlier theologies centred on the divine female, the earliest written
account of which, in Western civilization, is the collection of myths,
verse and hymns from Sumeria in 2,000 BC, concerning Inanna. The
relationship between Faith, Buffy and Angel seems to find resonances
with the longest of those hymns, *The Descent of Inanna*. In the Sumerian
account, the goddess Inanna turns her attention to her 'dark side', to
her sister-goddess, Ereshkigal: 'My Lady abandoned heaven and earth
to descend to the underworld.' Her entry into the underworld is a
process of progressive stripping of authority and power, and Ereshkigal
fiercely kills Inanna, and hangs her corpse on a hook, to rot.

At the pleading of her faithful woman-servant, Ninshubur, the gods allow Inanna to be rescued by tiny, cross-gendered creatures, the *kurgarra* and *galator*, who bring Inanna back to the world above. But Ereshkigal must have a sacrifice of some sort, and Inanna is pursued by the *galla*, demons of the underworld. In her place, therefore, Inanna first gives Ereshkigal her husband, Dumuzi, and then, on the lamentations of his sister, Geshtinanna, agrees that, for half the year, Dumuzi will dwell in the underworld and that, for the other half of the year, Geshtinanna will take his place.

The secular explanation for the myth is that it reflects the universal concern with the cycle of the moon – which goes into darkness each month for three days, as Inanna lies dead in the underworld – and the cycle of the seasons, with the earth lying fallow during Autumn and Winter. Its analogues with orthodox Christian belief are obvious – the three days spent in Hell by Christ, the theme of resurrection – and indeed, the same preoccupations with new life, death and resurrection form a central motif in Western theologies from Inanna onwards, with some of the same language: Inanna, like the Virgin Mary, was Queen of Heaven and Star of the Morning, and Dumuzi, like Christ, was the shepherd.

The *Buffy* series, too, echoes the same themes. Buffy must visit her 'dark sister', not once but time and again. Ereshkigal is represented most obviously by Faith, the Slayer-gone-bad, who figuratively kills Buffy by taking her body from her ('Who are You?' (4.16)), but that darkness is also represented by the First Slayer ('Restless' (4.22)), who haunts Buffy's dreams; by her negative reaction to Willow coming out as a lesbian, so that her 'sister' becomes sexually threatening ('New Moon Rising' (4.19)); by Glory, whose giant snake Sobek stands in place of the *galla*, pursuing Buffy's sister, Dawn ('Shadow' (5.8)); and most explicitly by the 'death-wish' which, Spike tells Buffy, led to the death of previous Slayers ('Fool For Love' (5.7)).

A similar journey towards understanding the hidden aspects of the self, as part of a necessary movement towards spiritual growth and wholeness, affects other key characters in the series: Willow first becomes aware of her lesbian identity when her 'dark side' enters the world as Vampire Willow ('Doppelgangland' (3.16)), while in his past, Giles was known as 'Ripper' and was a member of the dark cult of Eyghon ('The Dark Age' (2.8)). Angel perpetually holds in balance his dual identity as vampire and human, literally lives in Hell for an unspecified period of time and, on his return, finds it necessary to leave Sunnydale for Los Angeles, where he is joined by Buffy's sister-slayer, Faith, for whom he provides a release from her darkness, as Dumuzi does for Geshtinanna.

To move to a more generally familiar mythology, Buffy is like that Greek aspect of the moon-goddess which was personified as Artemis. Like Artemis, Buffy is a hunter, with the 'Scoobies' – named for the cartoon Great Dane – acting as the dogs which traditionally ac-company Artemis. Like Artemis, too, she is chaste – her primary relationship, with Angel, precludes sexual intercourse. As Artemis's slaying of animals represents the natural apotheosis of life, so Buffy's slaying of vampires restores them to the natural order of life and death.

Artemis has other aspects, as goddess of childbirth and as Hecate, death-hag of the crossroads, because she is a moon-goddess, repre-senting, like Inanna, the transformation of the moon from new to full to waning, darkness and re-birth. It is this transformative potential, this cycling through dark and light – enacted literally by Buffy's daytime school and college, and her night-time slaying – that is the theologically and philosophically important aspect of Buffy. Spiritually, it is what keeps her alive, where other Slayers die, since she is 'tied in' to the world of loving relationality, as Spike tells her: 'The only reason you've lasted as long as you have is you've got ties to the world . . . your mum, your brat kid sister, the Scoobies. They all tie you here but you're just putting off the inevitable' ('Fool For Love' (5.7)).

Archetypes

It is not that there are exact correspondences between the spiritual universe of *Buffy the Vampire Slayer* and either gnostic Christianity or goddess theologies. Rather, it is that the sensibilities of *Buffy* resonate far more convincingly with those earlier spiritual traditions than they do with orthodox Christianity. Indeed, it might be argued that the artefacts of orthodox Christianity – the Cross, Holy Water – belong more forcefully to the world of the vampires and demons, since they have an obvious effect on them, which is not extended to the Scoobies: Buffy and her team use these icons but they do not worship them, or attend a place where they are worshipped, any more than they worship the other esoteric artefacts which appear in the series, such as the Glove of Myhnegon or the Orb of Thesulah.

Rather, recognition of the virtuous nature of Christian artefacts and use of them, means that they take on an archetypal nature and are given universal significance. The orthodox Christian Cross and crucifix become translucent to the universal Tree of Life, the erica-tree of Osiris, the pine-tree of Attis, Odin's world-ash, the Shaman's journey, the Maypole of country ritual. Similarly, Holy Water becomes translucent to the tears of Christ, the Flood from which the world was reborn, the blood of the Grail, the Water of Life, which has represented the generative power of the natural world from the European Upper Palaeolithic period onwards.

Equally, the spiritual vision of *Buffy* is an immanent one, one which exists on earth, not a transcendent one in an unattainable heaven. The demons and monsters exist in the present, on earth, and although other dimensions are acknowledged their existence is parallel with, not separate from, the lived, daily one of Sunnydale. Sunnydale is, literally, the site of the Hellmouth, the point at which earth and other dimensions meet, and the regular fighting of monsters takes place on its streets. Spiritual pain and spiritual loss are perpetually present, just as spiritual grace is perpetually accessible, in the here and now. Transformation is achieved at an individual level, by the use of personal agency and, by the extension of that agency to others, through compassion.

A universal dimension of this is the resonance which the series sets up with earlier theologies than that of orthodox Christianity. Gnosticism was only one of the religious beliefs that the orthodox Church outlawed: its monotheism and its vigorous creation of a politically dominant, patriarchal structure, meant that all other beliefs were equally outlawed and ruthlessly suppressed. So, for example, another set of beliefs, at one time a dominant theology of the Western world, were the Eleusian Mysteries, sacred to Demeter and Persephone, enacting, like the *Descent of Inanna*, the lawfulness of the natural world and its cycles and supporting adherents in the human necessity of making friends with death. The little we know about them comes, in the main, from the attacks made on them by early Christian writers, before their final destruction. These mysteries were, therefore, part of the enduring consciousness of Western civilization, reappearing in many different forms, but always with the same principle of the numinous female at their centre, as Apuleius points out in the wonderful Eleusian invocation he provides in *The Golden Ass*.

The point is that Buffy represents a feminist spirituality, which locates the sacred in the personal, and which accepts personal responsibility, within a subjective, relational framework, for individual actions. By contrast, at the point at which Angel leaves Buffy, and moves to Los Angeles, he leaves his point of access to the immanent. His reason for leaving signals this: he does it because he is persuaded that it is for Buffy's own good, that is, he removes from her the reasonable right to speak for herself, to identify her own desires, and instead invokes some transcendent ideal of right behaviour – a paternalistic, 'daddy-knows-best' ideal of women as obedient to men – by which to guide his actions.

Angel demonstrates the limitations of the orthodox Christian ideas by which Angel the character then measures his conduct. He actively seeks atonement of what he now understands to have been his sins, hovering on despair and constantly thwarted in his attempts to 'earn' some mechanistic redemption, by one good act or another. Instead of the dark, inward journey Buffy takes, to meet her inner guide in the form of the First Slayer, her most fundamental self, when she believes herself unable to love ('Intervention' (5.18)), Angel is deluded into objectifying his inner dilemma as 'sin' and projecting it onto externalized others, whom he tries to save in the same way that he tried to 'save' Buffy – by his agency, not theirs. If the series runs true to the myth, then it will be only when Angel returns to the simple, human scale of values, that he will be redeemed.

[*Editorial note* – this part of the text is exactly as Zoe-Jane wrote it in January 2001, long before the broadcast of 'Epiphany' (A2.16), in which precisely this occurs – with the addition of his humbling himself to work for his former assistants.]

On Patrol, second shift: Political Significance

Citizenship

Politics may be understood, on the one hand, as the politics of public life, the state and political parties, with Sunnydale as a microcosm of Western democracy. On the other hand, though, politics may be understood as relationship, located less narrowly in the public sphere, and, in feminist interpretations, focusing on gendered systems, the distribution of resources and the location of power. These two ideas are conjoined in the notion of citizenship, which represents the relationship between public and private life. The issues of frontiers and boundaries, are important in all three ideas, both in physical terms of crossing borders, and in moral terms.

At the heart of the relationship between politics and citizenship, too, lies the question as to whether the citizen is conceptualized as merely a subject of an absolute authority or as an active political agent. The thrust of Platonic democracy, I have argued, is towards citizens as subject of an absolute authority, while the thrust of the Scoobies – especially Buffy and Willow – I shall argue, is towards citizen as active political agent. This agency, I wish to show, is demonstrated by their transgression of boundaries, their rejection of authoritarian systems of control, their exclusion from socially accepted norms and their creation of alternative ways of living.

Participation

Buffy herself is implicitly transgressive, because of her unique, embodied reconciliation of epistemology and ontology, and thus she provides an immediate political challenge to the order of life in Sunnydale. This political challenge is extended by the community formed by herself and her friends, which, like Gnostic communities, is based on a participative model rather than a hierarchical one. Leadership shifts, from Buffy to Giles to Willow to Angel to Oz to Xander to Riley, depending on who is functionally appropriate at any one time.

They form a group which, like that envisioned by Virginia Woolf, has no funds, no office, no committee and no secretary. Rather, each person is valued for different qualities, as the collaborative spell used to destroy Adam – the monster created by the Army and thus the personification of a male, hierarchical, authoritarian viewpoint – demonstrates, to which Willow contributes 'Spiritus' [spirit], Xander contributes 'Animus' [heart], Giles contributes 'Sophus' [mind] and Buffy contributes 'Manus' [hand] – 'Primeval' (4.21). This integrated, equal, participation provides a deliberate contrast to the political order represented by Adam: Buffy says 'You could never hope to grasp the source of our power,' as she pulls out Adam's mechanical power supply.

The Scoobies' contingent, contextualised, functional form of participative management is in strong contrast to the enforced, patriarchal, hierarchical structures which typify the series' evil leaders – the Master, Principal Snyder, the Mayor – and which is embodied in the terms of vampirism: vampires 'sire' other vampires, in a linguistic association of rape, insemination and kingship. The Master kills retainers who under-perform, as the Three did ('Angel' (1.7)). Principal Snyder rejoices in using his public position to violate the personal rights of individuals – 'This is a glorious day for principals everywhere. No pathetic whining about students' rights. Just a long row of lockers and a man with a key' ('Gingerbread' (3.11)) and the Mayor continues to seek power and control from beyond the grave, leaving a video-tape of instructions for Faith ('This Year's Girl' (3.15)).

Surveillance

As Foucault points out, it is by watching the worker, the mad or the imprisoned that authority maintains its power over them; you can only police what you can see. It is a surveillance arrangement such as this that Buffy explicitly refuses at the start of her relationship with Giles ('Welcome to the Hellmouth' (1.1)):

> Buffy: First of all, I'm a Vampire Slayer. And secondly, I'm retired. Hey, I know! Why don't you kill 'em?
>
> Giles: I, I'm a Watcher, I, I haven't the skill . . .
>
> Buffy: Oh, come on, stake through the heart, a little sunlight . . . It's like falling off a log.
>
> Giles: A, a Slayer slays, a Watcher . . .
>
> Buffy: Watches?
>
> Giles: Yes. No! (sets down the books) He, he trains her, he, he, he prepares her . . .
>
> Buffy: Prepares me for what? For getting kicked out of school? For losing all of my friends? For having to spend all of my time fighting for my life and never getting to tell anyone because I might endanger them? Go ahead! Prepare me.
>
> (They just look at each other for a moment. Buffy exhales, turns and leaves the library in disgust.)

Even when Buffy does quit, and retires to Los Angeles, her return is sparked off by a demon which enslaves humans into absolutely degraded labour – 'You work, and you live. That is all' – in a dark, brutalizing iron works, lit by vats of molten metal and flying sparks ('Anne' (3.1)), an image of industrialized Hell used from Charles Dickens onwards. That it is Buffy's agency which creates a different relationship from the usual surveillance one, rather than a quality implicit in Slayers, is made clear by the way in which Kendra accepts the surveillance and control of her Watcher, just as Faith does with the Mayor.

Kendra's self-abasement to authority, Faith's preparedness to sell herself to evil just to find acceptance from the fatherly Mayor, differ entirely from Buffy's constantly tested and negotiated relationship with Giles. Autonomy is available, but action is required to gain it: otherwise, Slayers and other citizens are merely pawns of an absolute authority. While Buffy provides an implicit political challenge, therefore, Willow provides the series' most explicit challenges. Her 'nomadism', her crossing of social and moral boundaries, is frequently underlined. She transgresses usual school social expectations by having an unusually able intellect, by being unfashionably dressed ('Welcome to the Hellmouth'(1.1)) and by dating a werewolf. She transgresses her family religious boundaries ('Passion' (2.17)):

> Willow: (nailing crosses around her French doors) I'm going to have a hard time explaining this to my dad.
> Buffy: You really think this'll bother him?
> Willow: Ira Rosenberg's only daughter nailing crucifixes to her bedroom wall? I have to go to Xander's house just to watch 'A Charlie Brown Christmas' every year.

and then goes through a deeply personal, inward journey, to find a further transgressive identity as a lesbian Wiccan. In this context, it is clear that Willow's Wiccan identification is a political one, rather than a religious one. As *Buffy the Vampire Slayer: The Monster Book* points out, Wicca 'is an established and legitimate religion' into which it would be an anomaly 'to keep throwing demons' since 'they do not believe in demons or the Christian mythology of devils.' Further, representations of Wicca in the influential works of Gerald Gardner and of

Vivianne Crowley, are fundamentally heterosexist, rather than lesbian, developing from a notion of a union of male and female principles, rather than one of female and female. Finally, Willow makes it clear that she is concerned with the alternative power-base that the craft offers, and it is that shared interest which attracts her to Tara (from 'Hush' (4.10) onwards):

> Willow: Talk! All talk: blah blah Gaia blah blah moon, menstrual lifeforce power . . . I thought after a few sessions we'd get into something real but . . .
> Buffy: No actual witches in your witch group.
> Willow: Buncha wannablessedbe's. It's just a fad. Nowadays every girl with a henna tattoo and a spice rack thinks she's a sister to the dark ones.

> Tara: I thought maybe we could do a spell – make people talk again. I'd seen you in the group, the Wicca group you were . . . you were different than them. I mean they didn't seem to know . . .
> Willow: What they were talking about.
> Tara: I think if they saw a witch they would run the other way. (She smiles and laughs.)
> Willow: How long have you been practicing?
> Tara: Always, I mean, since I um, was little . . . my, my mom used to, she had a lot of power, like you.

The political orientation of that power is demonstrated in 'Family' (5.6), where Tara's father tries to persuade her that she will become possessed by a demon when she becomes twenty-one, and that she should therefore give up her independent life in Sunnydale and return to keep house for the men of the family. It becomes clear that this demonization is a lie, aimed at the subjugation of women who have power, one through which Tara's mother was suborned, a literal piece of the patriarchy which Tara breaks.

That all of the Scoobies belong to Virginia Woolf's 'Outsiders' Society', by association with Willow, is demonstrated in 'Gingerbread' (3.11). There, Willow is linked to Buffy, through 'the monsters, and the witches, and the Slayers', to Xander via the generic 'freaks and losers', to Giles, who has his books confiscated and burned, and to the 'dozens of others [who] are persecuted by a righteous mob. It's happened all throughout history.'

Interestingly, though, the patriarchal authority which the mob are exercising in their witch-persecution is delusional, a product of a (literal) demonization which initiates the moral panic. In a political context, the episode seems to be suggesting that the subjugation of women is equally delusional, that the apparently 'objective' evidence collected by Principal Snyder by invading the privacy of students' lockers, has no truth in fact. Rather, a radical, feminist view of history, history as affinity, is foregrounded, in a process which 'refuses the various positions of detachment which define the historian' and 'values highly emotional, involved, "personal" pleasure and engagement'. Willow and Buffy are saved from burning by their friends, especially by Cordelia (whose swift action with a hose contrasts to Xander and Oz's clumsiness) who both share and refuse their demonization, and create both a counter-discourse to it and a counter-action.

Similarly, in 'Checkpoint' (5.12), the 'Previously on *Buffy*' recapitulation provides a montage of Giles objecting to Buffy's 'test' in 'Helpless'(3.12); of Buffy rejecting the Council in 'Graduation Day Part One' (3.21); and Buffy, Giles and Joyce discussing Dawn in 'Triangle' (5.11). These views of education, hierarchy and community are reiterated and extended in the episode, where Buffy advances 'a different perspective' of history and is publicly humiliated by her male teacher for doing so; the Council attempts to impose a surveillance model of management on the Scoobies by inspecting them; and Buffy understands and rejects this as power-play, and asserts an 'alternative government' of relationality, allowing willing Council members to join the group to fight Glory.

Back in the Library: Conclusion

In a world where woman is so abjected that she is virtually non-existent in political and psychological terms, *Buffy* may be read as an attempt to call her into being and knowledge. The struggle which takes place, the killing of vampires, then, is a political struggle, in which the spiritual, as well as the personal, is political. As simple allegory, the girl-Slayer fights against the problematics of growing up in a patriarchy, with her interior conflicts expressed as literal demons and vampires which she must slay. As more complex symbol, she reflects a Western culture in which successive waves of feminism have analyzed these problematics, where woman is now valorized, as having both knowledge and existence which is self-authenticating. The Slayer thus embodies the combination of knowing and being, and the challenge to Western male capitalism which this represents: Buffy's secret night-time slaying, done as well as her public attendance at school, stands for women's unacknowledged labour of reproduction, which provides a central feminist criticism of Marxist analysis.

Buffy herself is an embodiment of what Grosz calls the 'wayward philosophies', which refuse a mind/body split and insist on alternative readings of what it is to be human. It is not sufficient to construct an idea of 'woman' from that which exists already, since what exists already is objectified woman, as the robot, April, demonstrates: she is literally man-made, made by Warren to love and obey him, so that 'I'm only supposed to love him. If I can't do that, what am I for?' and 'if you call her and she doesn't answer, it hurts her' ('I Was Made to Love You' (5.15)). Rather, autonomy within relationality is required: as Buffy realizes in the same episode, 'I don't need a guy right now. I need me. I need to get comfortable being alone with Buffy'.

To return to Virginia Woolf, like her women's committee, Buffy and the Scoobies are all Outsiders. Individually, they all transgress established boundaries: Xander, a failure in the prescribed learning of state education, turns out to be a skilled craftsperson in adult life;

Willow is a lesbian and a witch; Angel a 'good vampire'; and so on.
Collectively, they form the Scoobies, the Outsiders' Society, and move
between the interpenetrating worlds of humans and demons, Heaven
and Hell, the sanctioned and unsanctioned social, political, spiritual
worlds. In relation to each other, they are almost always in a position
of forbidden love, between women, between demon and human,
between Slayer and vampire.

The solution of *Buffy* is inclusivity. What is required, is for
individuals to wish to enter, to want to become part of that community. Dawn, the Key, is as much a created being as is robot-Anna,
but she identifies at a fundamental, personal level with the Scoobies:
she is Buffy's political sister as well as her literal sister, standing up to
be counted in defence of Tara in 'Family' (5.6). This alternative
government, then, is one in which, in Irigaray's formulation, citizenship comes as a right of existing within the community, outside
hierarchies of money or birth. Thus, Anya is a vengeance demon, but
she may also lawfully join the alternative community of the Scoobies,
and Tara, rejected by her own father and brother for being a dis-
obedient female, is re-identified as part of Buffy's 'family'.

In terms of feminist theory, this position reflects the destabilization
of categories brought about by trans theory. For intersexed people,
gender identity can *only* be found through identification, at a personal,
essential level. The transitions made between male and female, in
response to that personal essentialism, has extended fundamentalist
'Fortress feminism' notions of what constitutes woman in terms of
sex, and what constitutes lesbian in terms of sexuality.

In spiritual terms, the transgression of boundaries is exemplified
by what Joseph Campbell calls 'the hero's journey':

> A hero ventures forth from the world of common day
> into a region of supernatural wonder: fabulous forces
> are there encountered and a decisive victory is won:
> the hero comes back from this mysterious adventure
> with the power to bestow boons on his fellow man.[3]

In this journey to the land below the sea, the world inside the mountain, the dark forest, the 'decisive victory' is one of will, not necessarily of action. Often, the hero fails to perform the task: she drinks what she should not, he cannot answer the question, or, like Buffy, there is an endless production-line of vampires, more than she could possibly ever kill. But the monomyth tells us that to try is enough, that intention rather than achievement is the measure of human relationality.

At the heart of this worldview lies the idea not of a fallen humanity separated from the godhead by inherited sin, but the idea of what radical educationist A.S. Neill called 'original good', the view that 'a child is innately wise and realistic.' Where it is accepted that the automatic impulse of people is towards their own happiness, through the love and friendship of others, then they may be judged by their intentions, the bond of the heart, by an intentionality which holds the actor's ethical position.

Finally, then, it is this essentially ethical standpoint, this continuous working-out of what individuals need to do and be in order to find personal apotheosis, which marks out *Buffy* from other beat-em-ups. Usually, the face-off is between the black hats and the white ones, with a decisive victory for the white hats. As early as the last scene of 'Lie to Me' (2.7), *Buffy* explicitly rejected any such easy conclusion. *Buffy* subverts set conventions, creating a new articulation of what it is to be autonomous woman. This is done in a context of inclusion, not separation from the world of men, on terms which refuse the dominant cultural ideologies of woman as secondary, sinful and subordinate.

Postscript: The First Slayer

When the First Slayer walked the earth, in the Palaeolithic period, a new sensibility appeared all across the world. Incised stone, engraved bone, carved figures and decorated cave walls testify to a new relationality, explored through art, which, in France's Dordogne, produced a remarkable sculpture and set of cave paintings.

The paintings show the myth of the hunter, the drama of survival: in one notable scene, a speared bison dies, while a rhinoceros shits the manure of new life and the shaman-hunter dreams their mutual interdependence.

Outside, a sculpture shows a woman, pointing to her pregnant belly with one hand and with the other, holding aloft a crescent-shaped bison horn, incised with the thirteen days of the waxing moon and the thirteen months of the lunar year. As above, so below, the figure indicates, as the moon waxes, wanes and is born anew, again and again, so is all life.

The painted myth of the hunter is about taking life as a ritual act in order to live; the sculpted myth of the goddess is about transformation, rebirth, and life in all its aspects. To a modern mind, the two instincts seem antithetical, the one about separation and survival, the other about relationship and meaning. How can Buffy both be a hunter, a Slayer, and live within the everyday relationality of her family and friends? Why does the First Slayer tell her 'death is your gift'?

To live only within the myth of the hunter is to live for survival, in time, where death is final and the experience of life, despair. It is Angel's tragedy that after leaving Buffy, denying their relationality, his sensibility is reduced to that. To return to her is to return to the sacred feminine, the Palaeolithic goddess that links the First Slayer with the last, through a myth which contains that of the hunter and places it in the larger continuum of relationship, an eternal image of recurrence, of the whole.

When one Slayer dies, another is called: when one moon goes into darkness, another becomes. Inanna's journey to Ereshkigal is re-enacted time and again, the necessary death and concomitant new life, transliterated into the Christian religion as the festival of the new child at winter solstice, darkness turning light, and as death at Easter, the pagan festival of fertility goddess Eostre, at the equinox where winter turns to spring.

The myth of the goddess contains the myth of the hunter, but the myth of the hunter cannot contain the myth of the goddess. Death is Buffy's gift in time when, as the Slayer, she hunts vampires for survival: but to stay there would be to share Angel's now tragic existence. Death becomes her gift in eternity, as the deepest part of her – the First Slayer – already knows, when she realizes that, as mother, she must go into the darkness to save Dawn, now her child, as Demeter did Persephone, as eternity must always redeem time. Together, Buffy and Angel rise again, made anew, as the moon does, as we all do, bound into a participative consciousness from the time of the First Slayer, a sense of eternity which vampires, those creatures caught in time, may disturb, but cannot end.

Inana and Ereshkigal are sisters: they are part and parcel of each other – the dark of the moon is still the moon. It will be interesting to see what is made of Buffy's next resurrection – the wonderful *noli me tangere* of the Christian myth or the terrible pursuit of the Assyrian? And what of her sex and sexuality, always something that becomes liminal in these circumstances? I think the aesthetic is pushing towards something simple and homely – not the Glory/God/Wonder Woman, so much as living eternity in time, zen without the moral ambiguity.

Notes

1. Virginia Woolf, *Three Guineas.*
2. Elaine Pagels, *The Gnostic Gospels* (Penguin, 1982).
3. Jospeph Campbell, *Oriental Mythology* (New York: Viking Press, 1962).

just a girl

buffy as icon

anne millard daugherty

Buffy Summers looks like a typical Californian teenager. She's cute, slender, not overly studious, and stereotypically preoccupied with her appearance. Though she might like to spend her evenings eating pineapple pizza and watching teen movies, instead she patrols for vampires and slays them.

It's not a life she chose; it chose her. Indeed, she's part of an age-old heritage of slayers. In this sense, Buffy represents all women throughout the ages who have become revered role models following a life-mission chosen for them, women like Joan of Arc, Rose of Viterbo or Mary, the Mother of Jesus. All are women of great strength who are called to give of themselves no matter what the cost.

Buffy is very much a woman of her time, too. She is a complex part of our popular culture and a product of it. She is a post-Madonna heroine, one who is liberated and believes she can be anything she wants. Just as the Biblical Madonna redeems the sin of Eve in the Ave/Eva dichotomy, so MTV's Madonna releases women from the constraints of Victorianism, encouraging them to be virgin and whore at the same time. Buffy protects her community, but she is also free to be a ditz as well. Buffy is indicative of the changing face of women on television. She typifies a post-feminist heroine. She is neither as overtly feminist as Murphy Brown nor as self-absorbed as Ally McBeal.

Buffy is a symbol of female empowerment. Many of the foes she faces represent both the hurdles women have overcome in the past and the hurdles that will constantly need to be faced. Buffy's challenges, struggles, and relationships represent many of the hazards that face all women, especially those who are young and impressionable.

Buffy as feminist spectator icon

Buffy first appeared in 1995, well after the 'male gaze' issue had been poked and prodded from many angles. Laura Mulvey's provocative 1973 article argued that traditional Hollywood cinema objectified women. Marcia Pally countered that far from being objectified, women enjoyed the power wielded as controllers of the gaze.

From the outset, it is clear that *Buffy* is a 'post-gaze' product. Women are obviously in control. In fact, Buffy is a feminist spectator's dream. There is, however, one major caveat – she is so very cute it is often difficult to get beyond her physicality.

Three 'looks' define the traditional cinematic male gaze: (1) onscreen men gaze at women in a way that objectifies them; (2) the spectator, therefore, is forced to identify with this objectifying male gaze; and (3) the camera contributes an original 'gaze' in filming. Ellis and Kaplan argue that the concept of the male gaze as outlined by Mulvey and others does not relate to television. Yet, the objectifying male gaze is so deliberately negated in the first episode of *Buffy* that it is worthy of comment.

The first episode, 'Welcome to the Hellmouth' (1.1), opens with a young couple entering a high school, their intentions obviously amorous. The male seems keener than the female, as traditional stereotypes might dictate. She lags behind, concerned about every little noise, worried that they are really alone. Once her fears are allayed, she turns on him and bites his neck.

The scene is reminiscent of the spate of slasher films (1978–1984) beginning with John Carpenter's *Halloween* (1978) and including many incarnations of *Friday the 13th*. As Wes Craven's *Scream* trilogy points out, teens indulging in sexual activity are begging to be mercilessly hacked to death by a madman. But not in *Buffy*. As the first scene pre-empts, it is the women who are in control here, at every juncture.

In that first episode, we meet three men who will be important to Buffy in the series. Each character is introduced with a deliberate collapsing of the traditional male gaze. Xander bobs and weaves his way through the crowd on his skateboard as Buffy walks up the steps to her new school. Upon seeing Buffy his reaction is typical male ogling – but his gaze is soon subverted when he fails to see the stair railing, promptly crashes into it and lands flat on his back.

Later, Xander gallantly dives to help Buffy rescue the contents of her scattered book bag. His attempts at conversation are less than suave. He begins with a stumbling 'Can I have you?' instead of, 'Can I help you?' and ends with 'Well, uh, maybe I'll see you around . . . maybe at school . . . since we . . . both . . . go there.'

This encounter, like their first, establishes that Buffy is in control; Xander is not. As she walks away, Xander looks at her longingly, rebuking himself for his poor language skills. He realizes that she has left something behind – her stake. He calls after her. But Buffy is out of earshot. Xander clutches the stake, symbolically representing the phallus, a traditional symbol of power. It very obviously belongs to Buffy, not to him. The scene suggests that Buffy is fodder for fetishists – those that Kaplan describes as desirous of finding the penis in a woman in order to grant themselves erotic satisfaction. However, the situation immediately negates any argument for fetishization. Buffy has been castrated, Xander has the phallus, but he has no clue what to do with it.

The next male Buffy encounters is Giles, the librarian. Giles wears glasses, indicative of his impaired gaze. Further, Owen opines that Giles is a feminized male, describing him as: 'Forty-something, speaks with a British accent, and is an expert on antiquities and arcane medieval mysticism; he is absent-minded, ambiguously gendered, fussy, and resistant to most late-twentieth-century technology.'

Giles is Buffy's 'Watcher.' His gaze, obviously neither sexual nor objectifying, is rather like that one would give to a new master. In fact, in Giles's early interactions with Buffy he is rather like an anxious puppy. He is eager to prove that he knows who she is, why she is there and so to win her approval. He is totally crestfallen when she rejects him.

The final important male character we meet is Angel. At first, Angel (like the camera) follows Buffy — watching her. The scene is reminiscent of the voyeuristic/scopophilic experience that Mulvey articulates in *Visual Pleasure and Narrative Cinema,* where male heroes control both evil and women (often brutally) and thereby reinforce their maleness. The scene again brings the slasher genre to mind — where young women are brutally murdered.

Buffy, however, overturns this image. She ducks into an alley and waits for Angel to follow her, then knocks him off his feet, demanding to know why he is following her. The traditional role is female as object of the gaze and likely victim, yet when Buffy later describes Angel to Giles as dark and gorgeous, he is the object of her gaze and, correspondingly, the object of our gaze.

Still, if Buffy is indeed reversing the male gaze when describing Angel, she certainly does not lose her 'traditional feminine characteristics – kindness, humane-ness, motherliness,' as Walters theorized would be the case. Rather, Buffy becomes the ultimate nurturer to Angel when she feeds him her own blood, insisting that he bite her neck and suck, in order to save his life ('Graduation Day Part 2' (3.22)).

For all the efforts taken to negate the traditional male gaze, Buffy's physical attractiveness is, in itself, objectifying. When Kuhn says the cultural construction of an ideal female – young, shapely, carefully dressed and made up, fashionable, glamorous – may be considered in itself as 'oppressive' because it proffers an image which many women feel it is important to live up to and yet is at the same time unattainable for most of us she describes Buffy perfectly. She is the quintessential American teenager – petite, blonde and always impeccably dressed – that few young women can live up to.

At least Buffy's physique is healthy. With role models like Calista Flockhart, Lara Flynn Boyle and Courtney Cox seemingly promoting eating disorders, Sarah Michelle Gellar is at least well proportioned. In a few outfits, one even detects that she has a healthy roundness to her abdomen. Buffy is obviously affluent. In five seasons, she has never worn the same outfit twice. She dresses in tight sexy clothes for school, usually with an eye-catching amount of cleavage and legs readily apparent to the viewer.

She rarely wears 'old' clothes. Often dashing home to change before going on patrol, she frequently slips into leather pants – in various shades and styles – which look comfortable and hard wearing but also convey a message of prosperity. She never has dirty hair. Indeed, there is a certain ridiculousness to her flowing tresses as she slays demons, although from a technical standpoint the tresses serve as convenient camouflage for the stunt double.

Buffy, however, is not a victim of her own appearance – she is not objectified by the onscreen males. She even mocks the gaze by matching words and garments as she selects an outfit to wear to the Bronze. The sexy black dress says: 'Hi, I'm an enormous slut!' while the blue floral number says 'Hello! Would you like a copy of the *Watchtower?*' Later we see she has chosen pants, with a white shirt over a white tank top.

She is the unquestionable hero of the show. All others bow to her wisdom and/or power. She is not fragile. She takes punches as well as gives them and occasionally shows signs of human frailty. In fact, Buffy manifests everything needed to countermand Aristotle's dismissal of the female as 'lacking.' Buffy has everything. Far beyond Aristotle's notion of woman as an 'imperfect man,' Buffy is everything the men would hope to be – Xander can but gaze at her in awe and

Giles knows that his role is to help guide her, for he will never have her power.

Jill Dolan describes three types of feminism – liberal, cultural and materialist. The liberal feminists aim for equality with men. The cultural, or radical, feminists believe they are far superior to men. The materialist feminists hope to establish a new order where competition between male and female is eradicated. Buffy might best be described as cultural feminist. As the Slayer, she is 'chosen', she is very special. Only one young woman can be the Slayer. Hence Buffy is part of a long line of chosen women. She represents her gender, herself and more.

Lest we think Buffy typifies the Slayer, two other examples have appeared in the show – Kendra and Faith. Kendra is a serious young woman who has no time for amusement or fun. Faith is her polar opposite. She has a little too much time for fun. The two are likely chosen for their extremes, representing the traditional Ave/Eva dichotomy of woman as virgin or whore. Buffy sits confidently in the middle somewhere, almost as if her position is normative.

Yet if Buffy is an obvious agent of privilege and power, she is not a snob. While she passes the cool test to become part of Cordelia's in-group, she rejects the offer. Rather, she seeks out the companionship of Willow. Willow, as Cordelia explains, is a 'loser.' Or, as de Beauvoir would describe it, Willow is the 'other' of the typical American high school. She is not popular and she at first dresses badly. Willow prefers to spend her time reading and is hopelessly tongue-tied in the proximity of boys. Buffy is drawn to Willow, however, and to her academic acumen. Buffy wants to succeed and knows that Willow can help her far more than popularity.

If Willow begins the series as the 'other', she quickly becomes indispensable to Buffy. Her computer skills and developing interest in witchcraft bring two sets of important skills to the group. Xander also might be categorized as an 'other' in the American high school. He is neither a sports hero, nor a rock star, nor an academic high achiever. Yet he too becomes an important member of the group, possibly more for comic relief than anything else.

One other important male figure in the first episode is the Master, a once powerful vampire who can be restored to his former greatness by drawing power from his minions on the night of the Harvest. The Master can then break through from his reality into ours. The French feminists of the twentieth century decry the phallogocentrism of Western culture as limiting women to 'other'. Buffy breaks through these traditional representations. She might be a high school girl, but she is a powerful and capable one. The Master hopes to return from his imprisonment and break into her reality. By feeding on the youth of America, he will be restored to his former power, maybe relegating Buffy to a 'sidekick'.

Finally, there is Angel, the vampire who will be Buffy's first lover. That Angel is also 'other' goes without saying. He is, after all, dead. He also becomes one of Buffy's most dreaded opponents.

'Beauty and the Beasts'

'Beauty and the Beasts' (3.4) is a thinly veiled morality tale about violence in relationships. The episode is framed by images of women as nurturers. The opening scene shows Willow baby-sitting Oz, who is in his werewolf phase and hence locked in a cage for protection. When Xander comes to relieve Willow, she gives him an update of Oz's status in deliberately mothering language: 'Now, he's had his 2 o'clock feeding, and uh, after sunrise, if he forgets where his clothes are, they're on top of the file cabinet in his cage.' At the end of the episode, Buffy comforts Angel on his return from Hell. The final image shows her watching as he sleeps on the floor. Her posture is protective.

The immediate story of the episode unfolds with some deaths that look like the work of werewolves. Oz is suspected, particularly after Xander falls asleep on duty, and the window in Oz's cage is found ajar. After an acceptable time to wonder if Oz is on the rampage, we discover that the monster is actually Pete, another senior, who has anger management issues, especially concerning his girlfriend, Debbie.

When we first meet them, Debbie and Pete look like an All-American high school couple. Debbie is blond and wears her hair in a bob. Her attire is modest. She opts for twin sets and skirts, and later a t-shirt and cardigan over cut-off pants. She clutches a bouquet of flowers that Pete has just given her. Pete's short hair and plaid shirt make him look like millions of other high school seniors.

Soon, however, we see the darker side of the couple. Pete pulls Debbie into a janitor's closet, kissing her passionately, until he notices a jar on the shelf that has a thin layer of bright green fluid at the bottom. Accusing Debbie of drinking the liquid, Pete flares into a rage and beats her. Pete's secret is that he imbibes a special formula to make him more of a man. Instead he is a monster, of Jekyll and Hyde proportions.

Debbie explains that she had poured the liquid out to help him. Pete counters that he does not need the formula any more, for he can transform into the monster just at the sound of her 'stupid, grating voice.' After Pete calms down, he apologizes, after a fashion, whispering 'You know you shouldn't make me mad. Huh? You know what happens.' She holds him in her arms and comforts him. Her action not only condones Pete's behavior, it also gives her some ownership of it.

Pete's anger is flared not only by her voice, but also by his jealousy. He turns on any males that get close to his girlfriend and kills them. At the climax of the episode, the three beasts – Angelus (newly returned from Hell), Pete, and Oz – all wearing their Jekyll suits of preference, face each other in a macho display that rivals world championship wrestling. The moves are just as choreographed, but the loser ends up dead.

Pete first fights Oz, whom he suspects has been giving more to Debbie than Physics notes. His timing is poor, however, since he attacks Oz just as Oz's own monster is emerging. Unable to defeat Oz, Pete attacks and kills Debbie in a classic castration/decapitation reaction. Pete then attacks Buffy, and is killed by Angel.

This episode originally aired on October 20, 1998. The National Center for Injury Prevention and Control, Division of Violence Prevention in the USA reported that in 1998 the average prevalence rate for non-sexual dating violence was 22% among high school students and 32% among college students (Sugarman and Hotaling). Studies have found that attacks occur when the male has sexually aggressive peers (Ageton; Adler; DeKeseredy; Gwartney-Gibbs and Stockard; Kanin), through heavy alcohol or drug use (Kanin; and Muehlenhard and Linton), and through the male's acceptance of dating violence (Gray and Foshee). Other studies reported that as the consumption of alcohol by either the victim or perpetrator increases, the rate of serious injuries associated with dating violence also increases (Makepeace).

The issue of dating violence is a serious one. Of course, the whole show is couched in terms of violence. Oz's penchant for violence is dealt with by establishing safety precautions for his protection and that of others. Buffy slays vampires on a weekly basis, with an average body count of three or four per episode. If we consider the vampire as metaphor of teenage angst, then Buffy's struggle to fight demons is now doubly complex. She has to fight demons, as specified in her job description, but she also has to fight the demons that grow out of her dealings with other people. Buffy's sexual encounter with Angel causes him to lose his soul. Pete wants to be more of a man for Debbie, and so takes performance-enhancing drugs that alter him so much that it leads to both their deaths.

The framing of the episode by Buffy's reading aloud of Jack London's *Call of the Wild* offers another perspective. It is through selfless devotion that the beast in man is tamed; it is his love for Buffy that has kept Angel sane during his season in Hell and it is love for Willow that enables Oz to put up with caging his wolf-self rather than letting it run free and wild.

'Family'

Absence of patriarchy is apparent throughout the series, but in 'Family' (5.4) the role of fatherhood – and patriarchy in general – is severely disparaged. At the beginning of the episode, Buffy tells Giles about her father and how he 'bailed' on the family to run off with his secretary. The fact that Buffy has never shared this information with Giles previously indicates its thematic importance now. Later, while helping Buffy move from her dorm room, Giles describes himself as taking on a patriarchal role, with 'lots of pointing and scowling.'

The immediate episodic issue concerns Tara McLay and her father. It is Tara's birthday, she will be twenty, and Willow has organized a party. Tara's father, her brother and her cousin, Beth, show up unexpectedly; they have come to take Tara home.

The portrayal of the McLay family as rednecks is probably deliberate. Her father is characterized as a stereotypical scowling patriarch, with a set jaw and the might of right firmly lodged in his attitude. The brother, Donny, sports a thin scrawny beard and bumpkin mannerisms. We first become aware of him in the store when he asks if Xander and Buffy are witches, turning people into frogs. His demeanour reflects belligerent ignorance. Cousin Beth looks as if she stepped right off the platform of the local 'Miss Nowheresville' pageant. Such stereotypical characterizations are deliberately menacing. This family is here to oppress Tara. They plan to whisk her back home so she can take care of her father and brother.

McLay pointedly reminds Tara that her twentieth birthday marks the emergence of her 'evil'. He says 'You're turning twenty. It's the same age your mother was when she . . .' The sentence is left hanging as a plot device to keep the audience wondering what Tara is about to become, but also to indicate that the words should not be spoken – they are too horrid to articulate and already well known to his daughter.

The message is simple. At twenty, Tara is at the eve of adulthood. McLay calls it 'evil.' A fully grown sexual female with a mind of her own and freedom to do as she pleases is evil and needs to be at home where her family can control her.

That McLay's wife became 'evil' when she turned twenty indicates that she either left him or began to indicate her discontent. In either case, it is clear that McLay married a very young woman, obviously younger than himself, and his pattern of patriarchal oppression is readily traceable.

Of course, we're aware that McLay is too late if he hopes to smother his daughter's sexuality. Tara is both lesbian and a witch. It's never clear to us which one McLay would consider the greater evil. It is apparent that the show's producers are nervous audiences will not accept overt lesbian sexuality. We're teased with images of Willow and Tara engaging in magic but almost never in sexual intimacy. (The two exceptions come late in Season Five – Tara kisses Willow to console her over Joyce's death and Willow kisses Tara in joy at having retrieved her sanity. In both cases, though the erotic is present, it is secondary to other emotions.)

The episode begins with Tara telling Willow a story about a cat – any mention of a feline inevitably leads to thoughts of pussy – and ends with the couple in an embrace that lifts them a foot in the air. In both cases the symbolism is apparent, but not overt. As Xander comments: 'When I think about two women doing spells, I have to go off and do a spell by myself.' ('Restless' (4.22))

Tara endeavors to hide her impending transformation into a demon by casting a spell on her friends. The result is that they are blinded when subsequently attacked by evil forces. Tara's attempt to hide her supposed evil from others also represents a societal pressure to hide the natural bodily functions of women. The Bible called menstruating women 'unclean'. Today products to absorb blood are called 'sanitary' and can be found in the 'feminine hygiene' aisle at the supermarket. Men hate buying them. Menstruation is a time of secrecy. Bloodstains are obviously taboo. As Gloria Steinem says in her hilarious article 'If Men Could Menstruate', men in a similar situation would boast about how many tampons they had filled.

Even *Buffy*, which obviously promotes female strength and power, still avoids open mention of menstruation, except during Buffy's row with her mother in 'Becoming Part 2' (2.22), when a general equation of Slaying and sexuality – 'Have you tried not being a Slayer' – includes as part of Buffy's list of Joyce's state of denial a mention of having to wash bloodstains out of Buffy's clothes. After discovering that Oz is a werewolf, he and Willow have to take precautions during his 'time of the month'. Such precautions include locking him up so he doesn't rip people to shreds, a nice play on women with PMS – Willow remarks that part of the month she is no fun to be around either. As Owen observes, in a show that is so much about blood and young women, it is odd that menstruation remains largely taboo.

There is a running 'joke' throughout 'Family' (5.6), one of some significance. While helping pack up Buffy's dorm room, Xander and Giles assure Buffy that she will be the victor in her next encounter with Glory, since they will all help her. Tara offers to 'introduce Glory to her insect reflection.' The rest of the gang fail to get the reference. Tara explains it is part of a Taglarin mythic rite and leaves the room highly embarrassed. Later, we see Tara and Willow enter the magic shop deep in conversation; Tara has relayed her suggestion about the insect reflection to Willow and the pair are laughing about it. Willow says 'Her insect reflection. That is so good.' Finally, at the end of the episode, during her party at the Bronze, Tara explains that the insect reflection represents one's insignificance. Anya nods in understanding, but declares that 'it's still not funny.'

Whether or not the insect reflection manoeuvre is brilliant or funny is never made clear. It may be that Willow loves Tara and so supports her every thought and idea. What is apparent, however, is the recurring theme of acceptance of the 'other' in the show. As established in the first episode, Willow is not 'like' the rest of the group. She is lesbian and Wicca and continues to follow a divergent path from her friends.

With the introduction of Tara, we see them constantly engaged in activities that are removed from mainstream and yet essential to the group as a whole.

The acceptance of difference is an important theme of 'Family'. Buffy and Xander bemoan the fact that they have to attend Tara's birthday celebration, worrying as to whether or not they will fit in with the 'swinging Wicca' crowd. But at the first indication that Tara is going to be forced to go home against her will, Buffy's response is immediate: 'You want her, Mr McLay? You can go ahead and take her. [beat] You just gotta go through me.' The gang then forms a united front against Mr McLay, emphasizing that they will all stand up for Tara's rights.

The plot, simplistic indeed, is reminiscent of countless other means of attempts to control women over the centuries – Ancient Chinese foot-binding, for example, or the current plight of women in Afghanistan, where they are beaten and stoned in public for not wearing the proper attire. Were it not for Buffy, Tara's father might have exercized his control over her and taken her home.

Like 'Beauty and the Beasts', 'Family' contains a strong message of female empowerment. Adulthood and freedom to be an individual are every woman's right. This essential message of the liberal feminists is rarely articulated today.

In the broader narrative structure, Season Five itself is also anti-patriarchy. Typical of the series' binary format, this season evidences both seasonal and episodic plot themes. In Season Five, the prevailing evil is Glory, a god. She seeks Dawn, Buffy's supposed sister, but actually the Key to the underworld. The notion of difference is becoming increasingly significant with the unfolding of the mystery of Dawn. Buffy knows that even though Dawn is not really her sister, she should nevertheless protect her, no matter what the cost. It is significant that when Buffy stands up to be counted as Tara's protector, it is Dawn who is the first to second her; the creation of this family of the heart is a matter of mutuality.

Glory is a god, but a far cry from the traditional image of the Judaeo-Christian God, who is adamantly male and generally considered benevolent. Glory is outrageously female, obsessed with her own appearance, and evil, indeed she arguably represents the legendary great Hollywood divas who cared only about their appearance and desires. This combination of Glory and the debasement of fatherhood paints a striking picture that undermines patriarchy on every level.

'Buffy vs. Dracula'

In the previous three episodes examined in this paper, I have discussed attacks on female empowerment. In 'Buffy vs. Dracula' (5.1), we see another such attack. Dracula's designs on Buffy are sensual and romantic. He comes to seduce her, to make her long for his bite. But his intentions are no less subtle than the other attacks on the female domination apparent in Buffy. Dracula wants to control the Slayer, to put her in her place, and in so doing, to re-establish his own power.

'Buffy vs. Dracula' is the opener for Season Five. This episode is both playful and effective. For the most part, the episode serves to re-establish the characters. Only in the last minute is a new character introduced, one who will be vital to the rest of the season – Buffy's sister.

Significant in this episode is Buffy's need to be loved. It is a natural desire, indeed it may be the most human of desires. When the season opens we see that she is not fully satisfied by Riley. While he lies in bed sleeping (likely in post-coital bliss), she sneaks out to patrol. Only after hunting and slaying a vamp can she snuggle in Riley's arms and fall asleep. The message is clear, Riley is not meeting Buffy's needs.

Giles has come to a similar recognition. He is not meeting Buffy's needs, either. He decides to move back to England and 'get a life.' With two male characters leaving Buffy wanting, the stage is set for someone who will satisfy her. And that someone is Dracula.

There is a great deal of comedy in this episode. During their first meeting, Buffy doesn't know Dracula. He introduces himself, saying 'I am Dracula.' There's a beat, then she answers 'Get out!' She displays no awe, no wonder, just an abundance of curiosity, mixed with some good old American brashness. Xander is even more brash in his first encounter with Dracula. He refuses to obey Dracula's command and mocks him, asking 'Where'd you get that accent, *Sesame Street*?'

It is not long, however, before both Xander and Buffy change their manner to Dracula. Dracula makes Xander his minion, with an offer of eternal reward. Xander accepts the commission without a fight. Dracula then wafts into Buffy's room, with the romanticized trimmings of every Dracula movie.

He appears in a puff of steamy smoke, accompanied by music heavy on the harp and violins. Even the shot gets soft and fuzzy as Dracula weaves his magic over Buffy and she allows him to bite her neck. The camera zooms in on Buffy's face, the music reaches a climax as Buffy's eyes close in ecstasy.

Both characters display evidence of Dracula's 'thrall'. Xander eats spiders and flies, while Buffy hides her Dracula love-bite from her friends. When they meet again later, Buffy oscillates between being drawn to Dracula's charisma and trying to kill him. It is when he entices her to taste his blood that she recognizes that he is just another vampire and so tries to kill him.

As soon as he is dead, the comedy returns. Xander complains that Dracula made him his 'spider-eating man-bitch'. And when Dracula's dust reassembles, Buffy is right there to stake him, again and again. 'You don't think I watch your movies?' she asks. 'You always come back.'

At the very end of the episode, just as Giles is about to tell Buffy of his decision to leave, she tells him how much she needs him. She recognizes her need to discover more about her heritage and seeks Giles's help. Giles blossoms like a flower, overjoyed that he again has a purpose.

In 'Buffy vs. Dracula' Buffy is fighting not only the manifestation of the character Dracula, she also fights the Hollywood narrative tradition that would have a woman succumb to the power of Dracula. Dracula comes close to defeating Buffy, not through a display of force, but by appealing to the romantic side of Buffy's nature. He calls to the part of her that is unfulfilled and yearning for something more. She wakes up in time to realize that what he has to offer is not what she seeks.

Much is made of Dracula's eyes. His first appearance in the episode is a close-up of his eyes watching Buffy. Buffy describes the eyes as 'dark and penetrating' and later as 'hypno-eyes.' Perhaps Dracula's gaze comes closest to that which Mulvey describes as visual pleasure in classical narrative cinema. Dracula tells Buffy he has been looking for her. He creeps into her bedroom late at night and stands gazing at her. When she wakes he makes no apology for violating her privacy, he merely remarks 'You are magnificent.' The encounter is akin to a voyeuristic relationship.

Further, our heroine, who has always been in the subject position, finds it difficult to command the narrative. Dracula bids her do something and she is almost powerless to resist. Unlike all the other villains, Dracula is drenched in pleasure. He likes looking at Buffy and believes that he can enrich her life if she will only bow to his wishes.

It is significant that after Buffy glimpses what a life of evil might contain her resolve to fight for good is re-affirmed. She turns to Giles, seeking his assistance and counsel. She has grown up.

In 'Welcome to the Hellmouth' (1.1) Buffy shows that she is not swayed by the peer group. She rejects traditional stereotypes of the 'other' and the 'male gaze.' In 'Beauty and the Beasts' (3.4) we see women as the protectors of men. With a cute title, the message of the episode is grave. The absence of patriarchy is apparent throughout the series, but in 'Family' we're reminded of how controlling patriarchy can be for women. In 'Buffy vs. Dracula' the issue of the traditional male gaze re-emerges. The legendary vampire, Dracula, seeks out Buffy. He spends a lot of time looking at her, willing her to submit to his power. She is tempted, but ultimately rejects his advances as repulsive.

Buffy remains, as she began, an icon for female representation. Buffy Summers is not a prissy heroine. She is neither a stereotypical 'good' girl, nor a 'bad' girl. She is human. She punches and she rolls with the punches. Not the object of the traditional male gaze, Buffy is a popular icon and represents female empowerment. She kicks butt and so can we all.

Bibliography

Adler, C., 'An exploration of self-reported sexually aggressive behavior'. *Crime and Delinquency*1985;31: 301–331.

Ageton, S., *Sexual Assault Among Adolescents*. (Lexington, MA: Heath; 1983).

Simone De Beauvoir, H.M. Parshley (Translator), *The Second Sex* (Vintage Books, 1989).

DeKeseredy,W.S., *Woman abuse in dating relationships* (Toronto, CA: Canadian Scholars' Press, Inc.; 1988).

Dolan, Jill, *The Feminist Spectator as Critic* (Ann Arbor: U of Mich Press, 1991).

Ellis, John. *Visible Fictions* (London: Routledge and Kegan Paul, 1982).

Gwartney-Gibbs, P.; and Stockard, J., 'Courtship aggression and mixed-sex peer groups' in: Pirog-Good, Maureen A. and Stets, Jan E. (eds.) *Violence in Dating Relationships* (New York, NY: Praeger Publishers; 1989: 185–204).

Kanin, E. J., 'Date rapists: differential sexual socialization and relative-deprivation'. *Archives of Sexual Behavior* 1985; 14:219–231.

Kanin, E.J., 'Date rape: unofficial criminals and victims'. *Victimology: An International Journal* 1984;9(1): 95–108.

Kaplan, E. Ann., *Women and Film: Both Sides of the Camrea* (New York: Methuen, 1983).

Kuhn, Annette, *Women's Pictures* (London: Verso, 1982).

Makepeace, J. M., 'The severity of courtship violence and the effectiveness of individual precautions'. *Family Abuse and Its Consequences: New Directions in Research* (Gerald T. Hotaling, David Finkelhor, John T. Kirkpatrick, Murray A. Straus, eds.) 1988: 297–311.

Muehlenhard, C. L.; Linton, M. A., 'Date rape and sexual aggression in dating situations: Incidence and risk factors'. *J. Counseling Psychology* 1987;34:186–196.

Owen, A. Susan, 'Vampires, postmodernity, and postfeminism: Buffy the vampire slayer' in *Journal of Popular Film and Television* v. 27 no2 (Summer 1999) p. 24–31.

Marcia Pally, 'Object of the Game,' *Film Comment* 21.3 (June 1985), 68–73

Steinem, Gloria 'IF Men Could Menstruate' in *Outrageous Acts and Everyday Rebellions* New York: Henry Holt 1995

Walters, Suzanna Danuta, *Material Girls* (Berkeley: Univ California Press 1995).

concentrate on the kicking movie

buffy and east asian cinema

dave west

Buffy draws thematically on a whole tradition of East Asian cinema – the various sorts of popular and art house film that can together be called the martial arts film – while using those themes in a context very different from its sources. The single most important element in a martial arts film must be the act of performing martial arts for the camera. Further, the martial arts sequences in a genre film must serve an essential role in the narrative. If the fight sequences occur in breaks in the narrative and do not advance the plot, then such a film is not a martial arts film.

In a classic genre work, the central conflict in the narrative is invariably resolved through displays of martial skill – the combat performances are the externalization of the protagonist's inner conflict. In a pure genre work, the hero is defined by fighting skills, and the culmination of the narrative is invariably a duel in which these skills are sorely tested.

There are many sub-categories within the martial arts genre. In Japan there are the *chambara* (swordplay films) and *jidai-geki* (period dramas). In Hong Kong there are *kung fu* films, swordsman films invariably based on old novels, and what have become known as either 'hero films' or 'heroic bloodshed' movies, contemporary action films usually about triads (gangsters). What all of these have in common is their lengthy and elaborate detailing of combat, and a shared thematic core, to which we shall now turn.

In *The Samurai Film*, Alain Silver defines the Japanese word *shushigaku* as meaning: '(the) Sino-Japanese belief that a person's life is governed by the circumstances of his or her birth.' (Silver, 1977, p189) It is easy to understand how this concept permeates Japanese martial arts cinema. The vast majority of chambara are set during the Tokugawa dynasty (1600–1868 CE), during the period when Japan experienced national isolation and the strict enforcement of Shogunate power. The feudal system was so firmly enforced and obeyed that there was no escaping the class of one's birth. Under this system, society was divided into distinct classes and the samurai, the warrior class, found themselves divested of the means of earning a living.

When Japan had been at war, the samurai (which literally means 'retainer') could find employment in the service of a *daimyo* and hope to earn fame and fortune on the battlefield. With the arrival of peace, many samurai found their services were no longer required and, unable to lower themselves by becoming merchants or beggars, they became either *ronin* (masterless samurai) or outlaws. Their lethal fighting skills were irrelevant and anachronistic, but they were the only skills such men possessed. This notion, that one's fate is decided at birth and is inescapable, was explored throughout Japanese martial arts cinema and, as we shall see, it is ever present in *Buffy* too.

Akira Kurosawa's *Seven Samurai* (1954) explores shushigaku in the relationship between Katsushiro, the young ronin, and the farmer's daughter. Through the course of the story they fall in love, but at the conclusion of the film, they each return to their separate worlds – she returns to the rice fields; he does not go to her, but remains with the other two surviving samurai. The distance between their social classes is expressed visually with the samurai on the hill, and the farmers in the fields below. Despite the passion they shared, they are both resigned to the notion that the class system into which they were each born will not allow them to be together.

The parallels with Buffy and Angel are striking. Despite the love that they both feel, they are doomed to be apart by fate. If they ever re-consummate their feelings, Angel will lose his soul for a second time and become the demonic Angelus. There is nothing either of them can do about it. Fate is inescapable.

In addition to the impositions made upon them by the feudal system, samurai were bound by the code of *bushido*, the standards of behaviour to which the samurai were expected to comform. Whilst there has never been a definitive standardization of the code, Yamamoto Tsunetomo wrote in his book *Hagakure*, a revered bushido text, that: 'The Way of the Samurai is found in death.' Similarly, in Season Five, Buffy is told by the First Slayer that 'Your gift is death' and chooses to interpret this as her own death rather than killing her sister.

At the conclusion of *The Seven Samurai*, when the three surviving warriors look down upon the farmers, the leader of the group, Kambei says: 'And again we lose . . . We lose. Those farmers . . . they're the winners.' The truth of his words is reinforced by the closing shot of the four graves of the samurai who died defending the village. This is the fate of the ronin, trapped by shushigaku, unable to renounce his warrior status, doomed to live and die by the sword.

It is also the fate of the Slayers, Buffy, Faith and Kendra. Whilst each has their own personality, their own goals and desires, they are trapped in their role as Slayers. Their very birthright dooms them to lives of constant conflict, simultaneously branding them as targets and burdening them with the responsibility to fight battles the rest of the world knows nothing about until they die in that very conflict. Kendra's death in battle is as inevitable as it was heroic. Her sacrifice, like that of the ronin in *The Seven Samurai*, will pass unnoticed in the outside world, regardless of her personal bravery and devotion to her role as a Slayer.

The very notion that the Slayers are the Chosen Ones is indicative of the predetermined role that fate has given them. Buffy sarcastically refers to the Slayers as 'a long line of fry cooks who die before the age of twenty-five.' Indeed, Buffy herself dies in combat with the Master, an event that Giles claims is preordained. Although Xander revives her, in the aftermath of her conflict with the Master, one question remains hanging in the air – has Buffy cheated fate, or merely postponed it? She dies again at the end of Season Five, nor will any subsequent return be other than provisional.

This deterministic view of the world is further played out in Kurosawa's *Yojimbo* (1961), right from the very start of the narrative. In the opening sequence, the audience sees an unknown ronin, played by Toshiro Mifune, wandering along a path. When he reaches an intersection he throws a stick up in the air, and when it lands pointing in one direction, that is the path he follows. Fate leads him into conflict.

The same is true for Buffy. In the first episode of the series, 'Welcome to the Hellmouth' (1.1), Buffy tells Giles that she wants no part of any war with the undead, that she wants to be left alone. Giles's response is to tell her that fate has brought Buffy to Sunnydale, and subsequent events speak to the truth of his words. The town rests on the Hellmouth and is plagued by demons. Buffy is inevitably drawn into conflict as she saves Willow from a vampire and learns of the Harvest. The call of her destiny is too powerful to be resisted. Giles was right.

Later, in 'Anne' (3.1), Buffy has fled Sunnydale and is attempting to live a normal life, free from violence and fighting, under an assumed name. However, fate will not let the Slayer rest and she is slowly drawn back into battle with the forces of darkness when she reluctantly decides to help Lily search for her missing boyfriend.

In that same episode, Buffy explicitly reclaims her mantle when confronted by a demon that is trying to break her spirit. The demon tells all the captives that when asked who they are, they must reply

'No-one'. When it is Buffy's turn, she replies: 'I'm Buffy, the Vampire Slayer. And who might you be?' With this gesture of defiance, Buffy asserts both her unbreakable will and her re-acceptance of her role as the Slayer. Her attempt to assume another identity, to stop fighting, is futile. Fate will not be denied, and the responsibility is hers, whether she wants it or not.

In 'Anne', another important theme from martial arts cinema is explored – that of the conflict between *giri* and *ninjo*. We can return to Alain Silver's *Samurai Film*, which offers the following definitions of these two Japanese terms:

> *Giri* – right reason; the dutiful service which bushido
> directs the warrior to give to his family, clan, and
> lord. (Silver, 1977, pp. 186)
>
> *Ninjo* – man's will; the personal or conscientious
> inclination which is often opposed to or constrained
> by giri or duty. (Silver, 1977, pp. 188)

These concepts are explored throughout chambara cinema.

Buffy too, finds herself struggling to balance her sense of duty with her own desires. It is possible to see the Council in the role of feudal lords, issuing instructions that Buffy and Giles are expected to obey without question. The best single example of this regarding Giles is 'Helpless' (3.12), when he is ordered to rob Buffy of her powers and to imprison her in a house with the insane vampire Kralik. Giles initially follows the Council's instructions, but finds himself wracked with guilt for exposing Buffy to such an ordeal. Ultimately, Giles rebels against giri, and tells Buffy of the Council's plan. This leads to the Council relieving Giles of his role as Buffy's Watcher, but Giles is content that he has done the right thing.

His personal feelings for Buffy, his desire to keep her out of danger, his ninjo, is more powerful than his loyalty to his overlords. The parallels with the character of Sasahara from Masaki Kobayashi's *Rebellion* are apparent. Both are patriarchal figures, Sasahara is Yogoro's father, Giles is Buffy's substitute father. Quentin Travers, the representative of the Watchers' Council in 'Helpless' notices the close relationship between Giles and the Slayer, criticizing Giles for allowing his 'fatherly' feelings to interfere with his duties. It is these feelings for his charge that create the conflict within Giles between duty and desire.

Buffy's attempts to balance giri and ninjo are more complex. However, it is illuminating to compare the three Slayers in the light of this inner conflict. Kendra is completely consumed by giri. She is completely devoted to her calling, having been taken from her family and raised by her Watcher at a young age. In 'What's My Line Part 2' (2.10), Kendra tells Buffy: 'You talk about it as if it's a job. It's not. It's who you are.'

However, the drawbacks of this devotion quickly become clear. Kendra's social skills are under-developed, and she is so uncomfortable around boys, to whom she has never been allowed to speak, that she can scarcely even look at Xander. Further, it is possible to view Kendra's death as the inevitable result of her total immersion in the role of the Slayer; she succumbs to Drusilla's hypnosis, where the more wilful Buffy was ultimately able to resist that of the Master and Dracula.

Subsumed by her appointed identity, Kendra is unable to ever stop being 'the Slayer', to lay down her burden even for a moment. It is the only 'self' she has ever known. She was doomed to die in conflict, because, for a Slayer, it is the only possible release from the burden they have to bear. Faith has a similar problem, but with a different root, as we shall see later.

Buffy, in contrast with Kendra, attempts to balance her sense of duty and responsibility, with her desire to be a normal teenager. This desire was expressed most eloquently in 'Homecoming'(3.5), when Buffy says:

> I thought, Homecoming Queen; I could open a
> yearbook someday and say 'I was there. I went to high

school and had friends and for just one minute, I got
to live in the world.' And there'd be proof. Proof that I
was chosen for something other than this.

Whilst Buffy may not succeed in becoming Homecoming Queen, she
will not pass unnoticed. In 'The Prom'(3.20), Buffy is awarded the
title of Class Protector by her fellow high school students, who have
recognized her importance in their lives. Buffy's ability to interact
with her peers, to have a social life and an existence beyond merely
fighting, demonstrates her ability to balance her duties with her
personal needs. Where Kendra's sacrifice has no impact on the world
at large, Buffy's ongoing struggle has made an impression, if only on
the students of Sunnydale High, and it is with the help of these students
that Buffy is ultimately able to defeat the Mayor in 'Graduation Day
Part 2'(3.22). An isolated warrior, like Kendra, could never have
hoped to recruit her contemporaries, because on the most
fundamental level she doesn't have any.

Buffy's relationship with the Council brings to light her struggle
to balance giri and ninjo. When Angel is poisoned by Faith and the
Council refuses to help Buffy cure him, in 'Graduation Day Part 1'
(3.21), she finally renounces her allegiance to them once and for all.
Yet this is not a complete rejection of her responsibilities as the Slayer,
for after graduating from High School, Buffy consciously chooses to
remain in Sunnydale rather than study somewhere else. She may have
cast off the Council's authority, but Buffy is still driven by her own
strong sense of duty. Her decision to remain close to the Hellmouth
and to keep opposing the forces of darkness is a clear indication of
the continued presence of giri in her life. Buffy does not need the
Council to remind her of her place in the world. She knows who she
is and what she has to do. She has to kill vampires and Sunnydale is
the best place to do that. Ninjo leads her to reject the Council, but
giri ensures that the fight goes on.

Where Kendra is a victim of her sense of duty, and where Buffy
achieves a precarious balance between the conflicting forces in her

life, Faith is utterly driven by ninjo. We can find a useful parallel in Yuen Wo-Ping's *Tai Chi Master* (1993), which details the lives of two Shaolin monks, Junbao, played by Jet Li, and Tianbao, played by Chin Siu-Hou. Both are deadly fighters, but where Junbao is filled with a sense of loyalty to his fellow man, Tianbao cares only for himself and is willing to sacrifice anyone in the interests of material enrichment and self advancement. Tianbao epitomizes a warrior who has no sense of loyalty, as does Faith. Like Tianbao, Faith is prepared to betray her former ally, Buffy, in order to ingratiate herself with the Mayor. To use the language of the chambara films, Faith is a ronin whose skills are for hire to the highest bidder, which brings us to the next point.

Although one is devoted to serving the Council and the other only to serving herself, Faith and Kendra have one thing in common. They are totally defined by their status as 'Slayers'. In Kendra's case, this arises from her complete obedience to the edicts of the Council and to the regime imposed upon her by her Watcher. However, Faith's Watcher was killed by the vampirc Kakistos and she regards the representatives of the Council with contempt. Upon first encountering her new Watcher, Wesley, in 'Bad Girls' (3.14), Faith takes one look at him and says, 'Screw that', before walking out.

In *Yojimbo* Kurosawa compares the protagonist, Sanjuro, to a stray dog, both in the dialogue and visually. At the beginning of the movie, when the farmer sees Sanjuro he complains 'The smell of blood brings the hungry dogs.' Then as Sanjuro walks into town, he passes a stray dog carrying a severed hand in its mouth. The camera links the two of them together. Sanjuro the ronin is a stray dog, the conflict in the town provides him with a means to earn his living, through spilling blood. At the conclusion of the film, when all the gangsters are dead, Sanjuro does not stay in town, but immediately turns and heads back out to the open road. He has to for there is no one left in town for him to fight, and so unable to make a living with his sword by staying, he has no choice but to move on. He must find his next adventure, which of course he does in Kurosawa's sequel, *Sanjuro* (1962).

Faith has several traits in common with the ronin in *Yojimbo*. Both walk into towns where conflict is ready to boil over. For Sanjuro, this conflict is the territorial dispute between the two gangs, for Faith, it is the Hellmouth, always ready to spew forth demons hungry for blood. Both are skilled warriors for whom fighting is the only means of survival, necessitated by their status as outsiders.

The warrior as a stray dog, who wanders into town and into trouble, is an idea that has great resonance throughout many cultures. It can be found in the Western, in *Shane*, in dystopian visions of the future, in the *Mad Max* trilogy, and it has been a very popular concept in chambara films. In addition to *Yojimbo*, another pertinent example is the *Sword of Vengeance* series (1972–1973), directed by Kenji Misume. The protagonist here is Itto Ogami, Lone Wolf, a character whose extraordinary capacity for violence denies him membership in society and forces him to exist by his sword. When Itto's wife is killed by assassins sent by the Shogun to kill Itto himself, he sets out on what he calls 'the road to Hell' and goes about fulfilling his prediction that 'They will pay with rivers of blood.' The road to Hell is a lonely one, and the only person with whom Itto has any emotional connection is his infant son, Daigoro.

The pair are completely estranged from the rest of the world, as Itto is never able to relax around people, for fear they may be assassins sent by the Shogun. Even when he stops to bathe, his sword is always within arm's reach. This echoes the vital connection between man and weapon that was present in *Yojimbo*, demonstrated when Sanjuro is captured and beaten because for one moment he was caught without his sword in his hand. Like Sanjuro, Itto relies on his sword to keep him alive, financially, as he becomes a killer for hire, and existentially, as combat becomes his only means of interacting with other human beings. Alain Silver offers this eloquent description of Itto's predicament:

> If such a hero is ruthless, it is because survival is the
> only value he has . . . If such a hero cannot lay down

his sword, it is because he is locked into a time where
to do so is to perish. (Silver, 1977, pp. 183)

This might as easily be a description of Faith. In 'Revelations' (3.7),
the former Watcher Gwendolyn Post compares Faith to a Spartan,
the ancient race famed for their fighting skills and hard lifestyle. She
has no family that we know of, no friends, no past other than tales of
the battles she has won since becoming a Slayer. She is typical of a
stray dog chambara character. She walks into Sunnydale and violence
erupts in her wake. For Faith, combat is the source of her vitality and
it fuels her libido, seen when she has sex with Xander after an
unconcluded battle in 'The Zeppo' (3.12). Faith tells Buffy that fighting
makes her 'hungry and horny' — it makes her feel alive and it is an
affirmation of her 'self'. When Faith is in combat, she is consumed by
the thrill of the fight, for it is only in battle that she can confirm that
she has a place in the world. Yet Faith is aware that her status as a
Slayer casts her apart from the rest of society and this is her tragic
flaw.

Faith is acutely and painfully aware that she is an outcast. She
attempts to reconcile these feelings by claiming that as a Slayer she is
above the rest of society, as enunciated in this exchange with Buffy
from 'Consequences' (3.15):

> Faith: You're still not looking at the big picture, B.
> Something made us different. We're warriors. We
> were built to kill . . .
> Buffy: To kill demons. But it does not mean we get to
> pass judgement on people, like we're better than
> everybody else . . .
> Faith: We are better. That's right. Better. People need
> us to survive.

This is an excellent example of the stray dog as social outsider. Faith,
divested of any sense of duty or responsibility, believing herself above

the mores and values that govern civilized society, is a complete ronin, bound only unto herself:

> As a consequence the ronin's plight, for all its tragic potential, also entailed in its total ostracism a kind of liberation . . . As a yakuza ('gangster') or sanzoku ('bandit'), as an outlaw, he was as free as he dared to be . . . (Silver, 1977, pp. 18)

Faith has embraced this liberation, but she knows what it has cost her. Where Buffy may feel some envy to see Faith apparently unburdened by the weight of responsibility, Faith in turn is envious of Buffy's place in society. If Faith were not a Slayer, she would effectively cease to exist. Like Kendra, the Slayer identity is the only 'self' that has ever given meaning to Faith's existence. By contrast, Buffy is tied to society – and, as Spike points out to her in 'Fool for Love' (5.7), life itself – by her family and the Scooby Gang . If she were not the Slayer, Buffy would be a girl very much like Cordelia, popular, pretty and on the cheerleading squad.

Faith has no comparable connection to the world at large. Her attraction to the Mayor is readily understood in this light, because here at last is someone who values her, someone capable of fulfilling a parental role. This relationship can work because the Mayor alone relishes Faith's capacity for bloodshed.

Faith attaches considerable emotional weight to the dagger that the Mayor presents to her as a gift. Unlike Itto and Sanjuro, Faith's attachment to the weapon is emotional rather than existential. She views it as a symbol of affection, it is not her means of survival – though, when she loses it, it becomes the weapon with which Buffy puts her in a coma and through which she destroys the Mayor.

However, we can return at this point to the notion of shushigaku, because Faith's attempt to build a relationship with the Mayor is cut short and she is once again left alone in this world, a stray dog. Like Sanjuro and Itto Ogami, all she can do is move on to the next town, to the next battle that will be her only reminder that she is still alive.

Indeed, Faith possesses a powerfully nihilistic spirit, demonstrated very clearly in 'Bad Girls' (3.14), when she leaps blindly into a nest of vampires. It is possible to view Faith's behaviour as the unconscious expression of her desire to be free of shushigaku, to escape through death the responsibility that her birthright has bestowed on her – Spike explains later to Buffy that all slayers have this death wish. In this regard Faith is reminiscent of the kung fu heroes in the films of Chang Cheh, whose protagonists inevitably choose to participate in the hopeless fights that end their lives. 'Chang Cheh . . . does not seek inspiration in the archaic and the mystical; he is cynical and spikes his films with a spirit of contemporary rebellion. He places his emphasis on the young – toughness and the will and audacity to kill one's way out.' (Sek, 1980, pp. 32)

Faith is cast in the same mould. When waking from her coma in 'This Year's Girl' (4.15), she does not flee Sunnydale, or take time to recuperate and plan strategy. She immediately seeks out Buffy, the very person who put her in a coma in the first place, consumed by the desire to exact a bloody vengeance. Further, in 'Who Are You?' (4.16) when Faith has the opportunity to leave Sunnydale in Buffy's body, scot-free, she instead chooses to stay and fight the vampires that have taken hostages in a church. This is clearly not in Faith's best interests, but the desire for combat, the call of fate and her own nihilism, override all else.

Faith is drawn to the church partly by her love of combat, partly by the tentative re-awakening of her sense of what being the Slayer means – it is crucial that the woman she earlier saved in the Bronze thanks her. Nonetheless, the moment she and Buffy have killed the vampires, Faith attacks Buffy again – her redemption is not yet complete. Faith wants to be 'the Slayer' more than anything else in the world. She likes slaying, she is good at it and even though she is aware of the dangerous position staying in Sunnydale puts her in, she can never walk away from a fight. Her fate, like that of all the Slayers, is not in her own hands.

It is significant that as her arc continues in *Angel*, her redemption comes through her acknowledgement that she wants to die, that her atrocities – the torture of Wesley for example – were the pursuit of death at Angel's hands; by going to jail to save him, she renounces the active heroism of the warrior for passivity and contemplation.

So far, much of the comparative analysis here has been between *Buffy* the TV series, and Japanese chambara films. However, the vast majority of the action scenes in *Buffy* are demonstrations of unarmed combat, which is the cinematic province of the Hong Kong film industry. The most important point to make here is that the audience is not viewing a 'fight' itself, but a representation of a fight. This may seem obvious, but it is crucial because if one is to understand the problem of placing Eastern martial arts in a Western TV show, then it is essential to remember that each on screen 'fight' is composed of a series of movements signifying combat. Each punch and kick performed for the camera is a sign, standing in place for the real thing.

As noted in *A Study of the Hong Kong Martial Arts Film*: 'Certain forms specific to Chinese civilization are unique in world history. One such form is Chinese martial artistry . . . No comparable phenomenon exists elsewhere in the world.' (Sek, 1980, p. 27)

Indeed, one can add to his statement the contention that Chinese kung fu *is* Chinese history. The various forms of combat developed in China are all interwoven with the times that created them, they are all connected with the people and personalities that spread them. The interplay of fact, legend and kung fu style was explored throughout the martial arts films produced in Hong Kong, beginning with *The True Story of Wong Fey Hung* in 1949 and wrapping up around the time of *The Legendary Weapons of Kung Fu* in 1982. Over this period, the historical characters that either devised or popularized Chinese martial arts made the transition from myth to cinematic icons through a process of repetition.

Kwan Tak Hing played the legendary kung fu master Wong Fey Hung in over forty films, until eventually it was difficult to distinguish between Wong Fey Hung, the folk hero, and Kwan Tak Hing as the living embodiment of that hero. In the 1980s the traditional kung fu heroes were replaced by movies about gangsters or policemen, although there was a revitalization of the traditional heroes in the early 1990s, following in the wake of Tsui Hark's *Wong Fey Hung* series (called *Once Upon a Time in China* in English).

The point of all this is to make explicit the importance of Chinese martial arts to Chinese culture and folklore. A fight sequence in a Hong Kong martial arts film does not exist in a vacuum, but is viewed in the context of a society where the martial arts are an intrinsic and vital part of the surrounding cultural landscape. Each movement in a battle, each gesture, is decoded by the audience with the benefit of a shared knowledge of an enormous body of work featuring other fight sequences, other gestures and movements. A single pose or strike will carry many connotations that will inform the viewer about the character of the person performing that movement. A simple example would be in the innumerable movies made about the heroes of Shaolin, the best of which were choreographed by the team of Lau Gar Leung and Tang Chia. Lau himself was a direct kung fu descendent of Wong Fey Hung, so all the heroes in these films used the *Hung Kuen* style of kung fu. It was therefore possible to identify the heroes in these films by their use of this style alone.

However, to a Western audience, all this is largely meaningless. Whilst many people in the West may have an interest in martial arts, or may take a couple of *TaeKwonDo* classes, the martial arts are inherently alien to Westerners. They do not possess the same cultural significance and, leaving aside for a moment the extraordinarily low standard of most of the martial arts instruction available in the United States, the vast majority of the population will have no first hand experience of the martial arts. Therefore, the same gesture, the same punch or kick, will not necessarily have the same connotations to a Western audience as it would to an Eastern audience.

Many Hong Kong films play with parodies of Bruce Lee's screen fighting style, and rely on the assumption that the audience is sufficiently knowledgeable to instantly recognize when a performer's movements are replicating those of Lee. An excellent example of this is *Legend of the Dragon* (1991), when four characters simultaneously perform Bruce Lee's side-kick, or the film *Skinny Tiger, Fat Dragon* (1990) when one of the recurring jokes is how Sammo Hung's character, Fatty, constantly imitates Bruce Lee's fighting style. If the audience is incapable of instantly identifying which movements are parodies of Lee's and which are not, the humour is lost.

The problem that *Buffy the Vampire Slayer* presents is that the show is produced in the United States and principally aimed at an audience of young Americans. Their field of reference, with regards to the on-screen presentations of martial arts, is considerably less evolved that that of a typical Hong Kong film audience. Indeed, the principal question that arises when attempting any analysis of the presentation of martial arts in *Buffy* is why are they there at all. In the cinemas of Hong Kong and Japan, the presence of martial arts reflects their corresponding presence in the local cultures and society. The martial arts have no corresponding presence in American society, and thus they tend to appear inherently alien when they are transplanted to an American setting, for whilst the movements may be present, in the form of punches, kicks and so forth, the accompanying mise-en-scene that informed the meaning of these movements can not be so easily transposed from their native cultures.

The result is that Buffy's on-screen fighting style is composed of a series of punches, kicks and occasional throws, that have no particular 'form'. It is impossible to extract from Buffy's movements which fighting style or styles she is employing. Where Bruce Lee's screen fighting style was a collection of movements taken from a diverse array of systems, it was still possible to recognize the individual elements. When he battles Colt, played by Chuck Norris, at the climax of *The Way of the Dragon* (1972), Lee employs a huge variety of techniques. His footwork is akin to a boxer, his kicks a mixture of Savate and Northern Chinese styles, his hand strikes combine the straight fast punches of *Wing Chun* with haymakers thrown in for visual effect.

When Buffy fights, it is not possible to perform a similar analysis, for where Lee's style was a mixture of forms that maintained the coherence of each element, Buffy's style is a formless mish-mash of wildly thrown punches and kicks. For the first four seasons of the TV series, Buffy's fight sequences were performed by stuntwoman Sophia Crawford, who has said:

> I try to stay away from looking too 'kung fuey' as they call it here. That kind of thing works if you are Chinese and doing a costume drama, but not so much in the USA if you are a girl fighting demons on TV.

This makes apparent the inherent contradiction of staging the fights in *Buffy* using the martial arts, for if they do not want the movements to appear 'too kung fuey', then why use martial arts at all? Why hire a stuntwoman, like Crawford, who was trained in Hong Kong? The best explanation may be that the fight sequences are there to provide a visceral means of externalizing conflict in the show. The absence of recognizable forms in the movements reflects the fact that the primary audience for the show would be incapable of identifying such forms even if they were present.

The next point of note with regard to the treatment of fighting displays in *Buffy* is the very prominent presence of Sophia Crawford. In the martial arts cinemas of Hong Kong and Japan, actors invariably performed their own fight sequences. In an article from *Film Quarterly*, stunt man Craig Reid made this observation:

> In Hong Kong, the actors are actors first, and martial artists first. They blend both attributes so each

complements the other. They have a passion for fighting
and acting.

(Reid, *Film Quarterly*, Winter 1993–1994, p. 31)

This is central to the appeal of performers like Jackie Chan, Sammo
Hung and Bruce Lee. Their active participation in the fight sequences,
their willingness to accept the physical consequences of participating
in dangerous stunts, is a vital part of their screen personas. Jackie
Chan even goes so far as to include in the closing credits of his films
all the footage of the stunts that went wrong. The fact that the stars
perform their own fights allows the camera to capture their faces
during the battles, and to record the intense emotional and physical
bearing of the players.

Sarah Michelle Gellar does not perform the fight sequences in *Buffy*
and, as mentioned, for the first four seasons of the show, she was
stunt doubled by Sophia Crawford. The most immediate consequence
of this is that the camera must avoid 'Buffy's' face during battles, to
hide the identity of the performer. The stunt coordinator on the first
four seasons of the show was Jeff Pruitt, who made the following
comment about the staging of the fights:

> Normally what I do is just pick what the important
> things are in the story, like what happens at the end
> and what happens at the beginning, and then where
> there are pieces of dialogue that I have to fit in. Then
> [I] choreograph the fight around that to make whatever
> the intention is happen. (Holder et al, 2000, p. 393)

Of interest here is the fact that the movements of the fight are slotted
in around any dialogue that needs to be performed by the actors.
The vast majority of the fighting is carried out not by the principal
cast, but by their stunt doubles. The limits this imposes on camera
angles and editing severely curtail the potential visceral impact of
each fight. Since the performer's features are always obscured, the
viewer cannot see Buffy's face and can not read her emotions. Any

emotional content comes from dialogue and music rather than from the fights themselves.

Close-ups of Sarah Michelle Gellar are often inserted into the fight sequences, most commonly at the end of the fight, when she will finish off a vampire with a stake, but this is insufficient to build any real intensity into the performance. Reflecting the fact that the shots of Gellar have to be filmed separately from the shots of Crawford, the final act of plunging the stake into a vampire is invariably unconnected to the wider flow of the melee. This is borne out by this comment from an interview with Sophia Crawford:

> She [Gellar] didn't really have much knowledge of any martial arts before she started *Buffy*. She just picked up some things as we went along. We usually have her do a duck or a stake at the end of the fight. Maybe raise her leg or punch – but never a whole combination of moves.

It is illuminating at this point to compare the TV 'Buffy' with the 'Buffy' from the feature film that preceded the show. Kristy Swanson played Buffy in the film and she was very visibly performing her own martial arts. Two sequences are particularly worthy of comment. The first is the training sequence when Merrick puts Buffy through her paces. The movements performed by Swanson are impressive not for her technique, which is somewhat unpolished, but for the full physical and emotional commitment she gives to each blow.

Swanson is seen performing an exercise to condition her forearms, which involves banging them repeatedly against a board. This is typical of the training encountered in traditional, hard style systems in the Far East and it is very painful when first undertaken. The fact that Swanson is willing to accept the pain and to perform the exercise with such vigour, speaks to her commitment to the physicality of the role of the Slayer. The grimace on her face as she performs the exercise greatly enhances the emotional content of the training sequence.

Secondly, the displays of martial arts are more thoroughly incorporated in to the act of slaying. In the television series, Buffy frequently engages in rather extended bouts of fisticuffs with the vampires before she will pull out a stake to finish them off. In the film, Buffy has to physically drive the stakes through the vampires' hearts, which she accomplishes by first impaling them, then by driving the stake home with a kick. This is how she defeats Lothos at the film's climax and reflects the attempt by the film-makers to combine the martial arts with the act of 'slaying'.

One of the essential elements in any martial arts film is 'the Duel', the climactic battle that marks the culmination of the narrative. As conflict is the externalization of the protagonist's inner conflict, so the Duel marks the emotional high point of the story, when all the heroes' emotions pour forth to be manifested in combat. The main difference, structurally speaking, between *Buffy* and a martial arts film is the episodic nature of the television series. The dramatic structure of a weekly TV show is inherently different from that of a feature film. However, there have been attempts in *Buffy* to build up an emotional flow over the course of several episodes to culminate in one battle. The most obvious example is Buffy's duel with Angelus in 'Becoming Part 2' (2.22), and one can also pick out Buffy's fight with Faith in 'Graduation Day Part 1' (3.21).

What is absent from *Buffy* is any attempt to show an evolution in her on-screen fighting style that is an essential part of the Duel in kung fu movies. In *Drunken Master* (1978), Wong Fey Hung (played by Jackie Chan) has to develop his own kung fu form in order to defeat the villain played by Whang Jang Lee. In *The Way of the Dragon*, Bruce Lee's style evolves even as the viewer is watching. In the first handful of exchanges, Tan Lung (Lee) is overpowered by his opponent Colt (Chuck Norris). It is only after Lee adapts his style to become more fluid that he is able to out manoeuvre his more rigid opponent. Indeed, this development of the heroes' fighting abilities is indicative of their triumph over themselves, for as the battle is the externalization of the heroes' inner struggle, the triumph over oneself is inextricable from the victory over ones' opponent.

The absence of this evolution in *Buffy* is further indication of the lack of 'form' in the fight sequences. Buffy's manner of fighting possesses no coherent style, thus rendering it impossible for her combat skills to evolve. The fighting displays are the same whether Buffy is fighting Angel, the Master, Faith or whomever. The only occasion on which the television show has played with the notion of 'form' in a fight sequence is the skirmish between Xander and Harmony in the episode 'The Initiative' (4.7). The two combatants slap at each other ineffectually and childishly and the use of slow motion in the scene highlights the futility of the pair attempting to engage in combat at all.

It is perhaps in the treatment of the Duel that *Buffy* finally disqualifies itself from the martial arts genre. When Buffy fights Angelus in 'Becoming Part 2' (2.22), the emotional climax of the story is not part of the fight. Buffy defeats Angelus, but the emotional peak occurs when Angel's soul is restored and Buffy is still compelled to run him through with her sword. Whilst this is an excellent example of the conflict between duty and desire, giri and ninjo, and a deterministic view of fate, the story's apex is not related to a display of fighting skill, but to the unrequited romance between the two lead characters, which shows that the narrative heart of the show is to be found in matters of love, not war.

Bibliography

Berry, Chris (ed.), *Perspectives on Chinese Cinema* (London, 1991).

Chan T.C. Ng, H. Sek, K. et al, *A Study of the Hong Kong Martial Arts Film* (Hong Kong, 1980).

Cook, Pam, (ed.) *The Cinema Book* (London, 1985).

Holder, Nancy with Mariotte, Jeff and Hart, Maryelizabeth, *The Watcher's Guide Volume 2* (New York, 2000).

Mintz, Marilyn D., *The Martial Arts Films* (Rutland, Vermont, 1978).

Richie, Donald, *The Films of Akira Kurosawa* (California, 1984).

Silver, Alain, *The Samurai Film* (Kent, England, 1977).

Turnbull, Stephen, *Samurai Warlords – The Book of the Daimyo* (Yugoslavia, 1989).

Periodicals

Reid, Craig D., 'Fighting Without Fighting: Film Action Fight Choreography', in *Film Quarterly* Vol. 47, No. 2, Winter 1993–1994, pp. 30–35.

Gardiner, Joe, 'Double trouble', in *Bizarre* Issue 38, October 2000, pp. 72–75.

Internet

Source: http://websites.cable.ntl.com/~fraxis/the_ww/features/jeff_sophia.html

Date downloaded: 4 January 2001

Source: http://www.the11thhour.com/archives/052000/features/pruitt1.html

Date downloaded: 4 January 2001

Source: http://www.geocities.com/Hollywood/Theater/1229/sophiacrawford.html

Date downloaded: 4 January 2001

Source: http://www.usastunt.com/members/sophiacrawford/crawford.html

Date downloaded: 4 January 2001

staking a claim

the series and its slash fan-fiction

esther saxey

A Vague Disclaimer is Nobody's Friend: preliminary descriptions

Fan-fiction is creative fiction written around characters, scenarios or elements from pre-existing sources (usually TV series or films, often in sci-fi and action/police genres). Slash is a genre of fan-fiction in which relationships between characters (traditionally two males, such as Kirk and Spock) are developed along overtly loving and sexual lines. Stories can include explicit sex, or no sex at all, but are predicated on the characters being, or becoming, lovers.

Currently there are at least 100 websites devoted to slash stories on the theme of *Buffy the Vampire Slayer* (or of its spin-off series, *Angel*). There are also mailing lists of fan-fiction, with web rings and catalogue sites connecting the different areas. Sites are often devoted to a particular character or pairing (for example, *Laconic*, an Oz site, or *Shoot Me, Stuff Me, Mount Me* – Xander and Giles).

Historically, partly because of the rarity in the seventies of well-drawn women characters in action series, most slash pairings were male/male, even though most of the writers and readers of slash fiction were women. Most critical examination of slash has focused on this paradox, finding explanations that vary from the sublime –

male pairings are 'more noble' – to Katherine Salmon's Darwinian explanations. Many theorists have also analyzed the erotics of slash in terms of possible routes into the work, via desire and identification. With two male characters, who might the female reader want to be and who might they desire?

Several theories are offered: Spock, by virtue of his Vulcan side, is coded female; both characters are coded androgynously; the characters have the 'marker' of maleness, the penis, but they are performing a feminine sex act. Writers and readers enjoy identifying with one male character while desiring the other; or they identify with and desire both.

These debates themselves were attempts to open the question of identification in erotica. They proved by the example of slash that identification does not pass smoothly between reader and character, with a female reader identifying with the female character and desiring the male character. Although multiple strands of identification, desire and other forms of reading pleasure undoubtedly take place in more traditional forms of erotic writing (such as serial romance or pornography) traditional male/male slash upsets these assumptions in a more explicit way. There was necessarily a gap, fluidity, a crossing over of the emotional investment in the characters that passed across genders.

These debates on identification are fascinating studies of a female erotica. But this research is based in a set of information which cannot be assumed to be stable in current slash fiction. Two major changes have occured in the last decade: in the circulation of slash; and in the genre itself.

The distribution of slash has undergone enlargement through the medium of the internet. Henry Jenkins and Camille Bacon-Smith describe a fandom where introduction by mentor is common, with tight-knit groups and conferences predominating. Now, rather than selecting a fanzine by attending a conference, or through a catalogue (sending payment, receiving a 'zine') one can access a hundred sites in an afternoon through links pages, web rings and search engines. One need not look within a fandom, and then within fan-fiction, for slash (the route suggested by Bacon-Smith); one can stumble over slash through a search engine while looking for other material on a particular TV series.

And, destabilizing another slash 'certainty', slash is widening to include female-female pairings. This began most markedly in the *Xena: Warrior Princess* fandom, where the show itself used an implied sexual or loving relationship between the two major characters, Xena and Gabrielle, as a central dynamic. Popular debates around the characters and more focused discussion venues (such as the 'subtexts in Xena' newsgroup) contributed to an atmosphere where female/female slash could be produced.

At around the same time, *Star Trek: The Next Generation* and its partner series *Voyager* and *Deep Space Nine* placed interesting female characters in command positions and treated them with the same degree of characterization and plotting that male characters usually attracted. Now female/female slash in these fandoms are common. Captain Janeway, the captain of *Voyager,* has attracted much attention and is frequently slashed with Seven-of-Nine, an ex-Borg now travelling on the ship. As is common in slash, their often fierce disagreements and spiked exchanges, combined with a deepening attachment over the course of the series, have been taken as signs of sexual interest and developed accordingly in fan-fiction.

With these alterations, it seems that the next stage of criticism might try to construct a model of 'why slash works', which can incorporate male readers, or lesbian or bi female readers, and female characters. I am avoiding this approach for a number of reasons.

Firstly, these changes show up difficulties in an identification-based study of the appeal of slash. The internet is clearly not the playground of mobile identity it has been proclaimed to be – its middle-class Western slant is evident in that it costs a considerable amount to get online – but it does ensure that any number of readers could be accessing fan-fiction without revealing their gender. Of course, this uncertainty was true when slash circulated by zine subscription. But the paranoia-inducing implications of the internet – fears of contamination, infinite circulation – should give critics pause before making assumptions about a fan base. As with the telephone and other new technologies in the past, the new medium allows intimations of infinity to enter arguments.

It would be wrong not to recognize that the distinction is partly in the mind (all-female, deeply personal conferences and magazines versus the genderless, faceless internet). Fan-fiction on the web is not faceless; fiction is not only archived on websites but exchanged on mailing lists, often with linked conversation lists for more informal discussions: the site *A Slayer, A Hacker* also has two mailing lists (*Buffy Loves Willow,* for discussion of their relationship, and *Buffy Wants Willow,* for more 'adult' content). Many sites and lists set regular 'challenges' for slash writers to attempt; writing is not done in a vaccuum. Communities are still in operation. And the fanzine circulation of stories and artwork continues alongside the internet circulation, often involving the same texts. But the concept of the internet removes to an extent the guarantee of the gender of the readership.

And this mental shift from zine to internet levers open the assumption that reading practices can correlate neatly on the basis of gender alone. Although the original studies attempted to open debate on indirect identification, and although most critics stress the fluidity of identification involved, a continuation of this focus risks closing the debates around slash back down into the question of gender. Ultimately it risks reifying the idea it originally attacked, that erotic response can be determined by simple gender grids.

Finally, to return to the subject of why women enjoy male-male character erotica at this distance risks demanding that slash continue to explain itself, twenty-five years after its genesis. And just as the demand that other non-normative sexualities explain themselves in relation to the mainstream is a form of oppression, this demand may become an oppressive one. In longer studies of fandom the 'problem' of gender in slash is often only part of their consideration of the medium. But it is the aspect most frequently referred to in media considerations of slash – news articles, magazine columns. Slash is taken out of the context of fandom and fan-fiction in general, and is seen as a racy and unintelligible pastime; this fits neatly into the low opinion of fandom in general (see David Plotz charmingly titled 'Luke Skywalker is Gay? Fanfiction is America's literature of obsession').

Slash has many more aspects to it; to return to gender investigation risks continuing not only the interrogation of dissident sexualities, but of emphasizing gender in slash as the only feature of interest. Other aspects of equal interest might include the reworking of supplied material; the production of a creative community in which original character invention is no longer considered the highest creative form. Or the unusual degree to which readers of slash are also writers, or contribute to the writing community, in contrast to the usual division of producers and consumers in fiction.

Taking the existence of slash as a given, there are other questions to ask, and *Buffy* serves as a useful focus for them. For example, how might a TV series, slash source material, give a form of permission for the speculations involved in slash? Not in terms of legal waivers or recognition of the fan base, something companies such as Paramount and Fox have stubbornly resisted, but potentially in its structures and themes.

Some critics of slash complain that it distorts characters and lacks grounding in the series; as such, it is disrespectful and offensive to the series and its fans. Writers of non-slash fan-fiction sometimes defend their own marginal position by condemning slashers. Sometimes, in both these cases, this condemnation derives from a homophobia that is also unhappy with the canonical relationship of Willow and Tara. The most basic justifications of slash in respect to its source material is that many slashers do not randomly impose psychologically implausible sex on characters. They research and admire the plotlines, character development and coherency of the *Buffy* universe, approaching the series as fans, not as vandals, and creating new homoerotic storylines with considerable ingenuity – a teenage Joyce has an affair with the 1977 Slayer, Faith takes full advantage of residence in Buffy's body. Ultimately, slash needs no defending – what is interesting is the intense slash-friendliness of *Buffy*, the way it generates interest in the act of sexual speculation itself.

Good v. evil, closure v. deviation – slash dynamics in *Buffy*

> Readers do not have to respect closures . . . We can
> insist on our sense that the middle of such a text arouses
> expectations that exceed the closure.

Alan Sinfield's observation on the vagaries of viewing holds very true for *Buffy*. Readers, indeed, do not have to respect closure; or authorial intention, the moral universe of the given text, the historical sexual preference of characters, copyright restrictions. *Buffy* is dedicated to dwelling on those interesting 'expectations' aroused in the middle of texts, and ultimately the slavish respecting of closure – the actual pairings of the show, the declared motives of the characters – is not what the show's structure encourages.

Arousing expectations in the middle has a glorious history in texts of horror. Horror often operates on a narrative type characterized by a threat or irritation that arises to disturb the status quo. This is then explored during the text, and closure is achieved by the working out of this irritation or the overcoming of the threat. The simplest form of this is often the crime novel, where the irritant is the criminal, who during the course of the novel, is found and punished. The reader/audience is expected to enjoy both the transgressive explorations of the text – the middles – and the conclusion which re-establishes the moral order. *Dracula* is a prime example of a portrayal of evil far more interesting than the moral order it disturbs. The audience is free to enjoy the vampire's intruding and radically foreign sexuality, because it is placed back in a moral order by the death of the vampire. *Buffy* elaborates this structure with delight but, due to the medium of the TV series, closure is more problematic than a single final staking.

Serial television has a peculiar relation to closure. Narrative theorists have in the main focused on such one-shot genres as the novel, play or film; TV series clearly work differently. The simple horror format of threat and expulsion, irritation and restoration can also be seen in TV series. But here there is a lingering continuity absent from the film or novel – the same characters appear week after week. As with that slashed couple Holmes and Watson, or indeed Kirk and Spock, the audience knows more about them with every case.

Buffy seems akin to this simple routine of irritation and closure. Each week brings the invading forces of darkness, which Buffy must, on a more-or-less weekly basis, defeat. But the serial use of this plotline, the repeated narrative closure, leads to a loosening of the structure itself.

Buffy uses the cleansing of the forces of darkness (and as I will examine later, the resolution of personal angst) as a central plot dynamic. Indeed, the thematics of the first seasons involve a series of binaries which need to be restored in each episode: inside/outside, knowledge/ignorance. Monsters spatially invade 'safe' spaces, such as the school and Buffy's house, and threaten to destroy the world – or at least enlighten it to its tenuous safety in the struggle between good and evil. By the end of the episode, these monsters have been expelled and convenient amnesia settles over Sunnydale again. The closure is often a scene of teenage banality in the sunshine.

But the repeated iteration of this plot leads to a blurring of the distinctions that drive it. Part of the essence of the Slayer's role is the ongoing nature of the struggle; triumph is only ever temporary. What's more, the teenage banality is achieved only at the expense of heavy interaction with the forces of darkness. For example, Buffy's fragile home life and naive mother can only be protected by Buffy's strenuous

efforts, reversing the authority and protection involved in the usual
mother/child relationship. Confusions such as these to some extent
derail the alternation between banal, non-narratable closure (Buffy's
home and school life) and the irritation that causes the narratable
action (the supernatural).

Buffy and friends become more and more liminal, more deeply
involved in old books, arcane magics and big weapons. In the same
way, Holmes and other serial detectives are borderline figures, never
quite outside the criminal underworld, permeated as they are by the
knowledge of crime that they need to defeat criminals (it is left to
the less knowledgeable, less liminal Watson to recount the tales of
restoration to law and order).

What's more, while the happy times become transitory, the threat
becomes less threatening by the same process. The perpetual
prediction of the end of the world undermines its own plausibility.
The tension collapses into Joss Whedon's trademark dry irony. As at
the finale of Season Four, 'Restless' (4.22), when the gang have
accidentally angered a primal force, the First Slayer. Buffy suggests
that Giles might have warned them:

> Giles: I said there could be dire consequences.
> Buffy: Yes, but you say that about chewing too fast.

Giles's habits of overstatement and understatement overlap to produce
a meaningless level of perpetual semi-alarm. Buffy's mother, previously
the protected site of innocence, is now also in on the game:

> Joyce: I'm uh, guessing I missed some fun?
> Willow: The spirit of the First Slayer tried to kill us in
>   our dreams
> Joyce: Oh. You want some hot chocolate?

Not even Buffy's mother can be called upon to provide the right
degree of alarm; partly because nobody knows what that level might
be. Thus the narrative repetition that weakens the closure also lessens

the threat of the middle; they managed to triumph last week, and *Buffy* has always already survived (and probably so has Buffy) because it's on next week.

And in *Buffy*, as increasingly with the most popular television series, storylines extend over the confines of the weekly episode. The increasingly confused and lengthy 'Previously on *Buffy*' section can include vital plot information from three previous episodes and more than one season. (The 'Previously on Buffy' for the 100th episode 'The Gift'(5.22) crammed shots from every single episode into less than a minute.) Plots such as the hunt for Adam, or the meaning of the Initiative take weeks to resolve. Extended plotlines affect audiences in terms of the sheer weight of suspense. We have in *Buffy* a longer span than is usual in most series and a more delayed conclusion than is achieved in cinema.

The structure of viewing is different; not in a cinema for a certain finite period of time, but in one's home on a weekly basis. Viewers live between episodes, look forward to them, speculate on-line as to their content. Put simply, the audience is kept in suspense, away from resolution, for far longer. Not only is closure made more problematic by repetition, it is infinitely held off by both the medium and the extended plotlines of this particular series. A taste for the excitement of development, rather than the contentment of the conclusion, is engendered.

And if fighting evil is thus problematized, emotional plotlines are similarly extended and blurred. In romance terms, in a non-serial genre, the final kiss or marriage is the conclusion to the romance plot; if a sequel is made, all too often the hero's lover is replaced, without explanation, with another character and the romance process is re-enacted. The audience needs the sexual narrative arc – uncertainty, confirmation, consummation. TV series perform the same arc, but in a repetitive way. Kirk's sexual exploits are legendary but each girlfriend will vanish by the next episode in order to return to point zero at the beginning of the next episode.

Just as the repeated fighting of evil entails a blurring between the fight and the resolution, the repetition of love and loss can undermine the closure provided by romance structure. One of the original reasons given for slash is that the 'dead girlfriend of the month' provided little emotional satisfaction – perhaps even less when the girlfriend survives and is discarded with no explanation. Kirk is the central character, and the mainstream audience wants romance, but his perpetually brief involvements undermine the idea of romance itself; especially set against his ongoing interactions with other men. (To look at another mainly female-consumed genre, serial paperback romance: these deliver the kick of closure over and over, but with a different couple in each volume, thus not undermining the presumption of eternal love.)

Buffy's relationship with Angel is on and off for a reasonable period, in extremely inventive ways. She attempts to form new relationships, thus undermining both the idea of Angel as the love of her life and the probability that boyfriend II (Riley) will achieve this status either. If the point of love, as Buffy and Angel decided, was that it was forever, what does serial TV do to 'forever'? Will the demand of audiences reduce her to the point of Kirk, or James Bond, whose relationships are no more than icing on a cake of action and explosions?

Patently Buffy won't descend to Bond level, as the emotional plotlines also extend through the series. A key example is Willow's attraction to Xander, which was not abandoned during her involvement with Oz, and is still a wistful retrospective presence when she is committed to Tara and he to Anya:

> Xander: (looking at Anya) Smart chicks are so hot.
> Willow: You couldn't have figured that out in tenth
>   grade. . .?

Buffy's relationships take several episodes to develop. Unstable love is a huge ratings draw, as comedy-romance shows such as *Cheers*, *Friends* and *Frasier* have found. In *Buffy* romantic relationships are between people who get more air-time than the 'dead girlfriend'. Lovers interact within the group – Willow and Xander, for example – or their 'external' partners are brought into the group –Tara, Oz, Anya. Romance partners are characters in their own right, appearing over a number of episodes, rather than operating on the 'dead girlfriend of the month' system; this also extends the character base of *Buffy*, providing a higher number of fleshed-out characters, which evidently aids slash.

This means that emotional experiences of the lead characters are an essential part of the action of the series, far more so than in, for example, the original *Star Trek*. It is not a side effect of 'the mission' or a momentary distraction. Emotional needs and risks often power the basic *Buffy* plotline, with the supernatural elements adding intensification. To take three from dozens of examples: the perceived risks of finding love on the internet are enhanced by the existence of a demon in 'I, Robot – You, Jane' (1.8); the dangers of fraternizing with frat boys are enhanced by a snake demon cult in 'Reptile Boy' (2.5); Buffy's failure at 'burying' her past is given literalized backup when zombies attack her house in 'Dead Man's Party' (3.2).

In terms of closure, on a successful series the ending isn't in sight for years; *Buffy* is still being filmed as I write. Buffy's true feelings, and the fate of the world, cannot be decided until the series ends; the ultimate closure on any character's true love, or whether they survive the Hellmouth, will not arrive until the series concludes. As Peter Brooks writes, paraphrasing Walter Benjamin:

> . . . what we seek in narrative fiction is that knowledge
> of death which is denied to us in our own lives; the
> death that writes *finis* to the life and therefore confers
> on it its meaning.

The point of closure is that point at which no more can be added, no new information can undermine the established meaning of the text.

Buffy, and television series in general, give to the audience only small versions of this ultimate closure. Death is threatened in *Buffy*, but is usually held off; ultimate closure on any of these characters is not what the audience wants. Angel's return from monstrosity and Hell, Spike and Drusilla's return to Sunnydale, Darla's resurrection as human, and subsequent re-vamping, the extraction from, and return to, the moment of her staking of vamp-Willow, Dracula's endless reformation from dust – all of these complicate the notion of what closure might be. There was a time when a simple staking would suffice.

Thus, because of its extended plotlines and serial nature, enjoyment of *Buffy* is rooted in the extension and blurring of the structures and categories that power the plot. This leads to a viewer relationship with closure which, to some extent, in turn powers *Buffy* slash. To take one example put simplistically, because of the structure of *Buffy* as a series, any potential pairing is possible in the future, or in an alternate reality that suddenly rewrites the canonical – as in 'The Wish' (3.9) or 'Superstar' (4.17).

Because it is a series which encourages speculation with its extended narrative structures, any pairing will eventually be slashed by a curious fan. For example, Tara and Joyce meet at a local lesbian group before Tara and Willow meet. In an exploration of existing character motivation, Joyce rejects Tara after finding out her involvement in Wicca, due to issues around Buffy's role as the Slayer. These are two characters who haven't had air time together by the close of Season Four. One of the foremost examples of slash expanding on minor characters is the use of Devon (a member of Oz's band), who is much slashed; one site, Devon/Jonathan, features two blindingly minor characters, who have nonetheless caught the public's imagination.

All this raises an ongoing debate as to whether slash provides missing supplements to popular shows or allows fans to enjoy more of what the show already provides. Slash has a clear tradition of supplying readings absent in the text. As one slash slogan states, 'If Paramount won't give us a queer episode, we'll make it so.'

But slash also provides more of the same. While Kirk/Spock may be an attempt to extend character development and interaction beyond the 'point zero' which every episode returns to, *Blake's 7* slash responded enthusiastically to the longer narratives of that series. And if Kirk/Spock or Starsky/Hutch was written to infuse a sexually off-limits workplace with emotion, *Buffy* is already fusing emotional and action plotlines – yet is frequently slashed.

I wish to suggest that what *Buffy* slashers are most drawn to is not only that which is absent, or that which is supplied by the series, but particularly that which is thrown out of *Buffy*: themes dwelt on in the middle of episodes or plotlines, which are then abandoned or overcome as part of the plot dynamic. This means moving from a general understanding of *Buffy* as slashable, due to its episodic cycles and extended emotional plotlines, to considering what forms of slash this endlessly delayed closure might produce. Pain in fan-fiction occurred before *Buffy*'s heady cocktail of chains and personal dilemmas. The 'hurt/comfort' genre (h/c) is established, where the hero tends his suffering partner after graphic violence, with or without a slash conclusion; also the 'get' convention ('get Spock', 'get Kirk'), where the hero is put through extreme suffering without any subsequent comfort. Debates among critics and fans circulate around the emotional needs that the description of suffering heroes fulfil. Bacon-Smith concludes that hurt-comfort is a means for women to cope with the pain in their own lives:

> I didn't want hurt-comfort to be the heart of the community, I didn't want to accept that pain was so pervasive in the lives of women that it lay like a wash beneath all of their creative efforts . . .

Buffy fandom has clearly personalized this brand of infliction fiction. The torture plot device, which has surfaced memorably in 'Becoming

Part 2' (2.22) (Giles is tortured by Spike, Drusilla and Angel) and in 'The Wish' (3.9) (Angel is tortured by Willow's evil alter ego), has caught the imagination of slash writers. Explorations of these scenes or inventions occur in both this universe and the vampire-ruled 'wishverse', the world created by Cordelia's wish where vampires rule. There are web archives devoted to the genre, such as *Spike's Torture Slash*.

But alongside this there is a vein of psychological torment in *Buffy* fiction, which links in with the deeper characterization of a long story arc and other peculiarities of the show. *Buffy* slash psychological torment narratives come less often from their own hostile universe than from the internal fears of the characters as they interact in the non-supernatural worlds of high school and college. *Buffy*'s characters fear loss of friends and lovers, rejection from their peer group, lacking a role in life. As *Buffy* joined the gang as teenagers, many of these concerns are age-specific; Buffy-as-Slayer and her problems are often an exaggerated parallel of the concerns of Buffy-as-teenager.

These issues are often both developed over a long period of time, and used by the programme writers to peak in certain episodes. The conclusion, of the happy group reassembled and discussing the episode's events can only partially restore the ensemble calm. When pain is reprised so often, the closure cannot hope to tie up all the ends. And indeed, the programme itself leaves these ends untied, these issues unresolved; just as, though Buffy defeats darkness each week, the threat is never obliterated.

Some peaks in these underlying currents of mental turmoil occur in Season Four, in which the fears of each character are almost too systematically explored. Xander is insecure in his status as non-college kid, while Buffy, Willow and Oz settle into student life – especially noticeably in 'Beer Bad' (4.5). Giles worries about his role in life; no longer Buffy's Watcher, with Professor Walsh taking over as her mentor, he feels increasingly isolated from the group, which reaches a peak in 'A New Man' (4.12). Because of the wide character base and the multiple plotlines, episodes such as these avoid the two-dimensional pathos of, for example, Feel-Sorry-for-Fox (Mulder) episodes common in *The X-Files*. Interestingly, although female characters in Buffy also angst, it is the males who are persistently tortured by doubt in slash accounts, Xander's fears focusing on sexual inadequacy and ending up a joking nobody, Giles on growing old and becoming irrelevant, Oz on dealing with his wolf side. This essay lacks space for a fuller speculation as to why slash readers and writers wish to explore the suffering of these often sensitive, non-traditional male figures, when female characters more often enjoy less emotionally painful treatment.

Bringing together the strands of mental distress and slash, psychologically dismal sex also has a heritage stretching before *Buffy*. The range includes the prequel to, or aftermath of, *pon farr* (Spock's seasonal rut) consummation for Kirk and Spock, where misunderstandings and emotional withdrawals confuse; or *Blake's 7*'s male-male mistrust, where issues of dominance and suspicion hamper emotional communication. Zoe Rayne states that an intrinsic element of slash is danger, a risk to the two characters involved:

> In the 1970s, K/S was a dangerous concept simply because the writers put Kirk and Spock in a homosexual relationship. However, attitudes are changing in the 1990s. To paraphrase a fellow Escapade attendee, 'If Mulder and Krycek are having sex and Mulder's biggest concern is "Does this mean I'm gay?" then the writer needs to seriously re-evaluate their story concept.'

The dilemmas of *Buffy*'s characters *can* neatly segue into a coming-out story – just as Buffy-as-Slayer and Buffy-as-teenager can often stand in for Buffy-as-queer (her 'coming-out' scene with Joyce attested to this identity overlap: 'Have you tried not being a vampire Slayer? . . . It's because you didn't have a strong father figure . . .' – 'Becoming Part 2' (2.22). Xander in particular seems to come out often: but this is usually with relief, as the standard coming-out narrative offers movement toward a positive future life. Xander's problems as they are currently presented – worries about his role in life, struggles with his notions of masculinity, sex and relationships – don't contain within them a recognizable solution.

So other dangers are required to fuel slash. Rayne states her favourite examples of this are love/hate relationships, where mistrust dominates and must be overcome. This element of obstacle has been expanded in *Buffy* slash to whole stories in which mismatched misery abounds. In many cases, the sex is the point of contact for a pair of lovers whose own problems are too vast for them to find anything but transitory comfort. Differences of temperament, age differences, relationships with vampires, all fuel these productive differences and confusions.

Part of this is undoubtedly due to the focus of impossible romance in establishing the series. In a clear example of the privileging of development over closure, Buffy and Angel's relationship was predicated on a set of basic incompatibilities and impossibilities. She would die young, he would live forever, she saved lives, he was a mass murderer. Brilliantly, the moment of their consummation provided their most major break-up (another supernatural intensification, dealing with the teen fear that a boy won't respect a girl after sex). Clearly the completion of closure in this relationship holds less appeal, in an ongoing series, than uncertainty, delay, advance followed by retreat.

Slashers have extended this to relationships involving the distant, prematurely old Oz and the repressed, suddenly in love Giles: 'It was insane, and discordant, and so bloody perfect in its awkward, angular jarred harmony.' Or the basically mixed up Xander and the sarcastic Spike: 'But on the same wavelength as this thing between them, mostly unspoken save for barbs, and small moans in his parent's basement.'

There is also an interest in alternative universes or past and future settings, where more troubles assail the group: the 'wishverse' – 'The Wish' (3.9) and 'Doppelgängland' (3.16) – is a canonical feature picked up by writers. Projecting back in time before the series allows for amplifications of the past suffering of vampire characters, and projecting forwards allows for exploration of a grim future often including the aftermath of the death of key characters.

This strand of slash shows not the triumph of romance over a grim world view, but a little human contact amongst insurmountable problems. The problems and the romance set each other off and are ultimately of equal importance in highlighting each other. But the exploration of the pain reflects the interest that *Buffy* has in the problems of its characters. It offers partial closure, but never a complete reassurance that its characters won't continue to feel worthless or ignored, or be left by their partners and friends. The stories are in some ways an exploration, in some ways an exorcism of these concerns that slashers draw from their source material. What is of interest is that slash is clearly not only interested in exploring and extending the utopic moments of closure from the series, the heady group atmosphere, but picks up in the middle, the compelling suffering of the characters.

The other summoned apparition in *Buffy* that slash explores is kinky sex. I use the word kinky rather than SM, bondage or another signifier, because at points of the show the whole gamut of non-normative sexual expression is thrown together – gaydar, sexual knowledge, role-play, 'casual' sex – and made to signify in much the same way.

The moments of kink in *Buffy* function for a gleeful audience in similar ways to the queer recognition moments. To take Danae Clark's notion of gay 'window' advertising, which will be available to queer readings for an aware audience but not disturb a heterosexual reading, there is a definite kink window in *Buffy*. Angel spends a ludicrous amount of time in chains, shirtless. Angel's chains and Oz's cage are *double entendre* props which the show is happy to display for fighting evil, and occasionally utilize for sex: for example, when Oz's cage becomes the playground for his encounter with Veruca ('Wild at Heart' 4.6).

The verbal side is equally memorable. The wishverse, which seems entirely predicated on evil and black leather, has some of the best lines: vampire-Willow, who has proved a popular slash character, comments: 'In my world, there are people in chains and you can ride them like ponies . . .' – which has made its way into numerous signature files (the material automatically added to a sender's e-mail). And vampires in general, with Spike in particular, seem constantly to be sexually experimenting. This lends the torture strand decidedly sexual elements (for example, when vampire-Willow 'plays' with 'puppy' Angel).

The presentation works on many levels. On the simple side, there is the chained Angel; on the explicit, knowing level, Angel asks Faith if (when strangling Xander) she 'forgot the safe word'. There is both camp glee in spotting kinky sex potential in a TV show and a deeper ratification of its existence which slashers have not failed to pick up on.

Those engaged in kinky sex are often evil. The conversion of spaces and props, which is enjoyed in the middle of the show is rectified by the conclusion: as above, when the cage that contains Oz is not the site of sex with Willow (his love) but Veruca (the homicidal object of his lust) who dies. Whereupon Oz leaves town.

One episode in particular raises the spectre for audience to enjoy, then exorcizes it with force: 'Who Are You?' (4.16), part of a double episode that sees the return of Faith, the rogue Slayer, to Sunnydale. In this episode, she has exchanged bodies with Buffy. She opens the proceedings with a joke about prison lesbians which horrifies Buffy's mother: 'I'm sure there's some big old Bertha just waiting to shower her ripe little self with affection.'

She then engages Spike in an interesting conversation:

> I could ride you at a gallop until your legs buckled
> and your eyes rolled up. I've got muscles you've
> never even dreamed of. I could squeeze you until
> you pop like warm champagne and you'd beg me to

hurt you just a little bit more. And you know why I
don't?

She doesn't do it 'because it's *wrong*'. This is a phrase Faith has been
practising as she feels it encapsulates Buffy, a parody which draws
attention to the slightly sketchy nature of the moral universe of the
show. She then becomes the first character to recognize Tara and
Willow's relationship ('So Willow's not driving stick anymore'), and
she attempts to seduce Riley with a clear invitation to unorthodox,
fantasy-based role play sex:

> What do you wanna do to this body? What nasty little
> desire have you been itching to try out? Am I a bad
> girl? Do you wanna hurt me?

Aside from the seduction of Riley, there is clearly here an interest in
the subject of Buffy's body and her sexual persona; that the prospect of
sex using Buffy's body is as interesting to Faith as sex using her boyfriend.
(Most of these lines were cut from the early evening showing of this
episode in the UK on the BBC, and only appeared in a late night repeat).

Riley is horrified; they make love as Riley would with Buffy, without
obvious kink. This experience and the declaration of love that follows,
temporarily unhinge Faith into disorientation conveyed by jumpy
camera cuts. She flees the scene. Real love, real sex, are too much for
the kinky Faith. She concludes the episode mired in self-loathing,
smashing the head of her body (with Buffy inside) against the floor
shouting ambiguously aimed accusations – 'You're nothing! Disgusting!
Murderous bitch! You're nothing! You're disgusting!' She then leaves
town. Of course, in plot terms Faith has to go not only because she's
kinky, but because she's a murderer – but this is the pattern that has
already been established by Oz, linking casual sex with murder and
expulsion.

Clearly, the closure of this narrative cannot banish the pleasure
created by the presentation of Faith, her sexual knowledge and sexual
preferences. Faith performing as her more sexual self in Buffy's body

is gleeful and exposes her to the viewer in (again) black leather. Throughout she has been used to add spice to the Scooby Gang. But the attempt here is to titillate, then expel.

To enjoy being in the middle of *Buffy* is essential – one can't watch an entire series just for the depictions of happiness and contentment. But the audience shouldn't unashamedly enjoy the middles either – because it's *wrong*. Sometimes only the place of the theme or character in the plotline indicates its wrongness; the moral universe is massively supported by, and articulated through, plot structure. Faith is right to be sceptical.

I'm not calling here for *more* sex in a teen fantasy drama, and am uncertain that there is a solution; there is a pleasure in seeing characters like vampire-Willow which derives directly from their appearance in a mainstream vanilla-fest. And certainly, the series is making efforts to depict some kinds of non-mainstream sex. In Season Four, Willow and Tara become lovers and their relationship becomes more explicit in Season Five: the use of magic to suggest sexual close-ness usefully negotiates what is representable in a teen-orientated series. The only couple to engage in kink unproblematically are Xander and Anya, and significantly this is in the most entirely committed couple relationship the show offers. The show depends to some extent on the amusing spectacle of good sex fighting bad sex, with the definitions of each divided by a hair's breadth.

In response to these invited sexual speculations, and combined with the general *Buffy* interest in the middle of shows over their closure, slash fans have gone to town on kinky sex. To ward off the same criticisms that are levelled at slash in general: this is rarely the imposition of non-vanilla sex into an implausible environment. Writers work hard to assess the psychological and practical components of their work. Hints from the show have been developed into full narratives (such as the pre-series relationships between Angelus, Spike and Drusilla, or Ethan and Giles).

Emotional drama has been translated into sexual terms, as is popular in all slash. Here in *Buffy* fandom, there is an added interest in the sexualization of emotional suffering, which is that suffering is already so much part of the series and the slash. Writers combine these two ejected themes – suffering and kinky sex – and play them against each other. Conflicts are played out in sex, conflicts are created around sex which are played out in conversations. The two themes become interdependent, and scrupulous attention to the particular brand of suffering which bedevils each character creates yet more grounded and plausible sex.

And on a lighter note, the gamut of gadgets, supernatural aids and props have created very source-specific sex: including not only Angel's chains, but also spells and magical levitation. For instance, ongoing speculations as to whether Spike's head chip (which prevents him from hurting humans) could prevent him from consensual SM sex:

> Xander realised that Spike was testing the limits; when
> he began to suckle one of Xander's nipples, he grinned,
> but when he tightened his teeth around it, the vampire
> winced in pain and just as quickly let go.

The fun is in the play before the conclusion. This is what slashers know and what *Buffy* as a series supports. They explore the possibilities generated by the middle of the narrative, which closure cannot hope to tie up; in part because there are many more opportunities than could ever be covered by one series. As the myriad slash sites prove, the possibilities of each pairing, developed to include a sexual element, are too many for any show to even approach.

Many sites recognize this and present themselves as public services, assistants to the series. The ways in which slash views and presents itself open up another way in which source text and the fan-fiction draw together in a complex (slashy?) relationship. While initially the source might be viewed as the parent, the authority, and the slash its less mature offspring, there are more interesting dynamics at work. And this is appropriate to *Buffy* where parent/child relationships – and other relationships based on authority – are also more complex.

To conclude, I propose another motivating factor in *Buffy*: the relation of the series, and fan-fiction, to authority/authorship.

The disclaimers warding off Joss Whedon, the Fox Network and Mutant Enemy legal action have moved into a class of creative surreality all their own. Most whilst asking for clemency, implicitly argue why they should be allowed to write, using the idea of the characters as toys:

> DISCLAIMERS: I'm one of the few people in the world who do not own a piece of, or profit from, the characters of Willow & Tara (& Spike & MKF). I only borrow Mr. Whedon's wonderful characters for fun, disinfect them when I'm done, and put them back . . .

Whedon is referred to in the most affectionate terms (frequently as 'God', but clearly a god with a sense of humour):

> COPYRIGHT DISCLAIMER: Joss moves in mysterious ways. But, damn his eyes, he owns the two lovlies and their auras. He created them, made them what they are, and I bow to you . . .

There is a degree of subversive respect here which ill accords with the definition of slash as inherently disrespectful, ascribed to by opponents within and outside fan-fiction. And now subtextual speculation (at least on an imaginative, if not a literary basis) has been given the blessing of the aforementioned God, on the discussion board known as The Bronze:

> But then, I think that's part of the attraction of the Buffyverse. It lends itself to polymorphously perverse subtext. It encourages it. I personally find romance in every relationship [with exceptions], I love all the characters, so I say B.Y.O.Subtext!

Debates over an authorship which uses another author's primary materials are ongoing, in legal and creative terms. This may turn out to be one of the most interesting areas of fan-fiction as a literary production; the interplay with authority/authorship. *Buffy* also exhibits a problematic relationship with authority. Parental (Joyce and the robot-stepfather Ted), civic (the Mayor) and pedagogic/military (Professor Walsh) figures are invariably undermined in their authority or are evil. Both Buffy and Giles abandon the Council, the Slayer's traditional command organization. Buffy is always the maverick cop who doesn't play by the book, a standard of action drama.

Just as *Buffy* encourages romantic speculation and toys with angst and non-normative sex, it flaunts a renegade cop/hacker ethos of jaunty rebellion. The slash it produces, and the fact that it produces slash, is in many ways more compatible with the series ethos than its opponents recognize.

Slashers are deferential but playful towards *Buffy*, and the producers return the favour: Marti Noxon, an executive producer on *Buffy the Vampire Slayer*, says staffers on *Buffy* and *Angel* know better 'than to disrespect the creative process of any of these people . . . It's flattering because something you're creating – a universe you're a part of – has inspired people to go off and continue imagining.'

When relations between fans and those involved in the source series have traditionally been impossible to gauge, or downright hostile, this and the speculative sanction of Joss Whedon are massively encouraging and generous creative statements.

It would be stretching the mark to say that there is a direct relationship between the series and slash; that *Buffy* encourages speculation and deviation to the degree that it produces or condones slash. Many series are slashed; most lack *Buffy*'s interest in the central diversions over the closure, the extended plotlines and characterization. But it's stretching the mark to say that Spike and Xander's on-screen banter is a clear sign that their awkward but passionate affair is only hours away. I hope that suggesting this relationship is stretching the mark in a productive way which can add to viewer enjoyment, just as slash can; that this may be slash theory.

Bibliography

Camille Bacon-Smith, *Enterprising Women* (Philadelphia: University of Pennsylvania Press 1992).

Peter Brooks, *Reading for the Plot* (Harvard University Press, 1998) p22

Danae Clark, 'Commodity Lesbianism', *Camera Obscura*, 25/26 (1991): 181–201

Henry Jenkins, *Textual Poachers: Television Fans and Participatory Culture* (NY: Routledge 1992).

Alan Sinfield, *Faultlines: cultural materialism and the politics of dissident reading* (Oxford: Clarendon Press, 1992) page 48.

they always mistake me for the character i play!
transformation, identity and role-playing in the Buffyverse (and a defence of fine acting)

ian shuttleworth

Among far too many critics, notions of genre obscure those of quality; it is assumed that certain genres of work attract fans who consume indiscriminately. The leap of logic comes with the conclusion that therefore, all genre work, all SF, horror and fantasy, is in effect pulp; there's no point in judging for such an audience, runs the reasoning, therefore there's nothing to judge.

This genre snobbery extends past genre writers and directors to performance – unfairly, because the demands of genre often call for greater complexity of performance than do more naturalistic dramas. Performance and identity are more integral to the fabric of such works; granted, the appearance/reality trope has been common in drama since long before honest Iago and Shakespeare's other smiling, damnèd villains, but such tropes are matters of persona rather than person. We know that Iago and Richard Crookback 'really are' wicked, but we have no idea, say, which of MacReady's colleagues in John Carpenter's remake of *The Thing* 'is' the alien at any given moment . . . or even whether it is the viewpoint character of MacReady himself, as with Matthew Bennell in the final reversal-of-perspective scene in Philip Kaufman's remake of *Invasion of the Body Snatchers*.

I pick those examples deliberately to illustrate the idea which Carpenter once put forward of 'left-wing' versus 'right-wing' horror. Carpenter, though a card-carrying Republican, is a champion of the former approach, in which the evil to be battled does not take the form of an easily perceived Other but is, to all intents and purposes, located in ourselves. The term 'left-wing' has in this sense no political overtones: *Invasion of the Body Snatchers,* particularly in Don Siegel's 1956 original, is famously a near-rabid anti-Communist parable, but the narrative mode of its horror is left-wing – the pod-people are outwardly indistinguishable from us, and to many intents and purposes *are* us.

It is always more interesting for an audience to have to negotiate its own deals with and interpretations of identity, the identity of the viewpoint and other characters as they encounter forces which are more insidious than identifiably external baddies. It is also more interesting to see performers negotiate *their* own deals with the characters they play as they undergo such narrative topological transformations.

This complexity of identity forms a major thread in *Buffy* and *Angel*. In fact, virtually every principal character in *Buffy the Vampire Slayer* in particular has at one point or another undergone one or more major transformations, with the associated demands this makes on the actors concerned in terms of complexity of performance; in *Angel*, the continuities, divergences and tensions between 'Angel' and 'Angelus' are a primary basis of the drama. There have also been a number of episodes in which the entire world is changed around – or sometimes with – the central characters, from the sinister (the *Crucible*-in-Sunnydale of 'Gingerbread' (3.11), and the 'wishverse' dealt with below) to the comic (nebbish Jonathan Levinson's apotheosis in 'Superstar' (4.17), which spills over from the storyline into the opening title montage), but it is the instances of individual transmogrification that shed most light both on some of the series' thematic concerns and on the acting abilities of those who depict them.

In a wholly naturalistic series, we can judge the quality of the player's performances by the skill and subtlety they bring to their portrayals of developments on-screen and the ramifications these may have with various back-stories, whether the latter have previously occurred on-screen or are simply implied or recounted. In the Buffyverse, we also have the opportunity to judge how the performers integrate their 'true' characters with the frequent changes wrought upon them. Every actor in any role is in a sense routinely being at once him- or herself and someone else; the players in *Buffy* and *Angel* are further called upon frequently to invest their own characters with such a dualism, and thus to cope with a second order of 'elseness'.

Or sometimes even a third order: on various occasions, Sarah Michelle Gellar, Alyson Hannigan and David Boreanaz have each been asked not just to ring the changes on their character, but to play their principal character *pretending* to be a secondary character. Most prominently, in 'Who Are You?' (4.16), thanks to a magical body-swap, Gellar succeeds in playing Faith *pretending* to be Buffy, and pretending plausibly enough for those around her not to notice, but with enough discreet signals for the audience to be clear about the imposture; indeed, the body-swap is not even made verbally explicit when it takes place.

None of these twists and turns are revolutionary in themselves; indeed, as Shakespeare buff Joss Whedon is no doubt aware, one of their most famous antecedents is in *As You Like It*, when the exiled Rosalind, played by a boy and disguised as a young man, offers to 'pretend' to be Rosalind so that her suitor Orlando can 'woo' her/ him/her. But the regularity with which they crop up in *Buffy*, and to a lesser extent in *Angel*, lifts matters onto another plane: far from indicating a lack of ideas, with the same furrow being ploughed repeatedly, it demonstrates the very opposite – a deep and abiding preoccupation with senses of identity and role-playing as everyday parts of personality in all its forms. Just as palpably, this demands a range, precision and subtlety from actors which would astound those critics who automatically turn their noses up at genre works simply because they *are* genre works.

Xander seems exceptionally prone to refashioning, perhaps to compensate for his lack of a discernible individual 'shtick'; indeed, 'The Zeppo' (3.13) is concerned with his continuing attempts to define a role for himself in the Scooby gang. Xander's very ordinariness (as a friend remarked, 'In a Stephen King novel, he would be the boy who grew up to become the author'), and thus his greater potential for audience identification, makes his transformations implicitly more significant for the viewer. His possession by a hyena-spirit in 'The Pack' (1.6) is a hyper-exaggeration of the dangers of peer pressure within a closed group. When he becomes the 'army guy' of his fancy-dress costume in 'Halloween' (2.6), his coldness and control are not just a bleak gag for the single episode, but constitute the first manifestations of a hitherto latent side of his personality. After his reversion, Xander retains knowledge both of military hardware and of the layout of Sunnydale's army base, allowing him to raid its arsenal in 'Innocence' (2.14); more significantly for the character, though, he grows more fully into the 'heart' of the core Scooby quartet, becoming a confidant and voice of reason to both Riley and Buffy as their relationship begins to founder in Season Five.

This development may have been dictated by the more visible ageing of actor Nicholas Brendon in the course of the first five seasons: more thickset of body and face now, 29-year-old Brendon (as of Season Five) would be ever less plausible if his character continued to live in his parents' basement and generally be a menial-jobbing, 20-year-old dork – hence in part the establishment both of a permanent job and a nice apartment for Xander in his own right and the de-emphasis of the character's actual age. (In much the same way, moving Cordelia to Los Angeles and away from her supposed contemporaries has allowed Charisma Carpenter, aged 28 by the first season of *Angel*, to escape the formal reminders of her character's relatively tender years and thus to be permitted to develop a more mature portrayal.) Xander's proposal to Anya in 'The Gift' (5.22) sets the seal on the character's full adulthood at a time when it increasingly stretches plausibility to have Brendon continually playing a post-adolescent.

More immediately evident, though, is the simple fact that Brendon is in unobtrusive possession of the acting skills to carry such a progressively more rounded character. Consummate as he is with the delivery and timing of the one-liners which are Xander's forte, he is also capable of the increasingly greater range demanded of him. His brooding menace can just about stand comparison with David Boreanaz's Olympic standards when Xander is reinvented as the Master's vampiric lieutenant in a Sunnydale without Buffy in 'The Wish' (3.9); later, when split into two opposing personalities in 'The Replacement' (5.3), he can portray both 'Lame Xander' and 'Suave Xander' without ever approaching the crass eye-rolling of William Shatner's James T. Kirk in the similarly plotted *Star Trek* episode 'The Enemy Within'. (Brendon's twin brother Kelly Donovan – each twin uses his middle name as a professional surname – plays 'Suave Xander' only in shots in which both 'halves' are on screen.)

Xander's continuing tutelage of girlfriend Anya following her own transformation from a vengeance demon at the end of 'The Wish', as she re-learns what it is to be a mortal human, is often sardonic but above all loving: another demonstration of Xander's role as the 'heart' of the Scooby gang, which is made explicit when the core quartet's qualities are combined to form a 'super-Buffy' in the Season Four climax 'Primeval' (4.21).

Joss Whedon, in his audio commentary to the DVD release of 'Welcome To The Hellmouth' and 'The Harvest' (1.1 & 1.2), has rhapsodized about Alyson Hannigan's qualities of luminosity as an actress and her astonishing ability to command audience sympathy and even empathy in the role of Willow. As with Xander, most of Willow's transformations play against the primary type of her character. She is likewise 'turned into' her costume – a ghost – in 'Halloween', but this merely affects her corporeal solidity rather than her personality. What is notable, though, is that her clothing beneath the spectral sheet, her original choice of get-up (albeit at Buffy's instigation, to help Willow get Xander's attention), is unwontedly sexy.

Whilst the character is plainly uncomfortable with trying to be so openly alluring, this appearance sows the seeds of her next metamorphosis in 'Bewitched, Bothered And Bewildered' (2.16), in which (in common with every other woman in Sunnydale) she develops a spell-bound, outright predatory lust for Xander. (When he tries to repel her advances with the threat, 'Don't make me use force,' she purrs in response, 'Mmm . . . force is OK.')

This in turn reaches full bloom when Willow, like Xander, is vamped in 'The Wish', and more so when vampire-Willow returns in 'Doppelgangland' (3.16), having been accidentally summoned to Sunnydale proper to exist in parallel with the 'real' Willow. The remarks made in this episode about the polymorphously perverse proclivities of vampire-Willow (says 'real' Willow: 'so evil and skanky . . . and I think I'm kind of gay') and their possible basis in the character of the normally demure Ms Rosenberg are put into some perspective by Willow's comportment under previous trans-formations: while much heat and little light has been expended in various discussion about whether Willow is 'truly' gay by dint of her subsequent (and by now obviously committed) relationship with Tara, the more obvious point is that, however permanent her shift in sexual *orientation*, there have by now been numerous signs that in terms of her sexual *conduct* she can be both a kitten and a panther as the occasion seems to her to demand.

The 'teeth' which Willow occasionally shows, and her growing self-confidence, give depth to the aforementioned luminosity of Alyson Hannigan's characterization. Xander may be the metaphysical heart of the Scoobies, but Willow more regularly commands the hearts of the audience. Whedon himself is evidently not immune from this captivation, as indicated on the DVD audio commentary when he describes Hannigan as

> King of Pain – when anybody attacks [Willow], we learned early on, it opens up your heart . . . She's so good playing that vulnerability . . . She brings so much light and so much tenderness to the role, it's kind of extraordinary . . . I knew that [viewers] would respond to her on a level that they couldn't even respond to Buffy . . .

This last remark clearly refers not simply to the character of Willow, but to Hannigan's characterization of her; the 24-minute demo reel-*cum*-pilot of *Buffy*, in which Willow is played by Riff Regan, confirms the extent to which Hannigan's performance fits the character and reveals the qualities with which she imbues Willow.

Hannigan can play on audience heartstrings like a concert harpist, as Willow undergoes her succession of emotional travails: her unrequited love for Xander, her romantic and moral torments during and after her clandestine affair with him in Season Three, when each is already in a steady relationship, and the protracted, several-step break-up with her lycanthrope boyfriend Oz. As an actress she is a perfect interpreter in particular of the bare emotional directness which is the speciality of writer Marti Noxon.

Writing and performance in this vein mesh most completely in 'New Moon Rising' (4.19), in which Oz's return to Sunnydale throws into question Willow's deepening relationship with fellow witch Tara. The final-scene Tara/Willow exchange – 'I understand: you have to be with the person you love' / 'I am' – has a supreme truthfulness and economy and is the precise moment at which Willow's transition of sexual orientation is simply but definitively completed for any viewer not in denial. It is, I maintain, no exaggeration to say that the final movement of 'New Moon Rising' can look the corresponding segment of *Casablanca* in the face without shame. (In contrast, an example of Noxon occasionally overplaying her heart-on-the-sleeve predilection is the final act of 'Into The Woods' (5.10), which does not so much look *Casablanca* in the face as dress up in its clothes.)

It is convenient, though unfair, to consider Oz in this context as an adjunct to Willow. His werewolf nature – uncovered in 'Phases' (2.15) – particularly as regards his attraction to the likewise anthropically challenged Veruca – culminating in 'Wild At Heart' (4.06) – is an obvious metaphor for adolescent and young-adult coming to terms with 'the beast within' (a far simpler, far less theologically convoluted version of Angel's relationship with his vampirism) but its portrayal is strengthened by actor Seth Green's mastery of laconicism. When one watches the series as a whole, Whedon and his writing team are revealed to have gradually distilled Oz's initially general quirkiness down to a wryly sparing way with words and deadpan facial looks, in order to exploit Green's playing strength in this area. The fact that, when the character is fully evolved, Oz never wastes a syllable is again utilized by writers when putting him into serious emotional situations; the knowledge that every word counts lends his utterances, in Green's performance, an unfussy heft. This is of course shown powerfully in 'New Moon Rising', but the necessity of plot exposition here renders Oz uncharacteristically garrulous (in relative terms) for much of the episode until its climax; possibly a better example is the aftermath of the discovery of Willow and Xander's liaison in 'Lover's Walk' (3.08) until Oz and Willow's reunion in 'Amends' (3.10): there is simply no inclination to talk around the central issues.

Giles has at different points undergone both psychological and physical metamorphoses. The former occurs in 'Band Candy' (3.06), in which the adult population of Sunnydale is magicked by some evil chocolate back to their respective teenage selves. While Joyce Summers and Principal Snyder are revealed with differing degrees of sympathy as fundamentally lame teens desperate to find a way into the in-crowd, Giles becomes his earlier 'Ripper' self, described by

Buffy as 'Less "together guy", more "bad magic, hates the world, ticking time-bomb guy".' Conversely, the extent to which Giles has consciously mastered his Ripperish impulses and reinvented himself is discreetly underscored in 'A New Man' (4.12), in which, even though physically transformed into a particularly thuggish demon, he remains (barely) on top of the growing appetite for violence which his new physiology brings (with the delicious exception of taking a minute out to chase, growling, his sinister rival for the role of mentor to Buffy, Professor Maggie Walsh).

The Giles persona that we principally know is kept in place by force of constant will. There is little danger that Ripper will ever regain the upper hand, although the deliberate suffocation of Ben in 'The Gift' (5.22) is, as it were, an invocation of Ripper for the purposes of good. However, on a number of occasions Giles has taken to the bottle as the only practical means of escape from the doubts or griefs which assail him. Rather than stoop to the level of making his drinking an issue in itself, Whedon & co use it to signal unassumingly that Giles, too, realizes he is fulfilling a role, but one which sometimes grows too much for him in terms of its internal rather than external obligations.

The single most succinct example of this is in 'Forever' (5.17): a brief, wordless scene, the day after Joyce Summers' funeral, shows Giles at home, obviously drinking heavily and listening to one of his old rock albums. Nothing is said; actor Anthony Stewart Head is all but motionless; the significance and potency lie in the numbness being depicted, and in Head letting the soundtrack make the message explicit . . . for the song is Cream's 'Tales Of Brave Ulysses', the same track that his and Joyce's *faux*-teenage selves had listened to in 'Band Candy'.

Head – naturally, as the oldest of the principal actors by a couple of decades – has the longest and most varied dramatic *curriculum vitae* of the company, ranging from the romantic serial played out over several seminal television commercials for Nescafé Gold Blend (Taster's Choice in the US) to a UK national tour as Frank N. Furter in *The Rocky Horror Show*. His performance encompasses the strengths of several of the other players: like Hannigan, he quickly demonstrates the resources to sustain a character far more complex than the initial quaint Britisher of early Season One episodes (Alfred the butler, almost, with the library of Sunnydale High as the Batcave); his skill with the drily English one-liners complements Brendon's with the wacky ones; his precision of emotional nuance may have rubbed off to an extent on Sarah Michelle Gellar over the seasons, as she has acquired an eye for underplaying feelings to match the technical abilities she always possessed.

Giles's dramatic function is less as a protagonist or agent in himself than as someone who reacts to and supports developments around him. Head has nevertheless found in this essentially secondary role a current and eloquence of its own, particularly through Season Three's second half and Season Four. Deprived first of his formal position as Watcher by the Watchers' Council – in 'Helpless' (3.12) – and then of any purpose whatever for being in Sunnydale, as his librarian's cover job disappears with the destruction of Sunnydale High, and his position as informal mentor to Buffy is threatened by her new milieu at university and specifically by Maggie Walsh, Giles flounders – but does so, in Head's portrayal, quietly and discreetly. Without ever stealing the thunder of Buffy and her younger associates, Head builds up an aggregation of little signals that underline and extend the central metaphor of the series as a whole.

Buffy is, it has been said often enough, really about growing up and negotiating one's way in a world which persists in putting knotty and seemingly unnatural problems in one's way; Head's Giles, more even than the explicit allusions in the character of Joyce Summers, reminds us that the difficulties of growing up are not experienced solely by those who do the growing, but also leave their mark on those whose nests they fly. In this phase Giles, like Xander, needs to find a definition for himself; unlike the younger man, though, Giles does not even pretend to know how to fashion one, and privately comes close to despair until a series of events over the first half of Season Five – Buffy's request that he resume as her *de facto* Watcher, his purchase of the magic shop and finally his formal reinstatement by the Council – cumulatively offer him the salvation of a full role again, and grimly exceed it as his surrogate-father status becomes more and more necessary through Joyce's illness and eventual death. Thereafter, in thinking the unthinkable with regard to preventing Glory's plan to merge dimensions – that it might be necessary to kill Dawn – he makes the transition from the suffering of the abandoned parent to that of the involved and loving parent amid horrific life complexities.

A slew of supporting characters have their roles modified through transformation. Oz and Anya have already been mentioned; Cordelia's former Valley-bitch sidekick Harmony, following her vampification, attempts and fails derisorily to recreate herself as Buffy's arch-nemesis; Jonathan likewise tries without success to magick a valued identity for himself in 'Superstar' (4.17). Dawn finds that her entire existence rests upon an act of magic which has incarnated the unspecified but crucial Key as a 14-year-old girl – it is unjust simply to note in passing that Michelle Trachtenberg deserves fully as much kudos as any of the other regulars for finding an intensity and truth in her character, as 'Blood Ties' (5.13) and 'Forever' (5.17) amply demonstrate.

Cordelia and Wesley do not experience such literal changes until late in the game (we can discount transitory instances such as Cordy's temporary demonic-pregnancy-dementia in 'Expecting' (A1.12)) – indeed, in 'The Wish', Cordy remains irremediably herself as the entire world around her changes. Both Wesley and Cordelia change and grow once in LA, of course, but only to the extent that *Angel* generally expands and darkens the characters who appear in it. Life – in both shows but especially in *Angel* – is always fluid in its rules and markers, both in everyday mundane life and in the course of 'the good fight' – and they are affected by this.

However, when first Cordy and then her *Angel* associates are transported to yet another world, the Host's home of Pylea, in the final four episodes of *Angel* Season Two, this new environment sets the seal on transitions which both she and Wesley have been gradually undergoing. Cordy's dream of success and status is given the greatest possible realization by her installation as queen of Pylea, but of course turns out to be no kind of solution to her LA frustrations. Nor, though, is it the simple opposite, an unambiguous curse (although it is the 'curse' of her visions which confirms her on the throne); rather, it is simply the case that all the usual complexities of emotion, power structures and the inevitable villainies simply continue under a different sun (well, pair of suns); it may be a hard decision for her to return through the dimension portal with her comrades, but fundamentally there is no wrench of lifestyle involved. Wesley, meanwhile, finds in his explicit recognition by the Pylean rebels as their new general a validation of his status as the man in charge of things; he no longer suffers when such validation is unforthcoming from his father, as evidenced in the phone call home in 'Belonging' (A2.19).

Here's an indicator both of how fluid Buffyverse events can be and of the universality of this 'rite of transformation' in *Buffy*: when I began writing this essay, I noted that the sole unambiguous exception to the rule is Tara, who is nevertheless revealed in 'Family' (5.6), as *believing that she is about to* undergo such a metamorphosis when she comes of age and her alleged demon-nature asserts itself (as it did, we learn in the back-story of *Angel* Season One with the similarly half-human, half-demon Doyle at a similar point). However, as with Cordy and Wesley, Tara's identity grows and deepens on a purely human level through her association with Willow and thus the other Scoobies.

The week of the completion of my draft, however, saw the US and UK broadcast of 'Tough Love' (5.19), in which Tara, in Benson's words, 'suffers some brain suckage' by Glory. Amber Benson rises to the ongoing challenges and opportunities offered overall by the role of Tara. She finds a continuity of character even after a mapping which is the opposite of that normally undergone by figures in the Buffyverse. Where, for instance, Spike (and in many ways even the extreme example of Angel/Angelus) experiences transitions of temperament whilst retaining a relatively linear, if not fully fixed, sense of self, Tara to all intents and purposes loses her very identity for the better part of four episodes, to the extent that she needs even to be fed by others; yet Benson invests Tara's post-mind-wipe witterings with the same range of moods and quirks as her previous lucid remarks. Even though Tara in this phase cannot recognize herself, the way that the remains of her mind work indicate a continuing, albeit thoroughly ravaged, personality. How this may develop with regard to the character's overall sense of person subsequent to Tara's cure by Willow in 'The Gift' (5.22) remains, of course, to be seen.

Riley's innate nature is overridden both by the diet of chemicals fed to him and by the chip embedded in his torso. The chip business is frankly superficial, little more than a plot device, but the cumulative effect of the removal both of these additives and of his association with the Initiative is to make him another character in search of a role by which he can define himself. If he is to be more than an appendage to Buffy, he feels he requires some kind of experiential knowledge of the darker world she inhabits; this, even more than the issues he undoubtedly has about her former relationship with Angel, is behind his flirtation with vamp-victimhood. In the end, of course, he fails to find any such niche (as either the writers and Marc Blucas fail to find a sufficient distinctiveness for him or it becomes apparent that he was never intended to be a major locus of audience sympathy), and off he flies back to the uniformed bosom of Uncle Sam, where it is easier to slot into a team than to stand as an individual.

(Entirely by the by, and as an indicator of how vampire themes in general are modulated to give them a greater application to contemporary preoccupations, it is interesting to note the number of motifs shared with the 1998 UK vampire series *Ultraviolet*: both it and *Buffy* involve a special paramilitary unit in which one member in particular has a problematic relationship with official policies and command structure; in both, that member works closely with a more hard-nosed colleague who happens to be black and answers to a female scientist with an agenda of her own; like *Angel*, it raises a number of complexities both theological and in terms of how irredeemably evil vamps may or may not be; even the 'Big Bad' of the series is, like Angelus, a vamp who when mortal had been an Irishman.)

Faith's entire life, we learn from bits and pieces of back-story, has been a battle against those who would ignore or deny her the opportunity to find a place for herself, and an increasingly resentful and aggressive battle. She cannot properly complement Buffy, and so feels on some level that she has no alternative but to become her opposite. The extent to which she is living out a role she has assigned to herself is finally revealed by her breakdown during the climactic fight with Angel, in 'Five By Five' (A1.18), and her realization that she can rewrite her own script at the end of 'Sanctuary' (A1.19) is the beginning of her redemption and thus of her retrieval of self-definition. Eliza Dushku brings to the role a combination of breezy nonchalance and equally insouciant callousness, with insights into Faith's disturbing self-loathing.

This strength of identity, whether it be rooted in a fixed sense of self or an impassioned quest for it, may also go some way towards explaining why many viewers feel that the 'Big Bads' of Season Four didn't quite cut the mustard. All the other principal season villains have shown a certain flair in their self-allotted roles, which the respective actors could utilize: Mark Metcalf with the Master's subterranean stratagems in Season One, David Boreanaz as the newly liberated Angelus in Season Two, Harry Groener's gleeful mixture of homespun folksiness and demonic plotting as the Mayor in Season Three ('There's more than one way to skin a cat . . . and I happen to know that's literally true'), and Clare Kramer's revelling in Glory's consumer-frenzied near-omnipotence in Season Five (not just divine but a diva – if the painting on her apartment wall is intended to be an original Tamara de Lempicka, this puts Glory in the company of the artist's best-known collector, Madonna Ciccone Penn Ritchie). Put bluntly, neither Maggie Walsh nor Adam in Season Four has such a hook. Lindsay Crouse takes a dry pleasure in Professor Walsh's above-ground role as the assured bitch-queen of Sunnydale University (and incidentally, am I the only one who thinks that her lectures are consciously written in a pastiche of the style of Crouse's ex-husband David Mamet?). But for the Initiative-supremo side of her character, Crouse limited herself to playing mainly on Maggie's repressed quasi-incestuous feelings for Riley, and the problem with such a decision is that there has to be a sufficiently solid surface layer for such repression to abrade against. As Adam, George Hertzberg – perhaps constrained by his various prostheses leaving him only half a face to act with – is reduced to telling us that he is a super-bad assemblage of human, demon and machine, without being able often enough to *show* us . . . in his own portrayal, rather than simply in terms of the atrocities we see Adam has committed. Moments such as the chilling gleam in Adam's eye (singular) at the end of the 'Frankenstein in the woods' scene in 'Goodbye Iowa' (4.14) are all too rare. Both Maggie and Adam are little more than plot functions which happen to overlay people who neither are, nor are seen to be striving to be, sufficiently defined as individuals; Adam's desire to learn, again, is stated and occasionally shown only indirectly through his deeds rather than made dynamically manifest in his person. Conversely, Kramer's Glory shows that even Big Bads can suffer meaningful identity crises; the psychological and emotional confusion of the increasingly frequent spontaneous metamorphoses between Glory and Ben would not have worked at all if Glory in particular had not been invested, through Kramer's performance, with a firmly grounded identity in the first place.

Probably the most interesting of this second stratum of identity-seekers and role-players, though, is Spike. In one phase he, like Harmony, revels in his self-proclaimed status as 'the Big Bad', and (after an initial bout of success on Spike's part in Season Two) we snigger at the bollix he makes of it. In the next, inhibited from harming humans by an Initiative brain-chip – implanted in 'The Initiative' (4.7) – he tries to reconcile his confused and confusing hybrid status: barely tolerated but never accepted by the Scoobies, still hungering after their downfall but unable to do more than sow seeds of disharmony among them and yet paradoxically eager to join them on demon-hunts when he finds that his chip permits him to indulge his fondness for ultraviolence as long as it is perpetrated on inhuman creatures.

This taste for a good ruck is itself an invented part of Spike's self-definition, part of the new character he fashioned for himself after being vamped by Drusilla; 'Fool For Love' (5.7) reveals both this and the delightful if heavy-handed truth about his human existence as 'William the Bloody', putting his frequent incompetence as an evildoer into perspective and once again emphasizing that the reality of Buffyverse identity is more complicated than Buffy's specious reassurance to Willow in 'Doppelgangland' that a vampire's personality 'has nothing to do with the person it was'.

Much of this saga, even when Spike is at his most insidious – 'The Yoko Factor' (4.20) – is superior comedy and James Marsters is a superior comedian of the sort required; it's a gentle modulation from the black acerbity of early Spike in his Season Two double-act with Drusilla. However, both Spike's character and Marsters' growing characterization skills, nurtured by the ongoing requirements of the series, take off with his realization in Season Five that 'It's a thin line between love and hate': that his obsession with Buffy is rooted in a desire to get on top of her in an altogether more horizontal context, and that his previous lovey-dovey episode with Buffy when a spell of Willow's goes awry – 'Something Blue' (4.9) – is less a wild aberration than a pre-echo of a strain that has always been present in his personality.

Spike's admission of this, first to himself and subsequently to Buffy, the aid and protection he offers Dawn and his genuine mourning for Joyce as he acknowledges a collective and heartfelt regard for 'Summers women', constitute a further and almost conscious level of synthesis between his pre- and post-vamp senses of himself, and generate some passages of acting on Marsters' part which are quite as heartrending as Alyson Hannigan in full flow, such as the final scene of 'Intervention' (5.18). By the climax of Season Five, Spike has implicitly completed this aspect of his journey and become a full-fledged member of the Scoobies; this is evidenced not so much by the overt action of Buffy reinviting him into her home as by the casual comradeship of his exchanges with Giles and Xander, such as the 'Crispin's Day' allusion to *Henry V* which the two English characters grimly share on their way to the final showdown.

As with all of the principal players Whedon has assembled, it is not just a matter of being able to portray explicit suffering but of knowing when to *stop* performing, when to let camera and context do the work, even with a shot as prosaic as a pile of cigarette butts under the tree where Buffy has discovered Spike lurking – 'No Place Like Home' (5.5). The cast and creators of the Buffyverse series rapidly evolved their approach to a stage where they realized they could trust the audience; they know that it is better to show than to tell, and also know that showing two points is enough for the viewer not just to infer a line between them, but also to extrapolate it beyond those points. This is, in turn, exploited through subversion, by throwing curves into the narrative line when we least expect them. Conversely, it also manifests in that, to a surprising degree, the best of the copious amount of internet fan-fiction featuring characters from the series is set in the interstices between episodes and yet harmonizes fully with both prior and subsequent events on screen, leading the reader to re-evaluate the implicit penumbra of those events. Viewers of *Buffy* and *Angel* are gently but insistently asked not simply to be consumers, but to take an active part in a process closer to theatrical transactions of character and identity, to work *with* the players and characters as both the scope and the limitations of identity and role continue in dynamic flux.

As is natural in such a mode of operation, this is nowhere more apparent or indeed more necessary than in the case of the Slayer herself. 'The Slayer' is a distinct concept from 'Buffy Anne Summers', and indeed the meat of the underlying drama lies in her attempts to reconcile the two elements of the series title or to find an accommodation with both. In Buffy more than anywhere else, the fact that identity is a matter both of person and of role is constantly apparent – often implicitly, but increasingly so as she moves away from the structures first of formal schooling and then of a parental framework. The Season Four finale, 'Restless' (4.22), is more than an amusing coda to the previous episode's climactic battle with Adam and the invocation of a 'Super-Slayer' drawing both on the qualities inherent in Giles, Willow and Xander and upon a link to the primal well of Slayer-power. In Buffy's dream-confrontation with the First Slayer, it also lays the foundations for the following season's explicit quest by Buffy for a path by which she can be sufficiently true both to her human desires and obligations and to the duties and impulses of the Slayer.

Again, the metaphor for adolescence and young adulthood, with its conflicts of independence and bonds and its needs to define a self capable of dealing with such conflicts, does not need labouring. In Buffy's case the process explicitly begins only a little while after physical puberty, with Slayerdom foisted upon her at the age (one infers, from the relationship of the semi-canonical 1992 movie to Season One) of fifteen, and just keeps growing from there on in, until at 20 she finds herself on the one hand able to dictate terms to the Watchers' Council – 'Checkpoint' (5.12) – and on the other suddenly the head of the family, with both human and supernatural obligations to her sister Dawn.

During the high-school phase it is possible to discern passages in which, although each insists on interfering with the other, either the

Buffy or the Slayer element is foregrounded for an episode or so. Indeed, much of Season Three is a see-saw between the two. Buffy *qua* Buffy attempts a normal high-school life by running for Homecoming Queen – 'Homecoming' (3.5) – or flees Sunnydale altogether in a bootless attempt to shun her Slayer obligations, with which even her first name seems so bound up that she temporarily discards it – 'Anne' (3.1). Conversely, Buffy *qua* Slayer is given the grim surprise that attaining her majority means an increase in formal Slayer demands and severance from the surrogate fatherhood of Giles – 'Helpless' (3.12) – or experiences the temptation personified by Faith to set herself above the law by virtue of her Slayerness – 'Bad Girls' (3.14). One side or the other keeps gaining the upper hand.

Increasingly in Season Five, though, both sides of the teeter-totter are simultaneously weighed down, and Buffy's challenge is to bear the loads, always and together, without breaking at the fulcrum which is her sense of self. There is simply no let-up as these demands grow equally and oppositely intense; another attempt at flight, this time into herself in a state of catatonia, fails, and finally – like heroes and messiahs down the ages – she is forced to the realization that the only resolution lies in consummating both strands of obligation at once in a noble death.

Whedon's Season One DVD commentary acknowledges and praises Sarah Michelle Gellar's technical prowess in the mechanics of screen acting right from the first episode, whether it be her ability to eat a cocktail cherry at exactly the same moment for a series of re-shot masters and cutaways or her skill at mutely speaking volumes in the prolonged reaction shots during her first interview with Principal Flutie. As the series progresses, though, Gellar swiftly finds the core of Buffy, such that she can adroitly act on a number of levels at once. She can indicate the repressed fears beneath the flinty exterior in 'Anne' or 'I Only Have Eyes For You' (2.19) without recourse to quivering lips or frightened eye movements for the camera only to see. Of course, any actor must be able to play subtext, but it is in practice rather rarer to find one – let alone an entire cast – who can consistently do so without the subtext, in Giles's words in 'Ted' (2.11), 'rapidly becoming text.'

Indeed, in 'Hush' (4.10), the central company play for half an hour or so without any verbal text at all, after a group of demons steal the voices of the Sunnydale population: possibly in part a homage to the central movement of Jules Dassin's *Rififi*, more likely just Whedon once again subverting expectations and bouncing in an unexpected direction, as when he responded to complaints about the amount of violence in *Buffy* by creating an episode of almost non-stop sex – 'Where the Wild Things Are' (4.18).

Most impressively, Gellar can take on board the entire body language of another person, whether as the Buffybot in 'Intervention' (5.18) or as Faith-in-Buffy's-body in 'Who Are You?' (4.16), without veering into gross parody. (Eliza Dushku is almost as impressive as Buffy-in-Faith, but more of her screen time is conflict of one kind or another rather than character work.) It is also telling that, even when her body is inhabited by someone else, the outward figure of Buffy Summers cannot escape the ineluctable role of the Slayer: the Buffybot also engages in Slaying combat, most gloriously (no pun intended) in 'The Gift' (5.22), when she engages in the kind of banter which the fleshly Buffy is now too tired and burdened to maintain; and Faith-as-Buffy ultimately resigns herself to the Slayer's obligation to save a church congregation held hostage by vampires.

But more than offering multi-layered performances, Gellar comes to show a kind of zen acting power in making herself a *tabula rasa* for the camera and/or the audience to work on. It is tempting to speak of a Beckettian minimalism in her – and the entire ensemble's – performance in 'The Body' (5.16), but to take such a cerebral stance on the episode is to do it a gross injustice. It is simply one of the finest pieces of television drama, and the single finest depiction of bereavement in any medium, that I have ever seen. It achieves this phenomenal power by demanding of the cast that they simply go numbly through the motions in dealing with the death of Joyce, not even explicating their numbness but letting the gaping void at the heart of matters come through unmodulated even by so much as a note of incidental music.

If Slayerdom is a figurative curse upon a young woman in a natural search for a selfhood she can feel comfortable with, how much more complex is the literal curse upon the person of Angel. The double-edged malediction – first, that while remaining a vampire his soul be restored to him; second, that he live in constant peril of losing it for a moment's true happiness (however 'boinkily' that happiness may be defined) – is at every moment Angel's overriding motivation and self-definition.

His vampiric sire Darla, granted a similar (though not identical) possibility of redemption when restored to humanity, first tries to deny this change of identity by continuing on a path as evil as that of her vampire incarnation, and ultimately seeks to renounce it and return to the reassuringly known selfhood of centuries past by begging that Angel re-vamp her. (The fact that her eventual reclamation by Drusilla was performed by force is incidental; however conflictedly at first, Darla clearly welcomes the return to what she identifies as her true self.) But Angel embodies a paradox: while his condition is the central plank of his current identity, he seeks redemption, and thus true embodiment as a whole person, through devoting himself to the rescue of others and thus engaging in the most profound kind of self-denial.

All this despite the certain knowledge that, to put it bluntly, vamps have more fun. The vampire Angelus is clearly far more comfortable with himself and his role – he has a flamboyance in word and deed which comes with complete self-assurance. This assurance is not just conscious, but moral . . . within a soulless, vampiric morality. Angel, on the other hand, labours hard and painfully along his chosen (rather than predetermined) path. Even when he dismisses his associates Wesley, Cordy and Gunn – 'Reunion' (A2.10) – and embarks on a renegade crusade against Darla, Dru and Wolfram and Hart, 'dark Angel' carries a continuing awareness that he *is* renegade, that he *has* abjured the way of light. His suffering even as he rampages is reminiscent of the Catholic teaching that the greatest torment of the damned in Hell is the knowledge that they are denied heaven. (In this respect, note too that Angel's moral horror is almost greater still on discovering the utterly amoral atavism to which his fully demonic side can manifest in Pylea.)

Where *Buffy* is at heart a human drama, *Angel* targets a slightly older audience demographic in part by being more theologically complicated. However it may be populated by Powers That Be, Oracles and various species of demon, and however the 'hell' of Wolfram and Hart's home office may be revealed as this world – 'Reprise' (A2.15) – rather than the nether dimension to which Angel has previously been despatched at the end of Season Two of *Buffy* – 'Becoming Part Two' (2.22) – the cosmos of *Angel* is governed by forms of Judaeo-Christian, and specifically Catholic, concepts such as redemption through good works. (In detail, of course, it's even more closely akin to certain Catholic heresies, but that's another subject.) Angel's rejection of the Gem of Amara – 'In The Dark' (A1.03) – can be seen as denying himself an unearned (or not yet earned) illusion only of redemption, a kind of spurious indulgence. This is not to reject an immediate and direct relevance as well: this deep sense of moral duty is more than simply Arthurian, but continues admirably to live in a number of ordinary folk today. It is the acceptance that, as a Christian friend of mine once succinctly put it, 'God hurts.'

Angel is not noticeably a theist, but he bases his function, and his notions of both his past and future transformations, his current and his ultimate hoped-for identities, on concepts of divinity and damnation.

The word almost invariably used to describe Angel's usual mood and David Boreanaz's performance is 'brooding'. To be sure, the role certainly calls for one hell of a lot of it, but 'twas not ever thus. In his early appearances in *Buffy* Season One, Angel is positively playful, more like a vastly attenuated Angelus. This may be partly because at this point the viewer knows him simply as someone who appears periodically to give Buffy little pointers, and Whedon does not wish to make the truth too obvious too soon (although he professes surprise that so few viewers worked it out in advance of the revelation). On his first appearance, he describes himself simply as 'a friend' , and in this phase functions more or less like Hal Holbrook's character in the film of *All the President's Men* – as a kind of 'Deep Fang'. He is revealed to be a vampire only in the episode entitled 'Angel' (1.7).

Thereafter, he darkens rapidly, so that by 'School Hard' (2.3), it is not implausible when the newly arrived and at this point seriously menacing Spike says to him, 'You were my sire, man, my Yoda.' (In one of the series' most famous 'retcons' – retrospective continuity changes – this is later glossed as a metaphorical statement, since Angel is in fact Spike's grandsire.) By this stage, though, Angel is becoming a more imposing physical presence as well, probably due in part to Boreanaz's now regular workout régime: his body and jawline have beefed up so that he cuts a significantly more impressive figure when standing ominous in dim light. This has the incidental consequence that, by the time the flashback scene is shot in which he is vamped by Darla in Galway town in 1753 – 'Becoming Part One' (2.21) – the mortal Liam is noticeably thicker-set than Angel on his first appearances in Sunnydale nearly two and a half centuries later.

Boreanaz has also gained command of the role of Angel to the extent that, when he reverts to Angelus following his 'moment of true happiness' with Buffy – 'Surprise'/'Innocence' (2.13 & 2.14) – the actor can retain strands of continuity with the ensouled Angel as well as introducing diabolical contrasts. However, it is his season in Hell between the end of *Buffy* Season Two and his return in 'Faith, Hope and Trick' (3.3) that fully creates the character we subsequently come to know. The reminder of what Angel has to lose banishes the last vestiges of levity from his sense of himself. He may continue to crack deadpan one-liners – such as 'You can go to *hell*.' / 'Been there, done that' – 'Lonely Hearts' (A1.2) – or 'I thought I knew eternity' when watching Cordelia's supremely atrocious performance as Ibsen's Nora Helmer – 'Eternity' (A1.17) – but they are always tempered by the consciousness of who he is at root and what he must transcend. Boreanaz develops a seemingly throwaway delivery for such lines whereby Angel seems to disregard them but is in fact showing loathing of this half of his identity, as is made clear when he lends the same delivery to virtually every line Angel utters during his dark phase in *Angel* Season Two. Even after he returns to his senses, it is clear that (to paraphrase Geno Washington) it is not just the blues that walk with him, but the downright midnight blacks.

Buffy and *Angel*'s major characters are engaged in a constant process of negotiating and evolving identities and roles for themselves. Both series have also included a number of self-conscious, reflexive meditations on this process seldom seen outside post-modern comedies.

In *Angel*, 'Eternity' (A1.17) is superficially an opportunity for self-deprecating satire on the culture of TV series, as actress Rebecca Lowell finds herself a prisoner of her past long-time screen role, but on a deeper level she is confined by her status as an icon, her obligation to maintain *that* role (or at least its outward youthful trappings, by persuading Angel to vamp her) in order to hang on to her sense of who she is. Rebecca, like Angel, defines herself in terms of others, but of their perception rather than actual value to them; she has acquiesced in a self-definition that operates from the outside in. In many ways, Angel's temporary, drugged 'reversion' to Angelus operates the same way; as Wesley tries to point out to him, the Doximol in his champagne has given him only the *illusion* of happiness, but on some level Angel's identity sensors tell him that he is untroubled, therefore he must be evil, therefore he must be Angelus.

In *Buffy*, 'The Zeppo' (3.13) revolves around Xander's quest for a role within the Scooby gang which he can use as a source of self-esteem. The very title of the episode (in an epithet bestowed on Xander by Cordy) refers to the fourth — and redundant — Marx Brother. Xander attempts to carve a niche for himself as 'Car Guy', providing wheels for the gang; but when he drives up in his tacky Chevrolet BelAir and tells the girls, 'It's my "thing",' Buffy cuts pertly to another kind of identity prop altogether when she asks, 'Is this a penis metaphor?'

It is not just Xander who is overtly conscious of playing, or needing to play, a defined role within the outfit: the motif is woven through the episode, not just on a structural level with our tantalizing side-glimpses of the other Scoobies toiling away in their allotted place at the Hellmouth, but with a number of reflexive remarks tossed out by them in passing. In the pre-title sequence, Willow notes the periodic subversion of her usual character by declaring, 'Occasionally I'm callous and strange'; on the most banal level of all, Giles defines himself in relation to the gang's doughnut purchases – 'I always have jelly; I'm always the one that says, "Let's have jelly in the mix".'

'Restless' (4.22), too, is more than a kind of satyr-play to bring Season Four to an end and herald Buffy's search the following season for a personal synthesis between her human and Slayer roles. In each of the three others' magical dreams, their subconsciouses riff on their senses of self, past, present and might-have-been: Giles's appearance on the stage of the Bronze, delivering his instructions to the others in song; Willow not only experiencing the classic actor's nightmare but also indicating how precarious her growing self-confidence is by imagining herself before a high school class in exactly the same costume she wore in 'Welcome to the Hellmouth'; Xander reprising his soldier bit one more time as Captain Willard to Snyder's Colonel Kurtz in a delicious recreation almost shot for shot of a scene from *Apocalypse Now*. Indeed, they even illuminate in passing the roles of others: Xander's vision of Spike training as a Watcher prefigures the blond vampire's gradual but unambiguous cross-over to the forces of good in Season Five, and in Willow's surreal nightmare production of

Death of a Salesman, Riley proudly proclaims, 'I'm Cowboy Guy' – which, of course, he is: the nearest thing the series has ever had to an unambiguous white-hat.

To conclude with a return to John Carpenter's left-wing/right-wing analogy, it is evident that over the Buffyverse as a whole, the macro aspect of the narrative has moved consistently leftward. As the initial simplicities – demons are bad and soulless, vampires are quite unrelated to the former human persons in their vessel bodies – are steadily complicated (to keep pace with the metaphor of one's growing awareness of the complexities of the world in general), it becomes problematic almost to the point of futility to attempt to identify villains as alien, as Other . . . or even unequivocally as villains: witness the cases of Spike, of Lindsey McDonald in *Angel*, or of the Ben/Glory duality in *Buffy* Season Five.

At the same time, the micro-narrative within individual characters veers sharply leftward and then transcends such a two-dimensional model. Characters own and/or disown various aspects of their personalities, seek to create and/or destroy identities for themselves, to resolve and/or accommodate contradictions within their composition; sometimes these processes alternate more or less rapidly, sometimes seemingly opposite approaches appear to take place simultaneously. Each transformation, literal or figurative, makes matters ever more complex. This integral flux of character, role and identity moves several steps beyond virtually any comparable drama series, and central to its success are the abilities of the performers – abilities which perhaps they did not even know they possessed when first cast – to bear and portray such complicated persons, to keep all these plates of character spinning at once.

episode guide

Buffy Season One

1.1 **Welcome to the Hellmouth** *by Joss Whedon*
Buffy and Joyce arrive in Sunnydale. Buffy befriends Willow, Jesse and Xander rather than Cordelia, and tells Giles she is not interested in slaying. Angel approaches her and is cryptic; Buffy saves Willow and Xander from the girlish vampire Darla and monstrous Luke, who are gathering food for the Master, who is trapped in the Hellmouth, but she fails to save Jesse.

1.2 **The Harvest** *by Joss Whedon*
Luke is to conduct a massacre at the Bronze to make possible the Master's escape from the field of force that traps him in the Hellmouth. Buffy tricks and dusts him, saving Cordelia; Xander dusts Jesse.

1.3 **The Witch** *by Dana Reston*
Buffy tries out for the cheerleader squad; various magical mishaps occur to other members – Cordelia goes blind. Amy, daughter of past cheerleader Catherine, finally makes the squad when Buffy is poisoned by a death spell. Amy is possessed by witch Catherine; the spell and possession are broken and Catherine is trapped in her own trophy statuette.

1.4 **Teacher's Pet** *by David Greenwalt*
Xander fancies replacement biology teacher Miss French who is actually a virgin-eating giant mantis of whom even vampires are scared. Buffy rescues him from being eaten and disorients and destroys Miss French with a mixture of bat cries, bug spray and violence.

1.5 **Never Kill a Boy on the First Date** *by Rob Des Hotel & Dean Batali*

The Master organizes the creation of the Anointed One by slaughter of a busload of people. Buffy's date with senior classman Owen turns into a battle in the mortuary with a religious psycho turned vampire whom she assumes to be the Anointed and kills. She dumps Owen for being an adrenalin junky. The Anointed is actually a small child.

1.6 **The Pack** *by Matt Kiene & Joe Reinkemeyer*

During a zoo trip, a clique of school bullies and Xander are possessed by hyena spirits. They eat the school's pig mascot and (while Xander is caged after attempting to seduce Buffy) Principal Flutie. Buffy breaks the spell, cast by an evil zoo-keeper, and throws him to his beasts.

1.7 **Angel** *by David Greenwalt*

Buffy is rescued by Angel from the Master's three assassins; she discovers Angel is a vampire, cursed with a soul and trying to atone. Darla, Angel's sire and ex-lover, frames him for an attack on Joyce; Buffy cannot bring herself to attack him. Darla attacks Buffy with guns and Angel dusts her.

1.8 **I, Robot – You, Jane** *by Ashley Gable & Thomas A. Swyden*

The scanning of Giles's rare occult volumes with help from technopagan computer teacher Jenny Calendar frees the demon Moloch to possess the net. He befriends and seduces various bright kids, including Willow, and builds a robot body for himself. Buffy traps him in this and destroys him.

1.9 **The Puppet Show** *by Rob Des Hotel & Dean Batali*

Principal Snyder makes Giles direct the school talent show. A dancer's heart is cut out, by a demon that needs this and a brain to retain human form. Buffy suspects Morgan, a genius, with an oddly animated ventriloquist's dummy, Sid. Morgan is killed; Sid turns out to be a transformed demon hunter. Sid and Buffy save Giles from the demon's guillotine. Sid dies.

1.10 **Nightmares** *teleplay by David Greenwalt, story by Joss Whedon*

Everyone's nightmares start to come true, including the death and vampirization of Buffy. She and the others manage to find the source of this, a child beaten into a coma by his baseball coach, and wake the child up.

1.11 **Out of Mind, Out of Sight** *teleplay by Ashley Gable & Thomas A. Swyden, story by Joss Whedon*

Mysterious attacks on the popular culminate in an attempt to disfigure Cordelia. Marcie, a nondescript schoolgirl, has been ignored so long she became invisible. Buffy defeats her and Marcie is abducted to become a government assassin.

1.12 **Prophecy Girl** *written and directed by Joss Whedon*

Buffy learns of the prophecy that she will be defeated and killed by the risen Master; she tries to walk away. Xander asks her out, and she rebuffs him. When she realizes that Giles plans to confront the Master in her place, she knocks him out. She fights the Master, loses and dies. Xander finds her in time to resuscitate her and she kills the Master, closing the Hellmouth.

Buffy Season Two

2.1 **When She Was Bad** *written and directed by Joss Whedon*
Buffy returns from vacation in bitch-mode, flirting with Xander and snubbing Angel to an extent that causes Cordelia to rebuke her. The Anointed One has his minions abduct Willow, Giles, Jenny and Cordelia, who were physically close to the Master's death, to his new factory lair so their blood may reanimate him. Buffy rescues them and smashes the Master's bones.

2.2 **Some Assembly Required** *by Ty King*
Bright Chris has raised his dead footballer brother Darren from the dead and is trying to create a perfect mate for him – Cordelia is abducted to provide the head for this patchwork girl and Buffy and Xander save her. Darren dies again trying to save his headless bride from the flames. Giles and Jenny go on a first date.

2.3 **School Hard** *teleplay by David Greenwalt, story by Joss Whedon*
Spike and Drusilla arrive in Sunnydale. Buffy is obliged by Snyder to cater a Parent-Teacher evening which Spike and the Anointed One's minions attack. Buffy fights them off; Snyder's hostile comments to Joyce are discounted because of Joyce's admiration for Buffy's courage. It becomes clear Snyder is part of the great Sunnydale coverup. Spike kills the Anointed One.

2.4 **Inca Mummy Girl** *by Matt Kiene & Joe Reinkemeyer*
An expected male exchange student turns out to be female – actually, a mummified human sacrifice on show at the museum has risen and is buying herself life and beauty by sucking people dry. She falls for Xander, and cannot bring herself to kill him; Buffy, who feels empathy for her plight as a chosen sacrifice, destroys her.

2.5 **Reptile Boy** *written and directed by David Greenwalt*
Cordelia persuades Buffy to join her at an exclusive fraternity house party. Actually, the rich boys regularly sacrifice young girls to a reptilian demon for wealth and power; the killing of the demon by Buffy results in various alumni going bankrupt and to jail.

2.6 **Halloween** *by Carl Ellsworth*

Snyder conscripts the gang to chaperone young masqueraders; Buffy, Willow and Xander buy costumes from Ethan Rayne, which change their natures – Willow becomes a ghost, Xander a soldier, Buffy a drippy belle, various children monsters. Spike exploits the situation. Giles knows Ethan and smashes his Chaos idol returning things to normal. Oz notices Willow for the first time.

2.7 **Lie to Me** *written and directed by Joss Whedon*

Ford, a crush from Buffy's LA schooldays, arrives in Sunnydale; dying of cancer, he plans to betray Buffy and a crowd of vampire wannabes, including ditzy Chanterelle, to Spike to live forever as a vampire. Buffy outwits him and Spike and stakes him when he rises. Buffy learns of Drusilla's presence in Sunnydale and is jealous of Angel's past.

2.8 **The Dark Age** *by Rob Des Hotel & Dean Batali*

When young, Giles, Ethan and friends raised the demon Eyghon, possession by whom is a sexual high, and had to exorcize him. Eyghon returns seeking revenge – Ethan tattoos Buffy with Eyghon's mark, while Eyghon possesses Jenny. Eyghon is tricked into possessing Angel, whose own demon expels him. Jenny, by now in love with Giles, is alienated from him.

2.9 **What's My Line Part 1** *by Howard Gordon & Marti Noxon*

Spike plans to cure Drusilla and hires demonic assassins to kill Buffy, who has problems of her own – it is Career Week at school. Kendra, a slayer created by Buffy's brief death, arrives in Sunnydale and attacks Angel, leaving him to burn in sunlight.

2.10 **What's My Line Part 2** *by Marti Noxon*

Angel is saved by bar owner Willy and sold to Spike, who needs his blood to cure Drusilla, whom Angel sired. Kendra and Buffy bond. Besieged by a bug demon assassin, Xander and Cordelia bicker and then snog. Oz takes an assassin's bullet for Willow. Buffy rescues Angel and leaves Spike for dead. Drusilla rises renewed. Kendra leaves.

2.11 **Ted** *by David Greenwalt & Joss Whedon*

Joyce's forceful new suitor takes against his potential stepdaughter; they fight and she apparently kills him. He returns good as new and keen to kill her. Ted is actually a robot into whom his creator downloaded his mind and his fifties attitudes to women; Buffy and the gang rescue Joyce from his lair.

2.12 **Bad Eggs** *by Marti Noxon*

Buffy fights the Gorch brothers, cowboy vampires. In a child care exercise, pupils are given eggs to care for which are demonic and hatch spawn that possess everyone save Buffy and Xander. Buffy fights their progenitor, a Bezoar demon, which kills Tector Gorch.

2.13 **Surprise** *by Marti Noxon*

Spike, crippled in 2.10, gives Drusilla a celebratory present – parts of a demon, the Judge, who will burn all that is human. Willow starts dating Oz. Buffy and Angel steal the Judge's arm and Jenny, one of the gypsy tribe who cursed Angel, argues that Angel needs to take it far away. They lose it to vampires on the docks and end up having sex.

2.14 **Innocence** *written and directed by Joss Whedon*

The gypsy curse is broken by Angel's happiness and he becomes the demonic Angelus again, joining Spike and Drusilla in their apocalyptic plans. Buffy and Giles quarrel with Jenny; Willow finds out about Cordelia and Xander. Xander uses post Halloween soldier memories to steal ordnance from an army base. Buffy blasts the Judge, invincible to any weapon forged, with a rocket launcher.

2.15 **Phases** *by Rob Des Hotel and Dean Batali*

Oz, bitten by a young cousin, becomes a werewolf and the prey of hunter Cain whom Buffy humiliates. Willow makes clear to Oz that his lycanthropy does not matter to her. Angelus starts his campaign of mocking cruelty against Buffy and her friends.

2.16 Bewitched, Bothered and Bewildered *by Marti Noxon*
Cordelia dumps Xander to regain her friends. He blackmails Amy into casting a love spell which misfires, making every woman in Sunnydale, including Joyce and Drusilla, proposition him. A besotted Amy turns Buffy into a rat. Giles makes Amy break the spells. Cordelia decides she will date Xander 'no matter how lame he is'. Angelus flirts with Drusilla.

2.17 Passion *by Ty King*
Partly forgiven by Buffy and Giles, Jenny reconstructs her ancestor's curse; warned by Drusilla, Angelus kills her before she can cast it, destroying her computer. He leaves her corpse in Giles's bed. Giles attacks him, setting fire to the factory, and Buffy has to rescue Giles.

2.18 Killed by Death *by Rob Des Hotel & Dean Batali*
Hospitalized with bad flu, Buffy has to confront her memories of a dead cousin and realizes that there is a demon, Der Kindermord, who preys on children. She deliberately makes herself ill enough to see and fight it. Angelus attacks her in the hospital and Xander confronts him.

2.19 I Only Have Eyes for You *by Marti Noxon*
Supernatural events at Sunnydale High are caused by ghosts of a student who shot his teacher lover and himself in the 50s – Giles briefly thinks the ghost is Jenny. Buffy learns forgiveness. The attempted exorcism culminates in Buffy's possession by the boy, Angelus's by the woman; Angelus's invulnerability to bullets breaks the cycle of repetition and frees the ghosts.

2.20 Go Fish *by David Fury and Elin Hampton*
Experiments by the school coach turn several of his star swim-team into aquatic monsters; the coach tries to kill Buffy when she finds out and she throws him to his creations. Xander goes undercover as a swimmer but is not affected enough to change.

2.21 **Becoming Part 1** *written and directed by Joss Whedon*

Construction workers uncover entombed demon Acathla, which Angelus (whose turning by Darla, curse and falling for Buffy we see in flashbacks) steals in an attempt to wake Acathla and suck the world into Hell. Willow finds Jenny's backup disk; her recasting of the curse is interrupted by Drusilla who kills Kendra and abducts Giles for his knowledge of the Acathla ritual.

2.22 **Becoming Part 2** *written and directed by Joss Whedon*

Accused of Kendra's murder, Buffy is approached by Spike who offers help against Angelus in exchange for Drusilla's life. Giles resists torture, but under hypnosis tells Drusilla the ritual, thinking she is Jenny. Expelled from school by Snyder and thrown out by Joyce when she finds Buffy is the Slayer, Buffy fights Angelus as Acathla wakes. Willow's curse re-ensouls Angel. Buffy stabs him and sends him to Hell to save the world. Despairing, she leaves Sunnydale.

Buffy Season Three

3.1 **Anne** *written and directed by Joss Whedon*
Waiting tables in LA, Buffy meets the former Chanterelle, now Lily, whose boyfriend is abducted by social worker Ken, actually a slaver from a factory-like Hell, and returned old and dying. Buffy follows Lily to Hell and raises the slaves in revolt. Buffy gives Lily her job and second name, Anne, and returns home. The gang have fought vampires in her absence.

3.2 **Dead Man's Party** *by Marti Noxon*
The gang and Joyce are still furious with Buffy for not contacting them; this erupts into bitter argument during a welcome back party and is resolved by an attack of zombies raised by an African mask from Joyce's art gallery.

3.3 **Faith, Hope and Trick** *by David Greenwalt*
Faith, Kendra's replacement, arrives in Sunnydale pursued by her enemy Kakistos and black techie vampire Trick; she and Buffy are prickly before bonding to defeat Kakistos. Giles persuades Buffy to talk – she admits that Angel was re-ensouled when she stabbed him; she leaves her ring in Angel's mansion and Angel reappears, out of his mind.

3.4 **Beauty and the Beasts** *by Marti Noxon*
Violent deaths leads to suspicion of Oz, who has escaped the cage he locks himself in three nights a month. Buffy suspects the returned, feral Angel she has found in the woods. In fact, a fellow student with an abusive relationship with his girlfriend has taken a drug that changes him into the brute he thinks she wants. Angel kills him.

3.5 **Homecoming** *written and directed by David Greenwalt*
Trick sells tickets for a Slayer hunt. Buffy stands against Cordelia for Homecoming Queen and it is they, not Buffy and Faith, who are hunted and have to unite against their foes – a demon, the surviving Gorch, twin assassins. Trick is recruited by the Mayor. Cordelia faces Gorch down with sarcasm. Neither Buffy nor Cordelia wins the election. Willow and Xander kiss.

3.6 **Band Candy** *by Jane Espenson*

To create a diversion while babies are fed to a demon he has debts to, the Mayor has Trick hire Ethan to sell candy bars that revert all adults to their teens. Joyce and Giles make love, though Buffy thinks she has intervened in time. With help from a punk Giles and (briefly) a nerd Snyder, Buffy captures Rayne, saves the babies and kills the demon.

3.7 **Revelations** *by Doug Petrie*

Giles and the gang are furious that Buffy hid Angel's return. Faith's posh new watcher Gwen Post warns of a magic artefact, the glove of Mynegin, and she and Xander incite Faith to attack Angel lest he misuse it. In fact, it is Gwen who uses it – she has been expelled from the Council. Buffy severs her arm. Faith feels her trust generally abused.

3.8 **Lover's Walk** *by Dan Vebber*

Spike arrives in Sunnydale mad with grief that Drusilla has dumped him and kidnaps Willow to make him a love spell, with Xander as a hostage. Abandoned by him in the ruined factory, they are found making out by Oz and Cordelia; Cordelia is badly injured. The Mayor sends vampires to kill the disruptive Spike; Buffy and Angel help Spike who mocking them decides to torture Drusilla into loving him again.

3.9 **The Wish** *by Marti Noxon*

Cordelia, humiliated by Harmony and unforgiving of Xander, makes a wish to vengeance demon Anyanka and finds herself in a world where Buffy never came to Sunnydale, the Master rose, and Xander and Willow are vampires. She is killed but not before she tells Giles what has happened. A harder Buffy arrives and dies fighting the Master; Giles smashes Anyanka's necklace power centre and returns things to normal.

3.10 **Amends** *written and directed by Joss Whedon*

Angel is tormented by visions of those he killed, notably Jenny, and told he is damned and must kill Buffy. Buffy realizes that the source of this is the Prime Evil, a corrupting force, and confronts and kills its priests. Angel tries to commit suicide by facing the dawn, but it snows in Sunnydale, indicating that someone powerful is looking out for him. Oz forgives Willow.

3.11 **Gingerbread** *teleplay by Jane Espenson, story by Jane Espenson & Thania St. John*

Haunting by apparently sacrificed children sends Joyce and Willow's mother on a rampage against occultism. Snyder seizes Giles's books for burning and Buffy, Willow and Amy are condemned for witchcraft – Amy escapes by changing into a rat. Cordelia intervenes with a firehose and Buffy breaks the spell which enables a demon to pose as the dead children.

3.12 **Helpless** *by David Fury*

After meditation sessions with Giles, Buffy finds her powers weakening; he is putting her through a test ordered by the Council where she has to defeat a vampire by intelligence. The vampire turns his Council minders and abducts Joyce; Buffy tricks and kills him, passing the test, but Council boss Quentin sacks Giles for caring too much.

3.13 **The Zeppo** *by Dan Vebber*

Sidelined from the struggle against another apocalypse – we see this semi-parodically in background shots – and mocked by a vengeful Cordelia, Xander is befriended by, and has to defeat, zombie delinquents who plan to blow up the school. Along the way, Faith casually seduces him. Cordelia mocks him again and Xander is smugly cool.

3.14 **Bad Girls** *by Doug Petrie*

Faith talks Buffy into doing things her way – neglecting school to burn out vampires, taking silly risks, stealing weapons from a store, mocking new Watcher Wesley, dancing sexily together. The Mayor becomes invulnerable on schedule. Fighting the vampire minions of demon Balthazar, Faith accidentally kills Deputy Mayor Finch. Buffy is appalled. Faith does not care.

3.15 **Consequences** *by Marti Noxon*

Faith blames Buffy for Finch's death; Giles plans to deal with it quietly. Buffy and Faith see the Mayor with Trick; the Mayor realizes they know of his villainy. Xander reasons with Faith and she nearly kills him; Angel stops her and talks to her about bloodthirstiness. He is getting through when Wesley arrives with Council heavies, from whom Faith escapes. Buffy and she are attacked by Trick; Faith kills him, saving Buffy. Faith asks the Mayor for Trick's job.

3.16 **Doppelgangland** *written and directed by Joss Whedon*

Warned by Faith of Willow's hacking skills, the Mayor decides to kill her. Willow is tricked by Anya into helping retrieve Anyanka's necklace; Willow wrecks the spell; vampWillow is brought to Sunnydale. She beats up the Mayor's assassins who attack the Bronze, where she kills Sandy; she tries to seduce Willow who overpowers her. They impersonate each other, confusingly. VampWillow is sent back and staked.

3.17 **Enemies** *by Doug Petrie*

Faith tries to seduce Angel, failing which she casts a spell to bring Angelus back as her lover and the Mayor's ally. They trick and capture Buffy, and Faith boasts of the Mayor's planned Ascension, before discovering that she has been tricked by Angel into blowing her cover.

3.18 **Earshot** *by Jane Espenson*

Contaminated by the ichor of a demon, Buffy acquires the power to read minds, which starts to drive her insane, but not before she learns someone plans mass murder at Sunnydale High. Angel saves her; the gang, including Cordelia, eliminate various suspects. Buffy thinks wimp Jonathan plans a shooting: in fact, he plans suicide and she stops him. Xander discovers the would-be murderer is the cook. Buffy learns Giles slept with Joyce.

3.19 **Choices** *by David Fury*

The Mayor receives a box of demon beetles he needs to eat for his Ascension; Buffy steals them from the town hall, but Willow is captured and threatened by Faith. The Mayor offers a swap which Buffy accepts against Wesley's orders. Faith loses her knife, the Mayor's gift.

3.20 **The Prom** *by Marti Noxon*

Xander discovers Cordelia's new poverty and pays for her Prom dress. Anya asks him to the Prom. Angel decides to leave town. Buffy saves her schoolfellows from Hellhounds raised and trained by a social reject; she is acknowledged as Class Protector. Everyone dances.

3.21 **Graduation Day Part 1** *written and directed by Joss Whedon*
From Anya, they learn that Ascension means becoming a vast pure demon; the Mayor plans to speak at Graduation and eat the class. Faith poisons Angel with an arrow; Wesley forbids Buffy from seeking a cure and she mutinies. The cure is a Slayer's blood – Buffy fights Faith, whom she stabs with her own knife, but Faith throws herself from the building.

3.22 **Graduation Day Part 2** *written and directed by Joss Whedon*
Buffy makes Angel drink from her; in hospital comatose Faith tells her in a dream that the demon Mayor will be physically vulnerable and still have human emotions. Oz and Willow make love knowing they may die. At Graduation the Mayor turns, eating Snyder; the class fight back. Buffy taunts him with Faith's knife and he chases her into the library, which Giles blows up. Harmony is vamped. Angel leaves Sunnydale.

Buffy Season Four

4.1 **The Freshman** *written and directed by Joss Whedon*

Buffy, Willow and Oz arrive at university, where Buffy feels at sea; she dislikes her control-freak roommate Kathy. She meets her psychology professor Maggie Walsh and Maggie's TA, Riley. She is mocked and beaten by Sunday, a vampire whose band prey on unhappy students. Sunday steals her stuff, smashing the Class Protector parasol, and Buffy gets angry and kills her. There are commandos on campus tracking vampires.

4.2 **Living Conditions** *by Marti Noxon*

Everyone worries that Buffy is cracking up – her hostility to Kathy becomes unreasonable and deranged. In fact, her suspicions are right; Kathy is a demon who has been magically removing her soul in order that Buffy be dragged off when Kathy's father comes to take her home. Buffy's soul is restored; Kathy is taken; Willow moves into the room.

4.3 **The Harsh Light of Day** *by Jane Espenson*

Willow is attacked by Harmony, now a vampire and Spike's lover. He has returned to Sunnydale in search of the Ring of Amara, which renders vampires invulnerable to stakes and sunlight. Anya seduces Xander; Buffy sleeps with plausible Parker; Spike rejects Harmony when he finds the ring. Buffy defeats him and takes the ring. (See A1.3)

4.4 **Fear, Itself** *by David Fury*

The Scoobies attend a Halloween party; blood spilled on a mystic rune, part of the decorations, evokes a fear demon. Buffy is dragged into the depths; Willow's spell goes wrong; Oz starts to change; Xander becomes invisible. Anya who arrived late fetches Giles. Buffy accidentally releases the fear demon, which is small, so she stomps on it.

4.5 **Beer Bad** *by Tracey Forbes*

Moping over Parker, Buffy takes to hanging out in the bar with poseurs who are rude to bar staff – including Xander. Oz is attracted to Veruca. Buffy and her new friends start to devolve – they into Neanderthals, Buffy into a

Angel Season One

A1.1 **City of** *by Joss Whedon & David Greenwalt*

Angel is killing vampires in LA and is approached by Doyle, a half-demon gifted by the Powers That Be with visions accompanied by blinding headaches. Angel needs human contact if he is to redeem himself. His first attempt to save a starlet who is being pursued by vampire Hollywood magnate Russell fails; he ends up saving Russell's next victim – Cordelia, who is struggling in LA and decides to come and work for him. He kills Russell, affronting Russell's lawyer, Lindsey McDonald of Wolfram and Hart.

A1.2 **Lonely Heart** *by David Fury*

The trio make the round of bars handing out fliers for Angel Investigations and get mixed up in a series of eviscerations for which Angel finds himself suspected by cop Kate. A wormlike demon that burrows into people is using singles bars to pick up new victims; it takes a barman who abducts Kate. She and Angel escape, and burn the demon.

A1.3 **In the Dark** *by Doug Petrie*

Following 4.3, Oz arrives to give Angel the Ring of Amara and Spike pursues attempting to get it back; Spike abducts Angel and has him tortured by paedophile vampire Marcus. Cordelia, Oz and Doyle swap the ring for Angel; Marcus double-crosses Spike and steals the ring. Angel catches and kills him, and then smashes the ring as dangerous and contrary to the spirit of his redemption.

A1.4 **I Fall to Pieces** *by David Greenwalt*

Doyle's visions send Angel to Melissa, who is being stalked by control-freak Dr Meltzer – he stops her withdrawing money from her account by changing her PIN. He also has the ability to separate parts of his body and control them at a distance – Angel poses as a client and Meltzer tries to kill him. He attacks Melissa in Angel's apartment, and Angel kills him.

A1.5 **Rm w/a Vu** *by Jane Espenson*

Cordelia can no longer bear her roach-infested flat; Angel cannot bear having her stay with him. He agrees to help Doyle with demon debt-collector Griff if Doyle finds Cordelia a flat. The apartment is perfect, except for vengeful fetchingly monosyllabic Cave-Buffy. Parker tries to seduce Willow who mocks him. The barman brewed magic beer – the bar catches fire and Cave-Buffy saves the day.

4.6 **Wild at Heart** *by Marti Noxon*
Oz escapes from his cage and meets another werewolf, the amoral musician Veruca. He locks her into his cage with him next night and Willow finds them together. Willow tries to curse Veruca, who arrives at sundown to kill her; Oz attacks Veruca as they both change, and kills her. Buffy overpowers him. Oz decides to leave town.

4.7 **The Initiative** *by Doug Petrie*
Spike is captured by the commandos – the Initiative, a military/research unit, commanded by Maggie Walsh; Riley is the commando leader, his friends Graham and Forrest his subordinates. Spike escapes to Buffy's room where he tries to attack Willow but discovers that a chip in his brain prevents him. Riley and other commandos try to seize Willow and Buffy fights them off.

4.8 **Pangs** *by Jane Espenson*
Work on a new cultural centre uncovers the lost Sunnydale mission, where local Indians were imprisoned and died – a vengeance spirit kills a lecturer and a priest. Willow makes a case for his right to vengeance – Xander catches all the diseases the Indians died of. Spike takes refuge in Giles's apartment where the Scoobies are having a Thanksgiving meal; Angel arrives, and helps fight off the vengeful spirits, without Buffy knowing he is there until after his departure. (See A1.8)

4.9 **Something Blue** *by Tracey Forbes*
Riley and Buffy date. Depressed Willow casts a spell that enforces her will including her casual remarks. Amy is briefly de-ratted; Giles goes blind; Xander finds himself chased by demons; Buffy and Spike agree to marry. Willow is offered Anya's old job as vengeance demon by D'Hoffryn, but declines, putting things right before demons can overwhelm the gang.

ghost Mrs Pearson, who dislikes young women and tries to drive Cordelia to suicide. Cordelia fights back and drives her out allowing the ghost of Dennis, the son Mrs Pearson murdered, to stay.

A1.6 **Sense and Sensitivity** *by Tim Minear*
Angel helps Kate arrest gangster Little Tony, a W&H client who complains about his treatment. Kate and the rest are obliged to take sensitivity training, which is magically enhanced to a point where they cannot function. Kate breaks down at her father Trevor's retirement party and insults him. Angel visits the warlock sensitivity trainer, but is tricked by him. In spite of the effects of the spell, Angel stops Little Tony killing Kate.

A1.7 **The Bachelor Party** *by Tracey Stern*
At the point where Doyle first discovered his half-demon nature, he was married to Harry; he became irresponsible and their marriage broke up. Harry has become a demonologist and is about to marry Richard, one of a tribe of demons who are almost entirely assimilated except for the custom of eating the brains of the first husbands of women who marry them. Angel rescues Doyle and Harry is furious with Richard. Doyle has a vision of Buffy in danger.

A1.8 **I Will Remember You** *by David Greenwalt & Jennine Renshaw*
After the events of 4.8, Buffy arrives to tell Angel off for coming to Sunnydale and avoiding her. He is attacked by a demon assassin and gets its blood in a scratch. Suddenly he is human – he and Buffy make passionate love and have a day of bliss. He pursues the demon and realizes he is too weak to be a champion any more – Buffy kills it for him. Angel does a deal with the Oracles, servants of the Powers, who turn time back – only he will remember.

A1.9 **Hero** *by Howard Gordon & Tim Minear*
Doyle's secret crime is that he failed to protect other Brakken demons from the Scourge – demon racists who kill half-breeds. The Scourge are on the rampage after a tribe of Lister demons; the Listers think Angel may be their promised saviour. He infiltrates the Scourge and discovers that they plan to use a device which burns all humans and humanness. Doyle, after discovering Cordelia is prepared to consider dating him, kisses her and sacrifices himself to save everyone.

4.10 Hush *written and directed by Joss Whedon*
Fairytale monsters, the Gentlemen, arrive in Sunnydale and steal everyone's voices as a cover for harvesting hearts. Willow meets Tara at a Wicca group and together they magically fight off a Gentlemen attack, finding a connection almost at once. Buffy and Riley separately trail the Gentlemen to their lair and destroy them; they then have to cope with their recognition of each other.

4.11 Doomed *by Marti Noxon & David Fury & Jane Espenson*
Buffy and Riley come to terms with each other's true identity. Three demons assemble tokens – a heart, some bones, a talisman stolen from Giles – to open the Hellmouth and bring the Apocalypse; Buffy, Riley and the gang stop them, realizing just in time that the crucial sacrifice is the demons' own leap into the Hellmouth. A suicidal Spike is dragged along; he discovers he can kill demons and vampires which cheers him up.

4.12 A New Man *by Jane Espenson*
Feeling neglected, and patronized by Maggie Walsh, Giles goes for a drink with Ethan who warns him of Room 314, before changing him into a lumbering demon; only Spike can understand him and demands payment for help. Buffy, thinking the demon has killed Giles, attacks him in Ethan's room, but recognizes him in time. Ethan is interned.

4.13 The I in Team *by David Fury*
Buffy joins the Initiative, but irritates Maggie Walsh by asking questions about Room 314; when Buffy sleeps with Riley, Maggie is jealous. Willow, feeling neglected, spends the night with Tara. Spike is tagged by Forrest and goes to Giles for help; Giles makes him pay. Maggie sets up a demon ambush which Buffy survives, exposing Maggie to Riley. Maggie goes to Room 314 and is killed by her creation Adam.

4.14 Goodbye Iowa *by Marti Noxon*
Riley discovers the gang's protection of Spike and becomes distrustful. Adam dissects a child. Riley becomes disoriented; Maggie's 'vitamins' were something more. In room 314, Adam boasts to Buffy, Xander and Riley of his kinship with Riley, and then stabs Riley non-fatally. Tara sabotages a demon-seeking spell.

A1.10 **Parting Gifts** *by David Fury & Jennine Renshaw*

Cordelia discovers she has inherited Doyle's visions and headaches; Angel is hired by Barney, a demon who thinks he is being hunted. Wesley turns up, hunting a demon who kills other demons for their magical body parts. This proves to be Barney – who abducts Cordelia for her seer's eyes, which he auctions. Angel and Wesley save her; she kills Barney.

A1.11 **Somnambulist** *by Tim Minear*

Angel has disturbing dreams of killings – Kate realizes he fits the profile, as do Cordelia and Wesley. They tie him to his bed, but the killings continue. The killer is Penn, a vampire whom Angel sired – Angel and Kate track him together and kill him, but the knowledge that Angel is a vampire turns Kate against him.

A1.12 **Expecting** *by Howard Gordon & Jennine Renshaw*

Cordelia's new friends, party girls centred around Sarina, introduce her to Wilson with whom she spends the night. Next morning, she is hugely pregnant, as are all of Sarina's circle, with multiple non-human foetuses of whom she becomes highly protective. Angel and Wesley track down the huge Hacksall demon who used Wilson as his surrogate, and freeze it with liquid nitrogen. Cordelia smashes it to bits.

A1.13 **She** *by David Greenwalt & Marti Noxon*

A security guard at an ice plant is burned hideously; Angel tracks a mysterious woman, Jhiera, who proves to be a renegade princess from a demon dimension where men rule by clipping the spines in which female individuality rests. She is running an escape route and does not care who gets hurt in the process. Angel helps her against her male enemies but warns her against killing in his city.

A1.14 **I've Got You Under My Skin** *by Jennine Renshaw*

Strange goings on in the Anderson family are caused by possession of the boy Ryan by an Ethros demon. Wesley and Angel persuade the family to let them exorcise the child – which ultimately works, but the demon escapes. Angel tracks it, only to learn that the demon, whom he kills, wanted rescuing from the psychopath child. Ryan tries to kill his family, but Angel rescues them.

4.15 **This Year's Girl** *by Doug Petrie*

After dreams, Faith wakes from her coma; she confronts Buffy, but is hunted by the police. Watchers, warned by her nurse, come to town. Faith receives a videotape in which the Mayor offers her vengeance. She takes Joyce hostage; Buffy arrives and they fight. The Mayor's gadget switches their bodies; and Buffy-in-Faith is arrested.

4.16 **Who Are You? written and directed** *by Joss Whedon*

Faith-in-Buffy has fun with Buffy's body, taunting Spike, teasing Tara (whom she guesses is Willow's lover) and seducing Riley. She kills a vampire and is thanked; Riley's tenderness freaks her out. Buffy-in-Faith escapes execution by the Council and explains things to Giles. Vampires influenced by Adam seize a church; Faith leaves an airport queue to save the congregation. Buffy helps her; they fight; Willow and Tara reverse the body-switch. Faith leaves town. (See A.18)

4.17 **Superstar** *by Jane Espenson*

Suddenly Jonathan is a world-famous hero and Buffy his sidekick; everyone, male and female, is besotted with him. Buffy realizes something is wrong when Jonathan is weak against a demon that shares his tattoo; she realizes that he has changed reality with a spell and created an evil demon for balance. When he and Buffy kill it, things return to normal. Jonathan helps Buffy forgive Riley for sleeping with Faith.

4.18 **Where the Wild Things Are** *by Tracey Forbes*

Buffy and Riley's love-making triggers and sustains poltergeist activity which causes sexual shame and general weirdness; the source of this is children disciplined when the house was an orphanage. Xander and Anya rouse Buffy and Riley before they die of exhaustion.

4.19 **New Moon Rising** *by Marti Noxon*

Oz returns, cured of lycanthropy, until he smells Willow on Tara, changes and attacks her – and is captured and tortured by the Initiative. Willow comes out to Buffy. Adam asks Spike's help, promising removal of the chip. Riley is arrested for trying to free Oz; Buffy enters the Initiative, takes the new commander hostage and frees Riley and Oz. Oz and Willow talk, and he leaves town. Willow and Tara make up.

A1.15 **The Prodigal** *by Tim Minear*

Flashbacks show us Angel's poor relationship, when human, with his father, to whom he was a disappointment; killing his family did not help. He discovers that Trevor is corrupt, working with demon drug dealers; Trevor's vampire partners kill him. Even though he helps her avenge Trevor's death, Kate's bitterness against Angel becomes intense.

A1.16 **The Ring** *by Howard Gordon*

Angel is hired to protect Darin's gambler brother Jack; in fact, both brothers run a secret gladiatorial arena in which demons fight to the death. They enslave Angel, who refuses to fight; W&H lawyer Lilah offers to buy his contract, but he refuses. Wesley and Cordelia free the slaves.

A1.17 **Eternity** *by Tracey Stern*

Angel saves TV star Raven from her stalker; she hires him as bodyguard, but it turns out the whole thing is a publicity stunt cooked up because she is ageing. She cultivates Cordelia's friendship and discovers Angel is a vampire; she drugs his drink hoping to seduce him into turning her. He becomes, or thinks he becomes, Angelus; Wesley and Cordelia manage to subdue him.

A1.18 **Five by Five** *by Jim Kouf*

Faith arrives in LA, hospitalizes a pimp and takes his apartment; she goes wild in LA's clubs, in one of which she is picked up by Lilah and hired by W&H to kill Angel. She taunts him repeatedly, and eventually kidnaps Wesley, whom she tortures; Angel confronts her and she collapses – she took the contract because she wants Angel to fight back and kill her.

A1.19 **Sanctuary** *by Tim Minear & Joss Whedon*

Angel starts to rehabilitate Faith, interrupted by a demon assassin and then by Buffy, furious that he is helping Faith. The Watchers' Council hitmen turn up, and try to persuade Wesley to help them; he guesses that they plan to kill Faith and Angel and double-crosses them. Buffy helps Faith escape. Angel is arrested for harbouring her; Faith gives herself up to save him.

4.20 **The Yoko Factor** *by Doug Petrie*

Adam kills Forrest. On Adam's orders, Spike spreads hostility between the Scoobies, playing on Giles's and Xander's sense of uselessness and Willow's fear of rejection. Buffy storms out. Angel comes to town and he and Riley fight; Angel and Buffy quarrel. Riley is summoned by Adam. The Initiative has captured so many demons its cells are full.

4.21 **Primeval** *by David Fury*

Buffy guesses Spike is working with Adam; she persuades the others to get over their differences. Adam tells Riley he has a chip which Adam controls — he will join Adam and Forrest as cyberdemonoids after a battle between demons and soldiers gives him spare parts. Buffy and the gang blend into a super-Buffy which defeats and kills Adam with help from Riley and Spike, whom Adam double-crossed. The Initiative is shut down.

4.22 **Restless** *written and directed by Joss Whedon*

Exhausted, Buffy, Willow, Giles and Xander fall asleep in front of videos. In dreams which reflect their insecurities, each is visited by a man with cheese and attacked by a mysterious being; Buffy learns from a guide with Tara's face that this is the First Slayer, who has been angered by the spell in 4.21, and that she has changes ahead. Buffy defeats the First Slayer.

A1.20 **War Zone** *by Garry Campbell*

Angel helps millionaire David Nabbit, blackmailed over visits to a demon brothel. He meets Gunn, leader of street kid vampire hunters, who are disinclined to trust him; vampires kidnap and turn Gunn's sister, whom Gunn stakes. Angel warns the vampires to leave Gunn and his friends alone.

A1.21 **Blind Date** *by Jennine Renshaw*

Lindsey is defending blind Vanessa, a mystic assassin who traded sight for power; when Lindsey discovers that her next hits are children, he has an attack of conscience and approaches Angel. They steal files and a mysterious scroll from W&H, and Angel fights and kills Vanessa. Once the children are safe, Lindsey makes his peace with his boss Holland and accepts promotion.

A1.22 **To Shanshu in LA** *by David Greenwalt*

The scroll Angel stole contains prophesies of his coming death. Holland raises a demon priest, Vocah, who kills the Oracles, drives Cordelia mad with visions, steals back the scroll and blows up Angel's apartment, injuring Wesley. Angel disrupts a ritual, killing Vocah and slicing off Lindsey's hand when he tries to burn the scroll. Cordelia is restored and Wesley realizes that the scroll prophesies Angel's return to humanity. Meanwhile, it turns out that Vocah summoned Darla back from Hell as W&H's new agent.

Buffy Season Five

5.1 **Buffy vs. Dracula** *by Marti Noxon*

Dracula arrives and seduces Buffy into letting him bite her; his mind tricks turn Xander into his bug-eating servant who delivers Buffy to him. Giles and Riley raid Dracula's castle and Giles is groped by his Brides. After tasting Dracula's blood – at this point, he echoes the Tara of her dreams – Buffy fights free and stakes him; he repeatedly re-forms. At home, Buffy has suddenly always had a sister, Dawn.

5.2 **Real Me** *by David Fury*

Dawn writes in her diary how much she hates being Buffy's kid sister. Harmony's inept minions raid the Magic Shop for books on slayers; Giles thinks about taking up the lease. Dawn is harangued by a maniac. Harmony and her minions attacks the Summers' house ineffectually. Dawn is taken hostage by a minion; Buffy stakes all the gang except Harmony.

5.3 **The Replacement** *by Jane Espenson*

The demon Toth shoots at Buffy with a magic rod, but hits Xander. Suddenly there are two Xanders, one suave and confident, the other dorky and clumsy; both think the other is a demon. In fact, both are aspects of Xander and need to survive; Willow reintegrates them. Xander and Anya get an apartment. Riley confides in a sympathetic Xander that he knows how lucky he is – but Buffy does not love him.

5.4 **Out of My Mind** *by Rebecca Kirshner*

Harmony takes refuge with Spike. Joyce is taken ill, momentarily not recognizing Dawn; Riley's heart is under strain from Maggie Walsh's enhancements; Spike and Harmony kidnap Riley's military surgeon to remove Spike's chip. The surgeon plays along, faking the chip's removal; Buffy rescues him and he operates on Riley. Spike wakes from an erotic dream, realizing he loves Buffy.

5.5 **No Place Like Home** *by Doug Petrie*

Monks send a mystic key away before being slaughtered by evil ditzy Glory. After finding a magic sphere, Buffy suspects evil magic is making Joyce ill

Angel Season Two

A2.1 **Judgment** *teleplay by David Greenwalt, story by Joss Whedon & David Greenwalt*

Angel and the others are fighting evil out of Cordelia's apartment, and getting cocky. Angel misinterprets a vision and kills a demon who was in fact protecting a pregnant woman, and she refuses to trust him. He goes to the Host's karaoke bar Caritas and (humiliatingly) sings so that the Host can help him find her and become her champion in a trial by ordeal. Meanwhile Lilah, Lindsey and Darla plot his downfall; Angel visits Faith in jail.

A2.2 **Are You Now or Have You Ever Been?** *by Tim Minear*

In A2.1, Angel visited a derelict hotel, the Hyperion; he sets Cordelia and Wesley to investigating its bloody history – they discover he lived there in the 50s. Angel befriends thief Judy who is passing for white; threatened with lynching, she betrays him. Angel gives the hotel's staff and residents to the Thesulac paranoia demon that caused this. In the present day, he kills the demon and frees the aged Judy before moving into the hotel.

A2.3 **First Impressions** *by Shawn Ryan*

Gunn interrogates Jameel about Deevak a powerful demon; Cordelia has visions of him in danger. Angel is befogged with dreams of Darla; failing to get hold of him or Wesley, Cordelia takes Angel's car to Gunn, which gets stolen. Their search for it brings them into confrontation with Jameel who *is* Deevak; Angel arrives in time to help. Cordelia realizes the real danger to Gunn is Gunn. Angel's dreams of Darla turn out to be real visits from her.

A2.4 **Untouched** *by Mere Smith, directed by Joss Whedon*

Angel tries to help Bethany, who has killed two muggers with telekinetic powers; she grows suspicious of Lilah, who befriended her in order to recruit her as an assassin for W&H and moves into the hotel. Lilah sends Bethany's sexually abusive father to see her, hoping she will kill him and turn to evil; under Angel's influence, Bethany settles for sending him away.

A2.5 **Dear Boy** *written and directed by David Greenwalt*

Staking out an adulteress (who claims to be abducted by aliens whenever and goes into a trance to seek it out. She discovers Dawn is not real. Spike starts stalking Buffy. Glory, who sucks out people's minds, tortures a monk; Buffy rescues him after fighting the stronger Glory, but he dies, after telling Buffy that Dawn is the Key and all memories of her are false. Buffy decides that Dawn is her innocent sister even so.

5.6 **Family** *written and directed by Joss Whedon*

Buffy tells Giles about Dawn. Tara's redneck family arrive; her father claims she, like her mother, will turn demonic unless she abandons college and magic. Riley flirts with vampire Sandy. Tara casts a demon-obscuring spell which hinders the fight against demon assassins sent by Glory. The Scoobies, including Dawn, tell Tara's father that they are her real family; Spike proves Tara's humanity by hitting her – it hurts him. Willow and Tara dance.

5.7 **Fool for Love** *by Doug Petrie*

Injured by a minor vampire and concerned about the deaths of Slayers, Buffy interrogates Spike about how he killed two. In flashbacks, we see ineffectual poet William turned by Drusilla, his self-invention as Spike and his fights with Angel, his killing of a Slayer in China and of another in New York. Like them, he says, Buffy will be killed by her own death wish. Buffy spurns his advances. Joyce is hospitalized; Spike, who has come to kill Buffy, comforts her.

5.8 **Shadow** *by David Fury*

Joyce has a brain tumour. Glory turns a cobra at the zoo into a hunter which tracks the Key and identifies it as Dawn; Buffy kills it before it gets to Glory. Riley finds Spike in the Summers' house stealing Buffy's clothes; Riley lets Sandy bite him and stakes her.

5.9 **Listening to Fear** *by Rebecca Kirshner*

Ben summons a meteor-dwelling Queller which starts killing the madmen created by Glory's mindsuck; the tumour has made Joyce deranged – when she is allowed home for the night, the Queller follows her. Dawn fights it off; Buffy and Spike kill it. Joyce realizes the truth about Dawn, but, like Buffy, accepts her as her own. Joyce goes into surgery.

she wants a date) Angel catches sight of Darla – but she is human. She frames him by having the actor who is posing as her husband killed; Wesley persuades Kate that Darla is who Angel says she is. Angel abducts and confronts Darla, who begs him to come back to her.

A2.6 **Guise Will Be Guise** *by Jane Espenson*

Distraught over Darla, Angel goes to see a swami recommended by the Host; he gets good advice even though the man he talks to is actually an assassin. Bryce forcibly hires Angel to protect his daughter Virginia – what he gets is Wesley posing as Angel; in fact Bryce plans to sacrifice Virginia to his demon patron. With help from the others, Wesley rescues her.

A2.7 **Darla** *written and directed by Tim Minear*

In a companion to 5.1, we see Darla's past – her turning by the Master, her abandonment of the Master for Angelus, her slaughter of the gypsies who cursed Angelus, his brief return to her and her unpreparedness to accept any compromise on pure evil. Tortured by humanity and guilt, she seduces Lindsey and is threatened with execution by Holland; Angel rescues her and she asks him to turn her again. He refuses.

A2.8 **The Shroud of Rahmon** *by Jim Kouf*

Wesley is giving a statement to the police . . . Angel and Gunn go undercover to prevent the heist by human and demon criminals of a demon's shroud; it has the power to send people mad and affects everyone involved. Angel has to bite Kate and fake her death to save her from a homicidal demon; worryingly he enjoys it. He destroys the shroud.

A2.9 **The Trial Story** *teleplay by Tim Minear and Doug, Petrie story by David Greenwalt*

Darla is dying of the syphilis that killed her in 1609; she is desperate to be turned and Angel finds her cruising low-rent vampires. He takes her to Caritas and the Host suggests an ordeal whereby Angel three times puts himself in jeopardy to buy her a second chance. He succeeds, but is told she already had it. She accepts mortality – and is then forcibly turned by Drusilla.

5.10 **Into the Woods** *written and directed by Marti Noxon*

The tumour is safely removed. Graham asks Riley to join a unit fighting demons in Belize. Spike tells Buffy that Riley uses vampire whores – she sets fire to the brothel. Riley stakes Spike with a piece of plastic wood as a warning; they bond over drink and hopeless love for Buffy. Riley offers Buffy an ultimatum – he will be boarding a helicopter at midnight. She is attacked by the vampire pimps and whores, and kills them; Xander convinces her to ask Riley to stay, but she is too late. Xander tells Anya he loves her.

5.11 **Triangle** *by Jane Espenson*

Left in charge when Giles consults the Watchers, Anya bickers with Willow about magic experiments, alienating Tara and Xander, and accidentally releasing a troll, once Anya's boyfriend whom she transformed. He wrecks the Bronze and pursues both women to the shop where he threatens to kill them. He is impressed by Xander's courage in fighting him and offers to spare one woman – Xander refuses to choose. Buffy fights the troll and Willow sends it away, leaving its hammer behind.

5.12 **Checkpoint** *by Jane Espenson and Doug Petrie*

A delegation from the Council arrives, insisting that Buffy pass tests and threatening Giles with deportation. They interview the Scoobies and Spike. Glory confronts Buffy in the Summers' home and threatens her family and friends. Buffy is attacked by the Knights of Byzantium, fanatics keen to destroy the Key. Buffy tells the Council that real power rests with her – they tell her that Glory is a god.

5.13 **Blood Ties** *by Steven DeKnight*

Buffy tells the other Scoobies about Dawn; Dawn guesses from their behaviour that something is going on. Spike helps her break into the Magic Shop where she reads Giles's diaries. Distraught, she cuts herself and burns her diaries; she goes to the hospital where she confides in Ben, who transforms into Glory. Buffy and the others arrive and fight Glory who is easily beating them when Willow teleports her five miles into the air. Buffy tells Dawn that they both have Summers' blood. Dawn has no memory of Ben's transformation.

A2.10 Reunion *by Tim Minear and Shawn Ryan*

Angel is too late to stop Darla rising as a vampire; she and Drusilla bond and go on a rampage. Angel realizes they intend to attack Holland and other W&H lawyers, but when he gets there, lets the massacre happen. Rebuked by Wesley, he sacks his team.

A2.11 Redefinition *by Mere Smith*

Wesley, Cordelia and Gunn go to Caritas and find they can fight without Angel. Darla and Drusilla are trying to recruit an army; Angel trails and kills their recruits. Lindsey and Lilah, survivors of Darla's massacre, are put in charge of the Angel problem and told he must be corrupted, not killed. Angel ruthlessly sets fire to Darla and Drusilla, who only just survive.

A2.12 Blood Money *by Shawn Ryan and Mere Smith*

Anne, formerly Chanterelle and Lily, runs a homeless shelter which W&H fund as a charitable write-off. Angel tells her the money is tainted; Lindsey and Lilah hire Boone, an old demon enemy of Angel. Angel sneaks a video into a benefit – actually it shows Wesley and Cordelia having fun. Boone steals the money and Angel fights him for it. Wesley and Gunn kill a fire-breathing demon.

A2.13 Happy Anniversary *by David Greenwalt*

The Host comes to Angel – a man sang karaoke the night before and the Host saw the world ending. The man is brilliant physicist Gene who plans to stop time in his room before his girlfriend can leave him, and is being used by Lubber demons to end the world; Angel and the Host stop this. Meanwhile, Wesley solves a magic country house murder.

5.14 **Crush** *by David Fury*

Spike persuades Harmony to impersonate Buffy for sex games; Dawn tells Buffy that Spike loves her. An LA train full of corpses arrives in Sunnydale – Drusilla is back. Buffy investigates; Spike tells her of his feelings. Drusilla tells Spike the chip no longer works and takes him to the Bronze, giving him a fresh corpse to drain. They capture Buffy, then Spike takes Drusilla prisoner, offering to stake her to prove his love for Buffy. Buffy rejects him; Harmony shoots him and leaves; Drusilla gives up on him. Buffy bars him from the Summers' house.

5.15 **I Was Made to Love You** *by Jane Espenson*

Mysterious April arrives looking for her boyfriend Warren; she beats up Spike for chatting her up. Everyone realizes she is a robot built as Warren's girlfriend and abandoned when he found a real one. Buffy saves his fiancee from April and then sits with April as her batteries run down; realizing she does not need a man, she cancels a date with Ben. Spike orders a Buffybot from Warren. Buffy finds Joyce dead.

5.16 **The Body** *written and directed by Joss Whedon*

After a flashback to Joyce's last Christmas, Buffy calls an ambulance – Joyce is dead from a post-op aneurism. The Scoobies meet up to join her and Giles and Dawn at the hospital; Willow has a clothes crisis and Anya broods about mortality. Dawn goes to the mortuary where a vampire attacks her; Buffy saves her. They look at their dead mother.

5.17 **Forever** *written and directed by Marti Noxon*

Xander rebuffs Spike for bringing a wreath, which is unsigned. After Joyce's funeral, Angel consoles Buffy. Dawn asks Tara and Willow to raise Joyce; Tara tells her it is wrong, Willow leaves a book out so she can see the arguments. Dawn tries the spell – Spike takes her to sinister demon Doc, who sends them to fight a monster for its eggs. Dawn casts the spell and something rises; Buffy goes to welcome it and Dawn breaks the spell.

A2.14 The Thin Dead Line *by Shawn Ryan and Jim Kouf*
Wesley and Cordelia take on a small girl infected with a demon third eye. Anne's centre and Gunn's friends are threatened by violent cops; Wesley is shot by them and the centre besieged. Meanwhile, Angel discovers that these are zombie cops – Kate helps him get into the precinct station and smash the local captain's voodoo statue just in time to save everyone at the centre. He visits Wesley in hospital – Cordelia sends him away.

A2.15 Reprise (Part 1 of 2) *by Tim Minear*
W&H expect a review from a demonic senior partner; both Angel and Darla plan to disrupt this – Angel plans to travel to Hell and attack the Partners. Virginia breaks up with Wesley; Kate is sacked as a result of complaints from the captain in A2.14 and takes an overdose; Cordelia is ambushed by third-eye demons. Told by Holland's ghost that W&H rely on the evil of humanity, Angel despairs and, when he finds Darla at the hotel, has sex with her.

A2.16 Epiphany (Part 2 of 2) *by Tim Minear*
Discovering he still has his soul, Angel taunts Darla and sends her away; she despairs and leaves Lindsey's apartment. Angel saves Kate, allowed to enter her flat uninvited by the Powers. He saves Wesley, Gunn and Cordelia from third-eye demons who plan to impregnate them, in spite of being delayed by a fight with Lindsey. He offers to work for Wesley.

A2.17 Disharmony *by David Fury*
Wesley makes Angel grovel, a bit. Vampires are abducting humans and turning them, as part of a vampire self-motivation cult. Harmony arrives in town; she and Cordelia pick up where they left off, in spite of Cordelia's misapprehension that Harmony's interest in her is lesbian rather than vampiric. To everyone's irritation, Harmony decides to fight on the side of good, then betrays them to the cult, whom they slaughter. Harmony leaves town.

5.18 **Intervention** *by Jane Espenson*

Buffy goes to the desert with Giles to confront the First Slayer, who tells her that her gift is death. Spike takes delivery of the Buffybot, makes passionate love and goes out slaying with it; Xander and Anya think this is the real Buffy and are appalled. Glory's minions guess Spike is the Key and abduct him; Glory tortures him for the Key's identity. In the course of the rescue, the Buffybot is damaged; Buffy impersonates it to find out whether Spike broke and kisses him when she realizes he did not.

5.19 **Tough Love** *by Rebecca Kirshner*

Willow and Tara quarrel; at a fair by herself, Tara is tortured and mind-sucked by Glory. After promising Buffy to do nothing rash, Willow does darkest magic to fight Glory, on whom she inflicts serious pain before starting to lose. Warned by Spike, Buffy arrives in time to help her escape; Glory follows them. Tara inadvertently reveals that Dawn is the Key.

5.20 **Spiral** *by Steven DeKnight*

Buffy and Dawn escape. The Scoobies and Spike leave town; on the road they are attacked by the Knights of Byzantium who wound Giles seriously. They warn that Glory's use of the Key will destroy the universe by lowering the barriers between dimensions; they are prepared to kill an innocent child. Besieged in a service station behind a magic force-field, Buffy rings Ben to treat Giles; Ben turns into Glory and seizes Dawn. Buffy lapses into catatonia.

5.21 **The Weight of the World** *by Doug Petrie*

Willow takes charge of the retreat to town and sends Spike and Xander to interrogate Doc whom they fight and seemingly kill; Spike eventually conveys to the others the link between Ben and Glory which mortals cannot remember. Glory prepares for a ritual in which she will bleed Dawn dry to use the Key. Dawn briefly escapes, but is betrayed by Ben to whom Glory promises continued existence. Willow enters Buffy's mind and talks her out of her despair over a moment when she thought of killing Dawn. After reading Doc's scrolls, Giles says that killing Dawn is the only way to save the world.

A2.18 **Dead End** *by David Greenwalt*
The time has come for W&H to decide which of Lindsey and Lilah gets killed, which promoted. Lindsey is given a transplanted hand, which starts scrawling messages; he investigates, as does Angel. W&H punish former employees by using them as an organ bank. Lindsey and Angel free those who can be freed and mercy kill others; Lindsey mocks his superiors and Lilah, and leaves town.

A2.19 **Belonging** *by Shawn Ryan*
A beast comes through a portal from the Host's world as does his cousin Landok; we learn that the camp Host comes from a species of barbarian warriors. Cordelia has a vision of a librarian, Fred, who disappeared five years ago; she has never been found. One of Gunn's old team is killed by vampires and Gunn feels responsible. Together Landok, Angel and Wesley track the beast and kill it; Landok is wounded and has to be sent home, using the book Fred had in Cordelia's dream to open the portal. Cordelia is sucked through.

A2.20 **Over the Rainbow** *by Mere Smith*
Cordelia is enslaved by demons in a mediaeval world. Gunn joins Angel, Wesley and the Host on a rescue mission. Cordelia has a vision and finds herself tortured by priests. Angel is happy to discover he can bear sunlight in this world – he and the others are arrested and taken to the Princess, who proves to be Cordelia.

A2.21 **Through the Looking Glass** *written and directed by Tim Minear*
The priests are part of W&H; they plan to make Cordelia have sex with the handsome dumb half-human Groosalug in order to steal her visions, and then kill her. Wesley and Gunn escape and join the rebels; the Host and Angel rescue Fred from execution by the Host's relatives. Angel changes into a hideous demon that Fred manages to control. Cordelia decides to start freeing slaves and the priests put her in her place by beheading the Host.

5.22 **The Gift** *written and directed by Joss Whedon*
Determined that Dawn should not die, Buffy demands that other ways to
beat Glory be found. At Anya's suggestion, they use the Buffybot, the troll's
hammer, the monk's glowing sphere and a wrecking ball. Willow sucks Tara's
sanity back out of Glory and the others help Buffy wear her down until she
subsides back into Ben, whom Giles kills. Doc appears and starts bleeding
Dawn; reality begins to crumble. Buffy realizes that Dawn's blood and hers
are the same, and sacrifices herself to save her sister.

A2.22 **There's No Place Like Plrtz Glrb** *written and directed by David Greenwalt*

The Host is not dead – he just has to be reunited with his body and Cordelia, the Groosalug and Landok deal with this. Wesley and Gunn persuade the rebels not to execute them, and become their leaders. Boss priest Seth plans to explode the collars on all slaves – Cordelia beheads him. Angel challenges the Groosalug, changes into the beast, but manages to hold back. Cordelia passes up true love, ruling the world and passing the visions to the Groosalug, for her duty. Fred's formulae get them home – to find Willow waiting with bad news.